SCOTTISH SOLDIERS
IN
EUROPE AND AMERICA
1600-1700

David Dobson

CLEARFIELD

Copyright © 2021
by David Dobson
All Rights Reserved

Published for Clearfield Company by
Genealogical Publishing Company
Baltimore, Maryland
2021

ISBN 9780806359175

INTRODUCTION

At the beginning of the seventeenth century Scotland had a relatively small standing army as the Union of the Crowns in 1603 had eliminated any military threat from England. Prior to that all men aged between 16 and 60 were required to provide military service to the Crown if needed. Regular local 'wapinschaws' or musters were held to assess the ability and efficiency of such levies. Many men wishing to follow military careers went abroad, for example in the second half of the sixteenth century there were around 25,000 Highlanders in Ulster fighting with the native Irish against the Tudor English. At the same time there were thousands of Scottish soldiers of fortune in Flanders and the Low Countries supporting the Calvinist Dutch in their struggle against Spain during the Dutch Revolt. The Scots Brigade in Dutch Service functioned until 1782, though by that time it was no longer exclusively formed by native Scots. These troops were authorised by the Privy Council to be recruited in Scotland to serve 'in the defence of Goddis trew religioun agains the persecutiouris therof' and were forbidden to 'serve with Papistis agains Protestantis.'

Scottish soldiers, therefore, could be found in the Netherlands throughout the seventeenth century. Many were killed in action while some married and settled in Holland and Zeeland, as evidenced in civic and church records as well as the published register of the Scots Brigade. The great overseas trading companies, the Dutch East India Company and the Dutch West India Company, also employed some Scottish soldiers in their overseas possessions. In 1620 the Dutch sent 1,200 of their Scottish troops to help their Protestant allies in Bohemia. The Protestants of Bohemia had rejected the Catholic Hapsburg Holy Roman Emperor and by doing so began the Thirty Years War(1618 to 1648). Soon the King of Denmark-Norway, Christian IV sent military support to the Bohemians, including Mackay's Regiment, which had been raised in the northern Highlands.

Scandinavia and the Baltic lands had long established economic links with Scotland, which were strengthened with Denmark through the marriage of King James VI and Anne of Denmark in 1589. From the 1560s both Sweden and Denmark were permitted to recruit soldiers in Scotland. Mackay's Regiment was originally in the Service of Denmark-Norway but in 1629 it was transferred to Swedish Service. Gustav Adolf, King of Sweden, the Lion of the North, landed his army in Germany in 1630 to fight for the Protestant Cause. Gustavus Adolphus had been building his army since around 1620, and had a significant Scottish element, between 20,000 and 30,000 men. The Swedish Army fought throughout northern Europe, particularly in Germany, Poland, and Russia. In the aftermath of the Thirty Years War many Scots remained in foreign service or settled on the continent.

Since the medieval period Scottish soldiers could also be found in the service of France, for example during the One Hundred Years War between France and England. The seventeenth century saw Scots soldiers fighting for or against France. In 1627 King Charles I sent 2000 Scottish fighting men to aid the English in the defence of the Huguenot stronghold of La Rochelle, which was besieged by the French Army. Conversely, Scots Catholics could be found in French or Spanish armies of the period, such as those of Colonel Sir John Hepburn, or Lord George Gordon, Captain in Chief of Company of Men at Arms in the Service of King Louis XIII of France in 1625.

The Wars of the Three Kingdoms, 1639-1651 involved Scottish soldiers in action in Scotland, England, and Ireland. Many Scottish soldiers, with years of military experience, returned from Europe to form the backbone of the Covenanter Army that opposed Charles I. The religious policies of King Charles I led to the Bishops Wars of 1639-1640, when the monarch unsuccessfully attempted to invade Scotland, and the subsequent Scottish occupation of Newcastle, then the Irish Rising of 1641, followed by the English Civil War in 1642.

The Irish Rising, which was initiated by the native Irish but joined by the Catholic Old English of the Pale, turned into a Civil War that ended in 1653. As the Scottish settlers in Ulster were under attack, a Scots Army under General Monro was sent to defend the Scots settlers there between 1642 and 1644. In England, the Scots gave support to the Parliamentary Army in its struggle with the Royalists, notably at Marston Moor in 1644; however the execution of the king in 1649 was not approved by the Scots. In England, a Republic was declared while in Scotland Charles II was declared king. The king led a Scottish army south as far as Worcester where it was defeated by Oliver Cromwell's New Model Army in 1650. Many of the Scottish prisoners were sent to the American colonies as indentured servants. The following year Oliver Cromwell led an army north to subdue Scotland. He failed to break the defences around Edinburgh and retreated to the nearby seaport of Dunbar to return to England. The Scots Army pursued Cromwell, but, many of its most experienced soldiers were no longer among its ranks. (Many were purged by the kirk as being of dubious faith.) The Scots, now lacking experienced soldiers, attacked the battle-hardened Parliamentary Army on 3 September 1650 and were soundly defeated. Thousands of prisoners were taken, many of whom were banished to the American Plantations.

With the Restoration of the Stuart Monarchy in 1660, the king attempted to impose Episcopalianism on a generally Presbyterian population in Scotland. This resulted in the Covenanter Risings, mainly in the south west, which were opposed by the government troops led by Thomas Dalyell and William Drummond, who had just returned from Russian Service. As the rebels were mainly ill-armed peasants, they were no match for the king's men. Charles II died in 1685 and was succeeded by his brother James. James was a Roman Catholic, and his policies led to his flight into exile and his replacement as head of state by William and Mary in 1688.

The Jacobites were those who supported and fought for the return of the Stuarts to the thrones of England and Scotland from James II in 1688 until the death of Bonnie Prince Charlie in 1788. There were several Jacobite risings or rebellions in the British Isles during the late seventeenth century, notably in Ireland ending in the Battle of the Boyne in 1690, and in Scotland where the Battle of Killiecrankie was most significant. By the end of the seventeenth century the Scottish Military Establishment was working closely with its English counterpart. Scottish regiments would fight alongside English ones against common enemies, for example in the War of the League of Augsburg in the 1690s, which ended with the Treaty of Ryswick in 1697. Several of the Scots soldiers, formerly fighting in Flanders, were recruited by the Scottish Darien Company to defend its settlement on the Isthmus of Panama.

The political union of Scotland and England led to the birth of the British Army and soon Scottish soldiers were fighting under the Duke of Marlborough at the Battle of Blenheim in Bavaria. The Union of 1707 increasingly provided opportunities under the British Crown for Scottish soldiers as the Empire expanded, so the appeal of service in continental armies declined.

David Dobson, Dundee, Scotland, 2020.

REFERENCES

ANQ Aberdeen Notes and Queries, [series, Aberdeen]

APS Acts of the Parliaments of Scotland

BK Battle of Killiecrankie, [Warwick, 2018]

BPL Britain and Poland Lithuania, [Leiden 2008]

CA Regimental History, Covenanting Armies, [Edinburgh, 1990]

Cal.SP Col. Calendar of State Papers, Colonial

Cal.SP Ire. Calendar of State Papers, Ireland

Cal.SP Scot. Calendar of State Papers, Scotland

CBRD Charters & Writs of Dundee, [Dundee, 1880]

CF Chronicles of the Frasers, [Edinburgh, 1905]

CRD Church Records... Danzig

CFR Cockburn Family Records, [Edinburgh, 1913]

CMA Court Minutes of Albany, [Albany, 1926-1932]

DCW Dundee & the Civil Wars, [Dundee, 2007]

DSA The Scots Army, 1661-1668, [Edinburgh, 1909]

ETR Edinburgh Tolbooth Register

GAA Amsterdam Archives

GAR Rotterdam Archives

H Omitted Chapters from Hotten's, [Baltimore, 1983]

HG House of Gordon, [Aberdeen, 1907]

JSM Geschiche Der Koniglich Preussische See und Handelstadt Memel

KAS Krigsarkivet Stockholm

LLNV Lost Lives, New Voices, [Philadelphia, 2018]

MGIF Military Governors Imperial Frontiers, [Leiden 2003]

NRS National Records of Scotland

NS Northern Scotland, series, [Aberdeen]

NWI New World Immigrants, [Baltimore, 1979]

OB Historical Notices of Old Belfast,

RPCS Register of the Privy Council of Scotland, series

SCA Scottish Communities Abroad, [Leiden, 2005]

SCL Scottish Community in ... Lithuania, [Vilnius, 2019]

SGB Ships, Guns and Bibles 1350-1700, [East Linton 1700]

SHR Scottish Historical Review, series

SIG Scots in Germany, [Edinburgh, 1902]

SIS Scots in Sweden, [Stockholm, 1962]

SJC Selected Justiciary Cases, 1624-1650, [Edinburgh 1974]

SOP Scots in Old Poland, [Edinburgh, 1941]

SPAWI State Papers, America and the West Indies, series

SR Scots Armies of the English Civil Wars, [Oxford,1999]

SSA Scottish Soldier Abroad, 1247-1967, [Edinburgh, 1992]

STW Scotland and the Thirty Years War, [Leiden, 2001]

TFD The Triumph of Fraser's Dragoons, [Stroud, 2013]

TGSI Transactions of the Gaelic Society of Inverness, series

UStA University of St Andrews

VCS Virginia's Colonial Soldiers, [Baltimore, 2008]

ZA Zeeland Archives

SCOTTISH SOLDIERS IN EUROPE AND AMERICA, 1600-1700.

ABERCROMBIE, JOHN, a soldier under Colonel Edmond, married Geertruyd from Utrecht, Holland, there on 18 February 1606. [Utrecht Marriage Register]

ABERCROMBIE, JOHN, a prisoner in Edinburgh Tolbooth, was released to go to France under Lieutenant John McCulloch on 4 February 1676. [RPCS.IV.668]

ABERNETHY, ALEXANDER, a trooper, married Janneke Thomas from Vlissingen, [Flushing], in Utrecht, Holland, on 28 October 1617. [Utrecht Marriage Register]

ACHESON, JAMES, Quartermaster of Fraser's Dragoons, at the Battle of Marston Moor, Yorkshire, on 2 July 1644. 47]

ACHESON, PETER, a soldier under Lieutenant Colonel Balfour, married Mechtelt Gossens from Arnhem, Holland, in Gorinchem, Holland, on 2 March 1640. [Gorinchem Marriage Register]

ADAIR, ALEXANDER, Captain of the Earl of Lindsay's Regiment in Bangor, Ireland, in 1642 [TNA.SP.28.120]

ADAIR, Sir ROBERT, of Kinhilt, a Cavalry officer in 1643, in Ulster in 1646. [Cal.SPIre.]; fought at the Battle of Dunbar on 3 September 1650. [SR.37]

ADAM, JAMES, a prisoner of war who was captured at the Battle of Dunbar on 3 September 1650, transported via London to Boston on the Unity of Boston in November 1650, an indentured servant at Lynn Ironworks in 1650s, a member of the Scottish Charitable Society of Boston in 1657. [Suffolk Court Files.1226] [NEGHS][LLNV.246]

ADAMS, JOHN, a soldier under Captain Bruce, married Aeltien Dircks from Tiel, Gelderland, there on 18 December 1657. [Tiel Marriage Register]

ADAM, JOHN, from Ormidale, a soldier in Argyll's Rebellion was transported from Leith to Jamaica on 7 August 1685. [RPCS.2.329]

SCOTTISH SOLDIERS IN EUROPE AND AMERICA, 1600-1700.

ADAM, ROBERT, was admitted as a burgess of Stirling, having served in the burgh's company of soldiers, on 31 May 1648. [SBR]

ADAMSON, JAMES, a soldier from Edinburgh in Dutch Service, was bound aboard the Gent for the Dutch West Indies in 1638. [GAR.ONA.78.166]

AFFLECK, Lieutenant Colonel ANDREW, commander of a militia company in Barbados in 1679. [Hotten.2.148]

AGNEW, Lieutenant ANDREW, son of Sir Andrew Agnew in Wigtownshire, of Livingstone's Regiment of Dragoons at the Battle of Cromdale on 1 May 1690. [BK.177] [NRS.GD77.189]

AGNEW, NIVEN, a prisoner of war who was captured at the Battle of Dunbar on 3 September 1650, transported via London to Boston on the Unity of Boston in November 1650, settled in Kittery, Maine, in 1656, probate 16 September 1687, Maine. [LLNV.248]

AIKEN, JOHN, from Perth, a soldier under Captain Arians, married Tanneken Jans from Steken in Flanders, in Rotterdam on 1 November 1601. [Rotterdam Marriage Register]

AIKMAN, JAMES, Lieutenant of the Cameronian Regiment at the Siege of Dunkeld, Perhshire, on 21 August 1689. [BK.146]

AIKMAN, THOMAS, a Cadet of the Douglas Regiment in French Service in 1671. [NRS.NRAS.O.174]

AINEEL, NATHANIEL, from Newmiln in Perthshire, a soldier who was banished from Holland and Zeeland, in Leiden, Holland, in 1611. [Leiden Judicial Archives, vol.6, fo.234]

AIR, ALEXANDER, a soldier of Captain L'Amy's Company, married Joanna Tubbings in Hulst on 23 April 1659. [Scots Brigade Marriage Register]

AIR, ALEXANDER, Corporal of Captain Oliphant's Company of Militia in Leith, was admitted as a burgess of Edinburgh in 1669. [EBR]

AIR, GEORGE, a soldier of Captain Mowbray's Company, married Margriet Jans from Eindhoven, Brabant, on 9 July 1630. [Scots Brigade Marriage Register]

AIR, GILBERT, a soldier of Captain Balfour's Company, at muster in 1682. [Dalton's Scots Army, 1661-1688, fo.127]

AIR, PATRICK, of Nether Liff, Angus, a burgess of Dundee, Quartermaster of the Army of the Covenant, fought at the Battle of Marston Moor, Yorkshire, on 2 July 1644. [DCW][CA]

ALANSON, ALAN, from Bo'ness, West Lothian, a gunner's mate on the Zeeland warship Utrecht around 1665. [ZA.Rekennkamer.C.6994]

ALEXANDER, FERGUS, chaplain to Fraser's Dragoons in 1646. [TFD.47]

ALEXANDER, Dr JAMES, a militiaman in Captain Richard Vintner's Troop of Horse in Barbados in 1679. [Hotten.2/3.120]

ALEXANDER, JAMES, a prisoner in Edinburgh Tolbooth, was released to go to Holland as a soldier with Captain Sharp on 12 July 1689. [RPCS.XIII.585]

ALEXANDER, PETER, from Prestonpans, Midlothian, a gunner aboard the Dutch ship Neptunus on 1 May 1645. [ZA]

ALEXANDER, ROBERT of the Stafford County Horse Militia, Virginia, in 1701. [TNA.CO5.1312/2]

ALLAN, GAVIN, an officer of Mackay's Regiment, in Danish service in 1626, and in Swedish service by 1629. [TGSI.VIII.188]

ALLAN, JAMES, was admitted as a burgess of Stirling, having served in the burgh's company of soldiers, on 31 May 1648. [SBR]

SCOTTISH SOLDIERS IN EUROPE AND AMERICA, 1600-1700.

ALLARDYCE, ANDREW, a prisoner in Edinburgh Tolbooth, was released to go to Flanders as a soldier on 22 February 1621. [RPCS.XII.431]

ALLARDYCE, HENRY, a prisoner in Edinburgh Tolbooth, was released to go to Flanders as a soldier on 22 February 1621. [RPCS.XII.431]

ANDERSON, ALESTER, a prisoner of war who was captured at the Siege of Worcester on 2 September 1651, was transported via London to New England on the John and Sarah of London and landed in Boston on 13 February 1652. [Suffolk Deeds, 1/5-6]

ANDERSON, ALEXANDER, a Company Sergeant Major of Colonel Alexander Leslie's Company in Muscovite Service between 1630 and 1632. [STW.179]

ANDERSON, ANDREW, born 1587, a soldier who was granted a licence to travel to Zwolle, Overijssel, in 1614. [TNA.E157.2]

ANDERSON, ANDREW, a soldier who was granted a licence to travel to Amsterdam in 1631. [TNA.E157.15]

ANDERSON, ANDREW, from Kirkcaldy, Fife, a musketeer aboard the Dutch ship Vere in 1644. [ZA]

ANDERSON, ANDREW, born 1664, a labourer in Selkirk, Selkirkshire, a former soldier, emigrated as an indentured servant via London to Maryland on 5 August 1685. [CLRO/AIA.14/355]

ANDERSON, ARCHIBALD, a former prisoner of was employed at Lyn Ironworks in Massachusetts, died in 1661, probate 27 September 1662, Essex County Quarterly Files.7.38] [LLNV.248]

ANDERSON, DAVID, a prisoner of war who was captured at the Siege of Worcester on 2 September 1651, was transported via London to New England on the John and Sarah of London and landed in Boston on 13 February 1652. [Suffolk Deeds, 1/5-6]

ANDERSON, DAVID, a militiaman in Thornhill's Company in Barbados in 1679. [Hotten.2.151]

ANDERSON, DAVID, Lieutenant of New Kent County Militia, Virginia, in 1701. TNA.CO5.1312/2]

ANDERSON, JAMES, a militiaman in Lyne's Regiment of Foot in Barbados in 1679. [Hotten.2.99]

ANDERSON, Captain JOHN, in Kedainai, Vilnius, and Slutsk, Lithuania, between 1651 and 1706. [SCL.159]

ANDERSON, JOHN, a prisoner of war who was captured at the Siege of Worcester on 2 September 1651, was transported via London to New England on the John and Sarah of London and landed in Boston on 13 February 1652. [Suffolk Deeds, 1/5-6]

ANDERSON, JOHN, a soldier in Tidcomb's Militia in Barbados in 1679. [Hotten.2.133]

ANDERSON, JOHN, a soldier in Lewgar's Militia in Barbados in 1679. [Hotten.2.145]

ANDERSON, NINIAN, a former soldier in Edinburgh Castle, a letter dated 1693. [NRS.GD26.9.55]

ANDERSON, ROBERT, a weaver, who had gone as a soldier to aid in the relief of La Rochelle, France, in 1627, was admitted as a burgess of Glasgow in 1627. [GBR]

ANDERSON, THOMAS, a militiaman in Affleck's Company in Barbados in 1679. [Hotten.2.148]

ANDERSON, WILLIAM, a prisoner of war who was captured at the Siege of Worcester on 2 September 1651, was transported via London to New England on the John and Sarah of London and landed in Boston on 13 February 1652; a member of the Scots Charitable Society of Boston in 1657. [Suffolk Deeds, 1/5-6] [NEHGS]

ANNAN, ALEXANDER, Captain of Mackay's Regiment, in Danish service in 1626, and in Swedish service by 1629. [TGSI.VIII.186]; a Captain in Germany in the service of Gustavus Adolphus, around 1630. [SIG.282][SAA.120]

ANNAND, GILBERT, in Angus, of the Earl of Airlie's Militia in 1670. [NRS.GD16.53.39]

ANNAND, THOMAS, from Edinburgh, a gentleman of the King of France's Guard, a deed, 1664. [NRS.RD4.11.122]; testament, 28 June 1664, Comm. Edinburgh. [NRS]

ARBUTHNOTT, ARTHUR, a Lieutenant of Mackay's Regiment, in Danish Service in 1626, and in Swedish Service by 1629. [TGSI.VIII.187]

ARBUTHNOTT, ..., Lieutenant of the Angus Regiment at the Battle of Marston Moor, Yorkshire, on 2 July 1644. [DCW.78]

ARCHIBALD, Lieutenant JAMES, on the Eagle at Dunbarton in 1627 bound for Sir William Alexander's settlement in Nova Scotia. [Dunbarton Burgh Records]

ARCHIBALD, JOHN, born 1627, a prisoner of war who was captured at the Battle of Dunbar on 3 September 1650, transported via London to Boston on the Unity of Boston in November 1650, an indentured servant at Lynn Ironworks. [Suffolk Court Files .1226] [LLNV.246]

ARMISS, ..., a Captain of Mackay's Regiment, in Danish Service in 1626, and in Swedish service by 1629. [TGSI.VIII.186]; a Captain in Germany in the service of Gustavus Adolphus, ca.1630, wounded at Stralsund. [SIG.282]

ARMSTRONG, ISRAEL, a militiaman under Captain Robert Harrison in Barbados in 1679. [Hotten.2.103]

ARMSTRONG, JOHN, a militiaman under Captain Robert Harrison in Barbados in 1679. [Hotten.2.103]

ARMSTRONG, JOHN, a Lieutenant of the Earl of Donegal's Regiment of Foot in 1703. [IWD]

ARMSTRONG, SAMUEL, a militiaman under Captain Robert Harrison in Barbados in 1679. [Hotten.2.103]

ARMSTRONG, WILLIAM, a militiaman under Captain Robert Harrison in Barbados in 1679. [Hotten.2.103]

ARNOTT, Sir CHARLES, with 3 Troops of Cavalry, fought at the Battle of Dunbar on 3 September 1650. [SR.37]

ARNOT, WILLIAM, Lieutenant Colonel of Leven's Regiment at the Battle of Killiecrankie on 27 July 1689. [BK.95]

ARROT, WILLIAM, in Angus, of the Earl of Airlie's Militia in 1670. [NRS.GD16.53.39]

AUCHENLECK, ARCHIBALD, Captain of the Angus Regiment in 1644. [DCW.78]

AUCHENLECK, JAMES, in Angus, of the Earl of Airlie's Militia in 1670. [NRS.GD16.53.39]

AUCHMUTIE, THOMAS, a prisoner in Edinburgh Tolbooth, volunteered to go to Holland as a soldier under Captain Francis Scott on 27 January 1691. [RPCS.3/XVI.55]

AULD, Colonel ALEXANDER, was buried in Greyfriars, Edinburgh, on 17 December 1671.

AUSTINDIN, DAVID, Captain of the Scots Guards of France in the 1560s. [NRS.NRAS.0.143]

BAILLIE, DAVID, a Quartermaster of Fraser's Dragoons, in 1646. [TFD.47]

BAILLIE, JAMES, of Fraser's Dragoons in 1645. [TFD.220]

BAILLIE, JAMES, Captain of the Town Guard of Edinburgh in 1691. [NRS.RH15.49.2]; was buried at Greyfriars on 7 October 1698. [Greyfriars Graveyard, Edinburgh]

BAILLIE, JOHN, a Lieutenant of Colonel Buchan's Regiment in Flanders before 1697, emigrated via Leith on the *Rising Sun* to Darien in 1699, died there in February 1700. [APS.XIV.App.127]

BAILLIE, Colonel WILLIAM, in Germany in the service of Gustavus Adolphus, ca.1630. [SIG.282]; Lieutenant Colonel of the Angus Foot from 1644 to 1647 in the Army of the Covenant at the Battle of Marston Moor, Yorkshire, and the Siege of Newcastle in 1644. [CA.109]

BAILLIE, WILLIAM, of Hardington, Captain of Colonel Buchan's Regiment in Flanders, a marriage contract with Anna Johnston, 27 February 1697. [NRS.RH9.7.192]

BAILLIE, WILLIAM, from Blackbie, a soldier who died at Darien, testament, 1707, Comm. Edinburgh. [NRS]

BAIN, LACHLAN, a Lieutenant of the Scottish American Company, a deed, 1699, [NRS.RD4.85.637]; died on the voyage from Darien to Jamaica in 1700. [DD.325]

BAIRD, ANDREW, a Cornet, a Jacobite captured at the Battle of Cromdale, Strathspey, on 1 May 1690. [RPCS.XV.304]

BALFOUR, ALEXANDER, a soldier under Colonel Edmond, married Dirckgen Dircks from Winssum, Groningen, in Utrecht, Holland, on 8 February 1606. [Utrecht Marriage Register]

BALFOUR, BARTHOLD, Colonel of Balfour's Regiment at the Battle of Killiecrankie, Perthshire, was killed on 27 July 1689. [BK.95/207]

BALFOUR, DAVID, a Captain under Leslie in Germany, dead by 1636. [SAU.ms36220.682]

BALFOUR, Major HENRY, of a Scottish regiment in the Service of the King of France in 1688. [DSA.159]

BALFOUR, Captain HENRY, of Livingstone's Regiment of Dragoons at the Battle of Cromdale, Strathspey, on 1 May 1690. [BK.177]

BALFOUR, JOHN, son of Patrick Balfour in the Canongate, a prisoner in Canongate Tolbooth, was released to go to Germany as a soldier under Colonel Sinclair, in June 1628. [RPCS.II.333]

BALFOUR, JOHN, a lance corporal in Danish Service in 1628. [SAA.ii.110]

BALFOUR, THOMAS, a Corporal under Colonel Balfour, married Blancefloer Gedde from Denmark, in Utrecht, Holland, on 29 December 1633. [Utrecht Marriage Register]

BALFOUR, Lord, of Burleigh, General of the Artillery, fought at the Battle of Dunbar on 3 September 1650. [SR.37]

BALLENDINE, JAMES, Captain of the Lifeguard of Horse in Carrickfergus, Ireland, in 1642. [TNA.SP16.539.1/105]

BALLANTYNE, JAMES, Lieutenant of the Earl of Angus's Regiment of Foot [the Cameronian Regiment] at the Siege of Dunkeld on 21 August 1689. [BK.146], later in Flanders, a burgess of Ayr in 1692. [ABR]

BALLANTINE, Colonel W., in Germany in the service of Gustavus Adolphus, around 1630. [SIG.282]

BALLANTINE, Captain, of the Cameronian Regiment at the Siege of Dunkeld on 21 August 1689. [BK.146]

BANKE, JOHN, a prisoner of war who was captured at the Battle of Dunbar on 3 September 1650, transported via London to Boston on the Unity of Boston in November 1650, an indentured servant at Lynn Ironworks in the 1650s. [Suffolk Court Files.1226][LLNV.240]

BANNATYNE, Lieutenant Colonel Sir JAMES, of a Scottish regiment in France in 1641. [NRS.GD1.1120/7]

BANNERMAN, ALEXANDER, Captain of Lord Sinclair's Regiment, in Newry, Ireland, in 1642. [TNA.SP18.120]

BARBOUR, ..., a Lieutenant of Mackay's Regiment, in Danish service in 1626, and in Swedish service by 1629, was killed at Brandenburg. [TGSI.VIII.187]

BARBOUR, JOHN, a soldier in Edinburgh, was buried in Greyfriars, Edinburgh, on 5 February 1672.

BARCLAY, Lieutenant Colonel ALEXANDER, father of Anna Maria Margaretta, who was baptised in the Reformed Church of Peter and Paul in Danzig, [Gdansk], on 16 March 1638, also of son Alexander baptised there on 16 June 1639.

BARCLAY, ALEXANDER, Major of the Earl of Glencairn's Regiment, in Carrickfergus, Ireland, in 1642. [TNA.SP.18.120]

BARCLAY, Sir DAVID, routmaster of Collairnie's Troop of Horse, fought at the Battle of Philiphaugh on 13 September 1645. [CA.124]

BARCLAY, GEORGE, Major of Major General Robert Monro's Regiment, in Carrickfergus, Ireland, in1642. [TNA.SP.18.120]

BARCLAY, Colonel HARRY, of Barclay's Regiment of Horse in the Army of the Covenant Army of the Covenant in 1644, fought at the Battle of Philiphaugh on 13 September 1645. [CA.117]

BARCLAY, HENRY, a Corporal in Marpa's Company of Erskine's Regiment in Danish Service in 1628. [SAA.117]

BARCLAY, WALTER, in Forbes of Tullich's Company in Danish Service in 1628. [SAA.II.121]

BARRIE,......., an officer of Mackay's Regiment, in Danish service in 1626, and in Swedish service by 1629. [TGSI.VIII.188]

BARRY, JAMES, a prisoner of war who was captured at the Battle of Dunbar on 3 September 1650, transported via London to Boston on the Unity of Boston in November 1650, settled Kittery, Maine, in 1656. [LLNV248]

BARRY, JOHN, a prisoner in Canongate Tolbooth, was released to go to Holland as a soldier under Captain Robert Reid of Bonakettle, on 18 June 1690. [RPCS.XV.713]

BARTHOLEMEW, WILLIAM, a soldier from Linlithgow, West Lothian, who married Lizbeth Bowens from Oudewater, Holland in Schiedam, Holland, on 27 April 1635. [Schiedam Marriage Register]

BARTLES, JOHN, a soldier in Edinburgh Castle, was buried in Greyfriars, Edinburgh, on 12 January 1690.

BATES, WILLIAM, from Glasgow, a musketeer aboard the Dutch ship Sandenburch in 1645. [ZA]

BAUGHAN, Captain JAMES, at the King's camp, Londonderry, Ireland, in 1689. [NRS.GD26.9.217]

BAXTER, JAMES, from Kirkcaldy, Fife, a gunner aboard the Dutch ship Neptunus on 1 May 1645. [ZA]

BAYNE, JOHN, a militiaman under Captain Robert Harrison in Barbados in 1679. [Hotten.2.103]

BAYNE, WILLIAM, a prisoner of war who was captured at the Siege of Worcester on 2 September 1651, was transported via London to New England on the John and Sarah of London and landed in Boston on 13 February 1652. [Suffolk Deeds, 1/5-6]

BEALL, NINIAN, born in Largo, Fife, in 1625, a prisoner of war after the Siege of Worcester in 1650, was transported to Barbados, an indentured servant in Maryland by 1652, later a militia officer in Upper Marlboro, Commander of the Maryland Rangers in 1699, died at Fife's Largo in Maryland around 1717, [SPAWI.1698-1699]; probate 28 February 1717, Maryland.

BEALL, Captain THOMAS, of the Richmond County Militia, Virginia, in 1701. [TNA.CO5.1312/2]

BEAMES, WILLIAM, a prisoner of war who was captured at the Siege of Worcester on 2 September 1651, was transported via London to New England on the John and Sarah of London and landed in Boston on 13 February 1652. [Suffolk Deeds, 1/5-6]

BEATON, Lieutenant ANDREW, of Livingstone's Regiment of Dragoons at the Battle of Cromdale, Strathspey, on 1 May 1690. [BK.177]

BEATON, FRANCIS, a Jacobite soldier captured at the Battle of Cromdale, Strathspey, on 1 May 1690. [RPCS.XV.304]

BEATON, GEORGE, in Angus, of the Earl of Airlie's Militia in 1670. [NRS.GD16.53.39]

BEATON, JAMES, an archer of the Scots Guards of France in the 1560s. [NRS.NRAS.O.143]

BEATOUN, JOHN, a Captain of Mackay's Regiment, in Danish service in 1626, and in Swedish service by 1629. [TGSI.VIII.186] [SAA.120-121]; a Captain in Germany in the service of Gustavus Adolphus, around 1630, was wounded at Stralsund. [SIG.282]

BEATSON, DAVID, a Lieutenant of the Earl of Dunfermline's Regiment in France, a deed in 1676. [NRS.RD4.39.796]

BECK, ANDREW, a Quartermaster of Fraser's Dragoons, in 1646. [TFD.47]

BECK, RICHARD, a Quartermaster of Fraser's Dragoons, in 1646. [TFD.47]

BELL, ADAM, a Lieutenant of the Earl of Dunfermline's Regiment in France, a deed in 1676. [NRS.RD4.39.796]

BELL, ANDREW, Major of the Earl of Eglinton's Regiment, in Bangor, Ireland, in1642. [TNA.SP.18.120]

BELL, Captain JACK, a soldier from Linlithgow, West Lothian, married Margriete Engelbachs from Deventer, in Schiedam, Holland, on 28 November 1637. [Schiedam Marriage Register]

BELL, JOHN, a Lieutenant of the [Darien] Company of Scotland, a deed, 1699. [NRS.RD3.91.567]

BELL, PETER, a soldier from Duns, Berwickshire, married Jenneken Wouters from Hervert, in 's Hertogenbosch, on 16 May 1632. ['s Hertongenbosch Marriage Register]

BENNET, Major George, born 1615 in Musselburgh, Midlothian, a soldier in Lithuania between 1650 and 1677, led 200 dragoons at the Battle of Khotyn in 1673, and was naturalised and enobled in Poland in 1673. [STW.211] [SCL.46/159/254] [BPL]

BENNET, JAMES, from Kirkcaldy, Fife, a gunner aboard the Dutch ship Arms of Zeeland in 1644. [ZA]

BENNET, ROBERT, son of Reverend William Bennet in Edinburgh, a Lieutenant of the King's Army in Poland, a deed, 1672. [NRS.RD4.32.255]

BENNY, JAMES, a prisoner of war who was captured at the Siege of Worcester on 2 September 1651, was transported via London to New England on the John and Sarah of London and landed in Boston on 13 February 1652. [Suffolk Deeds, 1/5-6]

BENNY, JOHN, a prisoner of war who was captured at the Siege of Worcester on 2 September 1651, was transported via London to New England on the John and Sarah of London and landed in Boston on 13 February 1652. [Suffolk Deeds, 1/5-6][LLNV.248]

BEREERE [?], THOMAS, a prisoner of war who was captured at the Siege of Worcester on 2 September 1651, was transported via London to New England on the John and Sarah of London and landed in Boston on 13 February 1652. [Suffolk Deeds, 1/5-6]

BINNEY, ALEXANDER, a militiaman in Colonel Lyne's Company in Barbados in 1679. [Hotten.2.4]

BIRRELL, ROBERT, a wright, was admitted as a burgess of Stirling, having served in the burgh's company of soldiers, on 17 January 1644. [SBR]

BLACK, DANIEL, a prisoner of war who was captured at the Siege of Worcester on 2 September 1651, was transported via London to New England on the John and Sarah of London and landed in Boston on 13 February 1652. [Suffolk Deeds, 1/5-6]

BLACK, NEIL, from Melford, Glenbeg, Argyll, a soldier in Argyll's Rebellion, was transported via Leith to Jamaica in August 1685. [RPCS.11.329]

BIGGAR, Lieutenant JOHN, in County Down, Ireland, 1643. [SJC.III.793]

BLACKADDER, JOHN, born 1664, a Lieutenant of the Cameronian Regiment at the Siege of Dunkeld on 21 August 1689, died 1729. [BK.71/146] [NRS.GD77.189]; a Captain of Colonel James Ferguson's Regiment in Flanders, a deed, 1696. [NRS.RD2.79.838]

BLAIR, BRYCE, Captain of the Earl of Eglinton's Regiment, in Bangor, Ireland, in 1642. [TNA.SP.18.120]

BLAIR, JAMES, Captain of the Earl of Leven's Regiment, in Carrickfergus, Ireland, in 1642. [TNA.SP.18.120]

BLAIR, JOHN, was admitted as a burgess of Stirling, having served in the burgh's company of soldiers, on 17 January 1644. [SBR]

BLAIR, PATRICK, Major of the Earl of Balcarres' Regiment of Horse in the Army of the Covenant from 1646-1647. [CA.114]

BLAIR, ROBERT, Captain of the Earl of Leven's Regiment, in Carrickfergus, Ireland, in 1642. [TNA.SP.18.120]

BLAIR, Sir WILLIAM, Captain of Major General Robert Monro's Regiment, in Carrickfergus, Ireland, in 1642. [TNA.SP.18.120]

BOG, JOHN, an archer of the Scots Guards of France in the 1560s. [NRS.NRAS.0.143]

BOGUE, JAMES, from Edinburgh, a Corporal in Dutch Service in 1645, served in Brazil and Tobago. [GAA.NA1291.161]

BONAR, Colonel W., of Rossy in Fife, fought in Germany in the service of Gustavus Adolphus, around 1630, settled in the Duchy of Bremen, Military Governor of Stettin, [Szczecin], Prussia, in 1658, died in 1674. [SIG.283] [MGIF] [NRS.NRAS.2838, bundle 424]

BONAR, Lieutenant Colonel of the Angus Regiment at the Battle of Marston Moor, Yorkshire, on 2 July 1644. [DCW.78]

BORLAND, JOHN, a militiaman under Captain Robert Harrison in Barbados in 1679. [Hotten.2.141]

BORTHWICK, Lieutenant Colonel, in Ireland, 1648. [NRS.NRAS.332.M1186]

BORTHWICK, EDMUND, a Cornet of Fraser's Dragoons, in 1647 [TFD.47]

BORTHWICK, PETER, from Abercorn, West Lothian, married Jannitge Dircx Bled from Delft, Holland, in Schiedam, Holland, on 26 December 1637. [Schiedam Marriage Register]

BORTHWICK, THOMAS, Captain of the Earl of Lindsay's Regiment, in Bangor, Ireland, in 1642 [TNA.SP.18.120]

BORTHWICK, WILLIAM, Major of the Earl of Lindsay's Regiment, in Bangor, Ireland, in 1642. [TNA.SP.18.120]

BORTHWICK, WILLIAM, a Cornet of Fraser's Dragoons, at the Battle of Marston Moor, Yorkshire, on 2 July 1644 [TFD.47]

BOSWELL, Cornet GEORGE, of Livingstone's Regiment of Dragoons at the Battle of Cromdale, Strathspey, on 1 May 1690. [BK.177]

BOURK, TOBIAS, a prisoner in Canongate Tolbooth, was released to go to Holland as a soldier under Captain Robert Reid of Bonakettle, on 18 June 1690. [RPCS.XV.713]

BOUSTOUN, GILBERT, a Sergeant in Colonel Brewer's Regiment in Ireland, a deed, 1691. [NRS.RD4.69.871]

BOWIE, JOHN, a prisoner in Edinburgh Tolbooth, was released to go to Holland as a soldier under Captain William Douglas on 6 March 1683. [Edinburgh Tolbooth Records]

BOWMAN, GEORGE, born 1661, fought at the Siege of Londonderry, I 1689, and at the Battle of the Boyne on 1 July 1690, later in Flanders under the Duke of Marlborough........died in Stair, Ayrshire. In March 1768. [SM.30.165]

BOYD, GEORGE, a Captain of the Earl of Eglinton's Regiment, in Bangor, Ireland, in 1642. [TNA.SP.18.120]

BOYD, JAMES, Captain of Sir Charles Graham's Regiment in Dutch Service, father of Johanna Charlotta Boyd born 1694 in 's Hertenbosch, Brabant. [HS.XXVI.29]

BOYD, JOHN, Ensign of the Cameronian Regiment at the Siege of Dunkeld, Perthshire, on 21 August 1689. [BK.146]

BOYD, ROBERT, Captain of Sir Charles Graham's Regiment of Foot, in Flanders, a deed, 1696. [NRS.RD4.78.621]

BRABAND, ALEXANDER, a prisoner of war who was captured at the Battle of Dunbar on 3 September 1650, transported via London to Boston on the Unity of Boston in November 1650, an indentured servant at Lynn Ironworks in the 1650s. [Suffolk Court Files.1226][LLNV.246/262]

BRICE, Captain EDWARD, in Belfast, Ireland, in 1707. [NRS.GD109.2807]

BRISBANE, Captain WILLIAM, in Ireland, 1643. [NRS.NRAS.800.fr.3]; Captain of the Earl of Eglinton's Regiment, in Bangor, Ireland, in 1642. [TNA.SP.18.120]

BRICE, JAMES, Captain of the Earl of Eglinton's Regiment, in Bangor, Ireland, in 1642. [TNA.SP.18.120]

BROCK, ANDREW, from Glasgow, gunner's mate on the St Andrew from Leith on 14 July 1698 bound for Darien, testament, 1707, Comm. Edinburgh. [NRS]

BRODIE, JACK, a soldier under Colonel Brog, married Jannegie Cornelis from Utrecht, Holland, there on 27 September 1612. [Utrecht Marriage Register]

BROG, Sir WILLIAM, Colonel of a Scottish regiment in Flanders, a sasine, 1622. [NRS.RS31.IV.266]

BROUK, EDMOND, a prisoner in Canongate Tolbooth, was released to go to Holland as a soldier under Captain Robert Reid of Bonakettle, on 18 June 1690. [RPCS.XV.713]

BROUNFIELD, WILLIAM, an Ensign of Mackenzie's Company in Danish Service in the 1620s, [SAA.ii.124]; a Sergeant Major under Colonel Sir John Ruthven in Germany, a testament, 1637, Comm. Edinburgh. [NRS]

BROWN, GEORGE, of the Militia in Dundee in 1643. [DCW.13]

BROWN, Colonel JAMES, in Barbados, was created a knight baronet of Scotland on 17 February 1664. [RGS.XI.553]

BROWN, JOHN, a Scottish soldier serving under Colonel Brock, married Geertgen Jansdaughter of Leiden, Holland, there on 29 December 1606. [Leiden Marriage Register]

BROWN, JOHN, a Scottish soldier under Sir Henry Balfour, married Susanna Jans from Friesland in Aardenburg, Holland, on 26 April 1608. [Aardenburg Marriage Register]

BROWN, JOHN, a skinner, was admitted as a burgess of Stirling, having served in the burgh's company of soldiers, on 17 January 1644. [SBR]

BROWN, Sir JOHN, of Fordell, Fife, Colonel of Brown's Horse in 1643, of the Army of the Covenant, fought at the Battle of Annan Moor in 1645 and at the Battle of Dunbar on 3 September 1650. [SR.37][CA.118]

BROWN, JOHN, a prisoner of war who was captured at the Siege of Worcester on 2 September 1651, was transported via London to New England on the John and Sarah of London and landed in Boston on 13 February 1652. [Suffolk Deeds, 1/5-6]

BROWN, Major THOMAS, of a Scottish regiment in the Service of the King of France in 1688. [DSA.159]

BROWN, WALTER, from Musselburgh, Midlothian, a musketeer aboard the Dutch ship Vere in 1644. [ZA]

BROWN, Captain, a Jacobite captured at the Battle of Cromdale, Strathspey, on 1 May 1690. [RPCS.XV.304]

BROWNLEA, [BROUNELL], HENRY, a prisoner of war who was captured at the Siege of Worcester on 2 September 1651, was transported via London to New England on the <u>John and Sarah of London</u> and landed in Boston on 13 February 1652. [Suffolk Deeds, 1/5-6][LLNV.248]

BRUCE, ALEXANDER, in Angus, of the Earl of Airlie's Militia in 1670. [NRS.GD16.53.39]

BRUCE, Captain ANDREW, a Lieutenant of Graham's Troop in 1678, a Jacobite in 1678. [APS.app.xi.158]

BRUCE, JAMES, a soldier who married Elizabeth Bothwell from Edinburgh, in Utrecht, Holland, on 5 February 1643. [Utrecht Marriage Register]

BRUCE, JAMES, Captain of Leven's Regiment at the Battle of Killiecrankie, Perthshire, on 27 July 1689. [BK.96]

BRUCE, JOHN, of the Surrey County Horse Militia, Virginia, in 1701. [TNA.CO5.1312/2]

BRUCE, MICHAEL, a Captain of Fraser's Dragoons, at the Battle of Marston Moor, Yorkshire, on 2 July 1644. [TFD.47]

BRUCE, ROBERT, a Lieutenant of a Scottish Regiment in France, a deed, 1671. [NRS.RD2.31.406]

BRUCE, ROBERT, Major of Leven's Regiment at the Battle of Killiecrankie, Perthshire, was killed on 27 July 1689. [BK.95/207]

BRUCE, THOMAS, Captain of a Scottish regiment in France, a deed and a bond in 1675. [NRS.RD2.373/429]

BRUCE, WILLIAM, a Russian Army officer from 1647 to 1680. [SSA.56]

BRUCE, WILLIAM, Captain of Sir Mungo Campbell of Lawers' Regiment in Temple Patrick, Ireland, in 1642. [TNA.SP18.120]

BRUNTFIELD, WILLIAM, a Lieutenant of Mackay's Regiment, in Danish service in 1626, wounded at Stralsund in 1628, and in Swedish service by 1629, later a Major of Ruthven's Regiment. [TGSI.VIII.187][SAA.119]

BRUNTSFIELD, WILLIAM, a Captain of Mackay's Regiment, in Danish service in 1626, and in Swedish service by 1629, later a Major in Ruthven's Regiment. [TGSI.VIII.186]; a Colonel at Buxtehude, Germany, in the service of Gustavus Adolphus, ca.1630, was killed at Buxtehude. [SIG.282]

BRYDEN, ANDREW, Captain of Major General Robert Monro's Regiment, in Carrickfergus, Ireland, in 1642. [TNA.SP.18.120]

BUCHAN, Captain JAMES, a Jacobite captured at the Battle of Cromdale, Strathspey, on 1 May 1690. [RPCS.XV.304]

BUCHAN, JOHN, Major of Colonel Mackay's Regiment in Holland, a deed, 1687. [NRS.RD2.68.745]

BUCHAN, THOMAS, Captain of a Scottish Regiment in France, a deed, 1675. [NRS.RD2.40.429]; from Berwickshire, a Lieutenant Colonel of Colonel MacKay's Regiment in Holland, a sasine, 1687. [NRS.RS18.5.26]

BUCHANAN, DAVID, a prisoner of war who was captured at the Siege of Worcester on 2 September 1651, was transported via London to New England on the John and Sarah of London and landed in Boston on 13 February 1652. [Suffolk Deeds, 1/5-6]

BUCHANAN, Sir GEORGE, of Buchanan, an infantry officer who fought at the Battle of Dunbar on 3 September 1650. [SR.37]

BUCHANAN, JAMES, a wright, was admitted as a burgess of Stirling, having served in the burgh's company of soldiers, on 17 January 1644. [SBR]

BUCHANAN, JOHN, a prisoner of war who was captured at the Siege of Worcester on 2 September 1651, was transported via London to New England on the John and Sarah of London and landed in Boston on 13 February 1652. [Suffolk Deeds, 1/5-6]

BUCK, Captain THOMAS, a soldier in the Service of Lithuania in 1614. [SIP.35-37]

BUIE, [BOY], JOHN, [1], a prisoner of war who was captured at the Siege of Worcester on 2 September 1651, was transported via London to New England on the John and Sarah of London and landed in Boston on 13 February 1652. [Suffolk Deeds, 1/5-6]

BUIE, [BOY], JOHN, [2], a prisoner of war who was captured at the Siege of Worcester on 2 September 1651, was transported via London to New England on the John and Sarah of London and landed in Boston on 13 February 1652. [Suffolk Deeds, 1/5-6]

BUIE, [BOY], ROBERT, a prisoner of war who was captured at the Siege of Worcester on 2 September 1651, was transported via London to New England on the John and Sarah of London and landed in Boston on 13 February 1652. [Suffolk Deeds, 1/5-6]

BULLION, ……., a Captain of Mackay's Regiment, in Danish service in 1626, and in Swedish service by 1629. [TGSI.VIII.186]

BURGESS, ALEXANDER, a prisoner of war who was captured at the Battle of Dunbar on 3 September 1650, transported via London to Boston on the Unity of Boston in November 1650, an indentured servant at Lynn Ironworks in the 1650s. [Suffolk Court Files.1226] [LLNV.240]

BURGESS, Captain JOHN, of Grant's Regiment of Infantry at the Battle of Cromdale, Strathspey, on 1 May 1690. [BK.177]

BURN, WALTER, a Scottish soldier, married Jacquemijne van der Heijden of Leiden, Holland, there on 6 August 1618. [Leiden Marriage Register]

BURNET, J., a soldier of the 1st Company of Cockburn's Regiment in Swedish Service in 1609. [SIS.217]

BURNETT, JAMES, a Jacobite soldier captured at the Battle of Cromdale, Strathspey, on 1 May 1690. [RPCS.XV.304]

BURT, HENRY, Governor of Greifswald, Mecklenburg, in 1643. [MGIF]

BURT, JAMES, a soldier from Kirkcaldy, Fife, married Helena Moor from St Andrews, Fife, in Bergen-op-Zoom, Zeeland, in 1585. [Bergen-op-Zoom Marriage Register]

BUTCHART, ANDREW, Sergeant Captain of the Angus Regiment in 1644. [DCW.78]

BUTCHER, Captain WILLIAM, was sent to Scotland by Colonel James Douglas to recruit 300 men for service in France, in 1640. [NRS.GD109.1506]

CADDELL, ALEXANDER, a soldier of Thomas Mackenzie's Company in Danish Service, in 1628. [SAA.ii.124]

CADDELL, DANIEL, Sergeant of Major Whyte's company mustered in Glasgow in 1682. [DSA.128]

CALDER, Lieutenant, of the Cameronian Regiment at the Siege of Dunkeld, Perthshire, on 21 August 1689. [BK.146]

CALDWELL, JOHN, Captain of the Cameronian Regiment at the Siege of Dunkeld, Perthshire, on 21 August 1689. [BK.146]

CALDWELL, WILLIAM, a Sergeant of Colonel Buchan's Regiment in Flanders, dead by 1696. [NRS.CH2.751.8.135]

CALLENDAR, ALESTER, a prisoner of war who was captured at via London to New England on the John and Sarah of London and landed in Boston on 13 February 1652. [Suffolk Deeds, 1/5-6]

CALLENDAR, DAVID, a prisoner of war who was captured at the Siege of Worcester on 2 September 1651, was transported via London to New England on the John and Sarah of London and landed in Boston on 13 February 1652. [Suffolk Deeds, 1/5-6]

CALLENDAR, JAMES, a prisoner of war who was captured at the Siege of Worcester on 2 September 1651, was transported via London to New England on the John and Sarah of London and landed in Boston on 13 February 1652. [Suffolk Deeds, 1/5-6]

CALLENDAR, WILLIAM, son of Ludovic Callendar of Dorritur, a soldier in Flanders, a deed, 1695. [NRS.RD2.78.1170]

CAMERON, Sir EWAN, a Jacobite at the Battle of Killiecrankie, Perthshire, on 27 July 1689. [APS.IX.54]

CAMERON, EWAN, a prisoner in Canongate Tolbooth, released to go to Holland as a soldier under Captain Robert Reid of Bonakettle, on 8 June 1690. [RPCS.XV.713]

CAMERON, JOHN, a militiaman in Colonel Bayley's Regiment in Barbados in 1679. [Hotten.2.138]

CAMERON, JOHN, the younger, a Jacobite at the Battle of Killiecrankie, Perthshire, on 27 July 1689. [APS.IX.55]

CAMPBELL, ALEXANDER, a soldier of the 1st Company of Cockburn's Regiment in Swedish Service in 1609. [SIS.217]

CAMPBELL, Captain ALEXANDER, of Fonabb, Perthshire, a soldier at Darien in 1699. [NRS.GD406]

CAMPBELL, Lieutenant Colonel ALEXANDER, late of the Duke of Argyll's Regiment and of the Earl of Portmore's Regiment, later in Darien, 1699. [APS.XIV.174]

CAMPBELL, ARCHIBALD, Routmaster of Argyll's Life Guard of Horse in the Army of the Covenant in 1643. [CA.110]

CAMPBELL, ARCHIBALD, Captain of Sir Mungo Campbell of Lawers' Regiment at Temple Park, Ireland, in 1642. [TNA.SP18.120]

CAMPBELL, ARCHIBALD, Commander of Argyll's Life Guard of Foot in the Army of the Covenant in 1644. [CA.112]

CAMPBELL, Captain ARCHIBALD, in St John's, Barbados, in 1679. [Hotten.2.68]

CAMPBELL, ARTHUR, soldier under Captain Balfour, married Barbara Veylens from Antwerp, Flanders, in Leiden, Holland, on 25 August 1601. [Leiden Marriage Register]

CAMPBELL, COLIN, Captain of Sir Mungo Campbell of Lawers' Regiment at Temple Park, Ireland, in 1642. [TNA.SP18.120]

CAMPBELL, COLIN, Captain of the Marquis of Argyll' Regiment at Dunluce, Ireland, in 1642. [TNA.SP18.120]

CAMPBELL, Colonel COLIN, with 80 soldiers were sent to Little Cumbrae, Bute, on 28 April 1652. [NRS.GD3.9.4.17]

CAMPBELL, COLIN, son of Reverend Patrick Campbell in Kenmore, Perthshire, a soldier at Darien, died in Jamaica in 1699, testament, 1707, Comm. Edinburgh. [NRS]

CAMPBELL, DANIEL, a soldier of Kerr's Company at the Battle of Killiecrankie, Perthshire, on 27 July 1689, was captured by the Jacobites. [RPCS.XIV]

CAMPBELL, Captain Dhu, of the Cameronian Regiment at the Siege of Dunkeld, Perthshire, on 21 August 1689. [BK.146]

CAMPBELL, DOUGALL, a militiaman in Colonel Lyne's Regiment in Barbados in 1679. [Hotten.2.103]

CAMPBELL, DUNCAN, a soldier, was granted a pass to travel to the Low Countries in 1617. [TNA.E157.3]

CAMPBELL, Sir DUNCAN, of Auchenbreck, Lieutenant Colonel of the Marquis of Argyll' Regiment at Dunluce, Ireland, in 1642. [TNA.SP18.120]

CAMPBELL, DUNCAN, of Dunans, Captain of the Marquis of Argyll' Regiment at Dunluce, Ireland, in 1642. [TNA.SP18.120]

CAMPBELL, DUNCAN, of Inverliver, Captain of the Marquis of Argyll' Regiment at Dunluce, Ireland, in 1642. [TNA.SP18.120]

CAMPBELL, DUNCAN, formerly an Ensign of the Earl of Argyll's Regiment, died in Darien in 1699, testament, 1707, Comm. Edinburgh. [NRS]

CAMPBELL, GILBERT, a militiaman in Colonel Lyne's Regiment in Barbados in 1679. [Hotten.2.103]

CAMPBELL, HUGH, a militiaman in Colonel Bayley's Regiment in Barbados in 1680. [Hotten.2.35]

CAMPBELL, Sir JAMES, of Lawers, a Brigade commander, who fought at the Battle of Dunbar on 3 September 1650. [SR.37]

CAMPBELL, JAMES, a prisoner of war who was captured at the Siege of Worcester on 2 September 1651, was transported via London to New England on the John and Sarah of London and landed in Boston on 13 February 1652. [Suffolk Deeds, 1/5-6]

CAMPBELL, JAMES, a soldier from Aberdeen, married Aneka Ranckes, widow of Pieter Narne, [Peter Nairn?], in New Amsterdam in the New Netherlands, on 1 March 1659. [Dutch Reformed Church Register]

CAMPBELL, JAMES, a Captain of the Earl of Dunfermline's Regiment in France, a deed, 1675. [NRS.RD4.39.200]

CAMPBELL, JAMES, in Angus, of the Earl of Airlie's Militia in 1670. [NRS.GD16.53.39]

CAMPBELL, Captain JAMES, of Fordie, Commissary of the Train of Artillery in Scotland, 1686. [DSA.166]

CAMPBELL, JAMES, Ensign of the Cameronian Regiment at the Siege of Dunkeld, Perthshire, on 21 August 1689. [BK.146]

CAMPBELL, JAMES, a militiaman in Colonel Thornhill's Regiment in Barbados in 1680. [Hotten.2.148]

CAMPBELL, JOHN, a soldier in Spanish Service in Antwerp, Flanders, in 1588, husband of Margaret Burnet. [NRS.GD1.382.959]

CAMPBELL, JOHN, Captain of the Marquis of Argyll' Regiment at Ballycastle, Ireland, in 1642. [TNA.SP16.492.58]

CAMPBELL, JOHN, a prisoner of war who was captured at the Siege of Worcester on 2 September 1651, was transported via London to New England on the <u>John and Sarah of London</u> and landed in Boston on 13 February 1652. [Suffolk Deeds, 1/5-6]

CAMPBELL, Sir JOHN, late Commissary of the Scots Army in Ireland, 1651. [NRS.NRAS.258.2.16.1]

CAMPBELL, JOHN, a militiaman in Colonel Lyne's Regiment in Barbados in 1679. [Hotten.2.106]

CAMPBELL, JOHN, a militiaman in Colonel Bate's Regiment in Barbados in 1679. [Hotten.2.179]

CAMPBELL, JOHN, from Dunalter, Kintyre, Argyll, son of Walter Campbell, a soldier in Argyll's Rebellion, was transported via Leith to Jamaica in August 1685. [RPCS.11.329]

CAMPBELL, JOHN, from Auchenchrydie, Cowal, Argyll, son of Donald Campbell, a soldier in Argyll's Rebellion, was transported via Leith to Jamaica in August 1685. [RPCS.11.329]

CAMPBELL, JOHN, from Lochwoar in Lorne, Argyll, son of Robert Campbell, a soldier in Argyll's Rebellion, was transported via Leith to Jamaica in August 1685. [RPCS.11.136]

CAMPBELL, JOHN, from Carrisk, Lochfyneside, Argyll, a soldier in Argyll's Rebellion, was transported via Leith to Jamaica in July 1685. [RPCS.11.329]

CAMPBELL, JOHN, a Jacobite soldier captured at the Battle of Cromdale, Strathspey, on 1 May 1690. [RPCS.XV.304]

CAMPBELL, MATTHEW, Captain of the Marquis of Argyll' Regiment at Ballymoney, Ireland, in 1642. [TNA.SP16.492.58]

CAMPBELL, NEIL, a prisoner of war who was captured at the Siege of Worcester on 2 September 1651, was transported via London to New England on the John and Sarah of London and landed in Boston on 13 February 1652. [Suffolk Deeds, 1/5-6]

CAMPBELL, Lieutenant Colonel ROBERT, in Bellicastle, Ireland, a deed, 1649. [NRS.RD4.584.]

CAMPBELL, ROBERT, a militiaman in Colonel Thornhill's Regiment in Barbados in 1679. [Hotten.2.156]

CAMPBELL, Captain ROY, of the Cameronian Regiment at the Siege of Dunkeld on 21 August 1689. [BK.146]

CAMPBELL, WILLIAM, a soldier, married Lijntgen Plattevoets from Poperinge in Flanders, in Leiden, Holland, on 21 November 1604. [Leiden Marriage Register]

CAMPBELL, Captain WILLIAM, in Danish Service in 1628. [SAA.ii.111]

CAMPBELL, WILLIAM, Major of the Marquis of Argyll' Regiment at Ballycastle, Ireland, in 1642. [TNA.SP16.492.58]

CAMPBELL, WILLIAM, Ensign of the Cameronian Regiment at the Siege of Dunkeld in August 1689. [BK.146]

CAMPBELL, WILLIAM, a soldier who died at Darien in 1699, testament, 1707, Comm. Edinburgh. [NRS]

CAMPBELL, Lieutenant, in Killeleagh, Ireland, 1653. [OB.83]

CAMPBELL, ..., a Lieutenant of Mackay's Regiment at the Battle of Killiecrankie, Perthshire, on 27 July 1689. [BK.96]

CANCANEN, BRIAN, a prisoner in Canongate Tolbooth, was released to go to Holland as a soldier under Captain Robert Reid of Bonakettle, on 18 June 1690. [RPCS.XV.713]

CANT, DAVID, a trooper in Lyck, Eastern Prussia, in 1682. [SIG.263]

CANT, Lieutenant John, died in Danzig, [Gdansk], buried in St Elisabeth's there in 1652. [CRD]

CARMICHAEL, ARCHIBALD, a prisoner in Dundee Tolbooth, was released to go to Holland as a soldier under Lieutenant Alexander Murray of Skirling, on 13 September 1689. [RPCS.XIV.619]

CARMICHAEL, JOHN, a soldier from Dundee, married Anneken Jans in Heusden, Flanders, on 18 May 1636. [Heusden Marriage Register]

CARMICHAEL, JOHN, a prisoner of war who was captured at the Siege of Worcester on 2 September 1651, was transported via London to New England on the <u>John and Sarah of London</u> and landed in Boston on 13 February 1652. [Suffolk Deeds, 1/5-6]

CARMICHAEL, THOMAS, in Lanark, sometime Adjutant of Lord Carmichael's Regiment of Dragoons, testament, 12 December 1709, Comm. Lanark. [NRS]

CARMICHAEL, WILLIAM, Lieutenant Colonel of Clydesdale's Foot, in 1643, fought at the Siege of Newcastle, and at the Battle of Marston Moor, Yorkshire, in 1644. [CA.122]

CARMICHAEL, WILLIAM, a prisoner of war who was captured at the Siege of Worcester on 2 September 1651, was transported via London to New England on the <u>John and Sarah of London</u> and landed in Boston on 13 February 1652. [Suffolk Deeds, 1/5-6]

CARMICHAEL, WILLIAM, Captain of the Earl of Leven' Regiment at Carrickfergus, Ireland, in 1642. [TNA.SP18.120]

CARMICHAEL, ..., a Captain of Mackay's Regiment in Danish Service in 1626, and in Swedish Service in 1629, was killed at Bredenburg. [TGSI.VIII.186]

CARMICHAEL, General, in Russian Service, Governor of Pskov, Russia, in 1570. [SSA.47]

CARNEGIE, Lord JAMES, Colonel of the Angus Regiment, was captured at the Battle of Preston, Lancashire, on 18 August 1648. [DCW.78]

CARNEGIE, JOHN, Earl of Southesk, commander of the Angus Regiment in 1644. [DCW.78]

CARR, Lieutenant ANDREW, in Lord Clanboyes quarter, Ireland, 1653. [OB.83]

CARR, Colonel GILBERT, with 2 Troops of Cavalry, fought at the Battle of Dunbar on 3 September 1650. [SR.37]

CARR, MALCOLM, a militiaman in Colonel Lyne's Regiment in Barbados in 1679. [Hotten.2.101]

CARR, ROBERT, a soldier under Captain Nesbit, married Anna Theunis, a widow from Amsterdam, in Haarlem, Holland, on 15 February 1594. [Haarlem Marriage Register]

CARRELL, JOHN, a prisoner in Canongate Tolbooth, was released to go to Holland as a soldier under Captain Robert Reid of Bonakettle, on 18 June 1690. [RPCS.XV.713]

CARSTAIRS, Major JAMES, served in the Radziwill Militia in Lithuania between 1651 and 1661. [SCL.159]

CARSTAIRS, ..., Ensign of the Royal Scots Guards of France in 1663. [NRS.GD29.42]

CARTER, NEIL, a prisoner of war who was captured at the Siege of Worcester on 2 September 1651, was transported via London to New England on the <u>John and Sarah of London</u> and landed in Boston on 13 February 1652. [Suffolk Deeds, 1/5-6]

CARVER, WILLIAM, from Dumfries, a soldier of Captain Buntin's Company, married Anneken Stoffel Steenhouwen, in Breda, Brabant, on 20 March 1598. [Breda Marriage Register]

CASWICK, WALTER, a prisoner in Canongate Tolbooth, was released to go to Holland as a soldier under Captain Robert Reid of Bonakettle, on 18 June 1690. [RPCS.XV.713]

CATHCART, ALLAN, a soldier who died at Darien in 1699, testament, 1707, Comm. Edinburgh. [NRS]

CATHCART, WILLIAM, Lieutenant of the Cameronian Regiment at the Siege of Dunkeld on 21 August 1689. [BK.146]

CAVILLE, Cornet, of Livingstone's Regiment of Dragoons at the Battle of Cromdale, Strathspey, on 1 May 1690. [BK.177]

CHAMBERS, Captain JAMES, was naturalised and enobled in Poland in 1673. [STW.211][BPL]

CHAMBERS, General JOHN, Commander of the Semionovsky Guards, in Russian Service, captured Narva, Estonia, in 1704. [SSA.55]

CHAMBERS, Lieutenant, of Balfour's Regiment, was killed at the Battle of Killiecrankie, Perthshire, on 27 July 1689. [BK.207]

CHARTERS, Captain ROBERT, a Jacobite at the Battle of Killiecrankie, Perthshire, on 27 July 1689. [APS.IX.55]

CHARTERS, WILLIAM, Captain of the Foot Guards in 1685, a Jacobite soldier in 1689. [APS.acc.ix.56]

CHEAP, WILLIAM, Ensign of the Earl of Orkney's Regiment in Holland, a decreet, 1708. [StAU.CRP.II.13.88]

CHEYNE, JOHN, a prisoner of war who was captured at the Siege of Worcester on 2 September 1651, was transported via London to New England on the John and Sarah of London and landed in Boston on 13 February 1652. [Suffolk Deeds, 1/5-6]

CHIRNSIDE, DAVID, Captain of Lord Sinclair' Regiment at Newry, Ireland, in 1642. [TNA.SP18.120]

CHISHOLM, JAMES, surgeon to the Army in Flanders, a deed, 1696. [NRS.RD4.79.1319]

CHRISTISON, ALEXANDER, from Dysart, Fife, a gunner on the <u>Lion of Zeeland</u> in 1631. [ZA]

CHRISTOWAL, EDWARD, a soldier from Glasgow, married Catelincken de Clerck near Middelburg, Zeeland, on 14 February 1615. [Arnemuiden, Zeeland, Marriage Register]

CLAPPERTON, SAMUEL SPENCE, born 1576 in Coldstream, Berwickshire, son of Reverend John Clapperton and his wife Joanna Spence, Colonel of Horse under Gustavus Adolphus, late Governor of Finland, died in Womar in 1622. [F.2.40]

CLARK, ALEXANDER, a soldier, father of John who was baptised in Lobenicht, Prussia, on 9 March 1636.

CLARK, JOHN, a prisoner of war who was captured at the Battle of Dunbar on 3 September 1650, transported via London to Boston on the <u>Unity of Boston</u> in November 1650, an indentured servant at Lynn Ironworks in the 1650s. [Suffolk Court Files.1226]; a member of the Scots Charitable Society of Boston in 1657. [NEHGS][LLNV.240/263]

CLERK, JOHN, a Captain of Balfour's Regiment, who was killed at the Battle of Killiecrankie, Perthshire, on 27 August 1689. [BK.207]

CLARK, WILLIAM, a merchant in Edinburgh, later Lieutenant of a Scottish regiment in France, papers from 1633 to 1647. [NRS.GD18.2278]

CLARKE, WILLIAM, Lieutenant of the Cameronian Regiment at the Siege of Dunkeld, Perthshire, in August 1689. [BK.146]

CLEGHORN, JAMES, a prisoner of war who was transported to New England around 1650 an indentured servant who settled at Martha's Graveyard. [NWI.I.159][LLNV.249]

CLEGHORN, JOHN, Ensign of the Cameronian Regiment at the Siege of Dunkeld, Perthshire, on 21 August 1689. [BK.146]

CLELLAND, JOHN, of Faskin, Quartermaster and Cornet of the King's Regiment of Horse, a Jacobite at the Battle of Killiecrankie, Perthshire, on 27 July 1689. [APS.IX.55]

CLELAND, WILLIAM, a Covenanter at the Battles of Drumclog on 1 June 1679, and Bothwell Bridge, Lanarkshire, on 22 June 1679, a soldier in Argyll's Rebellion in 1685, Lieutenant Colonel of the Earl Angus's Regiment, [the Cameronians], at the Battle of Killiecrankie, Perthshire, on 27 July 1689, was killed at the Siege of Dunkeld on 21 August 1689. [Dunkeld Cathedral gravestone] [CalSPDom.1689-1690,184]

CLELAND, Colonel WILLIAM, in Barbados in 1699, [SPAWI.1699.53]; probate 1719 Barbados.

CLERK, A., in Angus, of the Earl of Airlie's Militia in 1670. [NRS.GD16.53.39]

CLERK, RICHARD, born in Angus in 1604, a Vice Admiral under Gustavus Dolphus, King of Sweden. [ANQ.4.320] [SHR.IX.269]

CLERK, WILLIAM, Captain of a Scottish regiment bound for Sweden in 1607. [SHR.IX.268]

CLOUSTON, WILLIAM, a prisoner of war who was captured at the Siege of Worcester on 2 September 1651, was transported via London to New England on the John and Sarah of London and landed in Boston on 13 February 1652. [Suffolk Deeds, 1/5-6]

COATS, SAMUEL, a soldier of Robert Schogens' Company, married Marytgen Henricxdaughter of Leiden, Holland, there on 21 January 1604. [Leiden Marriage Register]

COBBAN, WILLIAM, Quartermaster of the Angus Regiment at the Battle of Marston Moor, Yorkshire, on 2 July 1644. [DCW.78]

COCHRANE, Lieutenant ARCHIBALD, in Antigua in 1678. [SPAWI.1678.741]

COCHRANE, BRYCE, Captain of the Earl of Glencairn's Regiment at Carrickfergus, Ireland, in 1642. [TNA.SP18.120]

COCHRANE, ELIAZER, a militiaman in Colonel Standfast's Regiment in Barbados in 1679. [Hotten.2.58]

COCHRANE, Lieutenant Colonel H., in Antrim, Ireland, in 1645. [SP.Ire.260/137]

COCHRANE, Lieutenant Colonel HEW, of Belican, County Down, Ireland, a deed, 1668. [NRS.RD2.21.678]

COCHRANE, Colonel Sir JOHN, born 1604, Ambassador to Poland, in Danzig, [Gdansk], a letter dated 1649. [NRS.GD220.3.191]

COCHRANE, WILLIAM, a soldier from Glasgow, married Jakelijne van Camme from Bomene, in Arnemuiden, Zeeland, on 9 March 1614. [Arnemuiden Marriage Register]

COCHRANE, WILLIAM, Major of Robert Home of the Heugh's' Regiment at Carrickfergus, Ireland, in 1642. [TNA.SP18.120]

COCKBURN, JOHN, a soldier from Jedburgh, Roxburghshire, married Anneken Hermans in Heusden, Flanders, on 22 April 1633. [Heusden Marriage Register]

COCKBURN, JOHN, Routmaster of the College of Justice Horse Troop, at the Siege of Newark in 1644. [CA.127]

COCKBURN, SAMUEL, born around 1574, a Captain of Foot in Swedish Service in Livonia in 1606, fought in Russia in 1610, a Major General of the Swedish Army, settled in Finland from 1616 to 1621, wounded and died near Riga, Latvia, in December 1621. [SIS.30][SNQ.IX.3.215][CFR]

COLBERT, WALTER, a Scottish soldier, bound for the Dutch West Indies aboard the De Witte Swaen in 1638. [GAR.ONA.293.117.139]

COLQUHOUN, JOHN, a prisoner of war who was captured at the Siege of Worcester on 2 September 1651, was transported via London to New England on the John and Sarah of London and landed in Boston on 13 February 1652. [Suffolk Deeds, 1/5-6]

COLT, JAMES, a Lieutenant of Ramsay's Regiment at the Battle of Killiecrankie, Perthshire, on 27 July 1689, was captured by the Jacobites. [BK.207]

COLTART, DAVID, Lieutenant Colonel of Mackay's Regiment at the Battle of Killiecrankie, Perthshire, on 27 July 1689. [BK.95]

COLZIER, Captain, in Dutch Service in 1665. [JCP.I.136]

CONNELL, JOHN, a prisoner of war who was captured at the Siege of Worcester on 2 September 1651, was transported via London to New England on the John and Sarah of London and landed in Boston on 13 February 1652. [Suffolk Deeds, 1/5-6]

CONSTABLE, W., a soldier of the 2nd Company of Cockburn's Regiment in Swedish Service in 1609. [SIS.217]

COOPER, ALEXANDER, a prisoner of war who was captured at the Battle of Dunbar on 3 September 1650, transported via London to Boston on the Unity of Boston in November 1650, settled in Berwick, Kittery, Maine, in 1656, died on 11 February 1684, probate, 28 February 1684, Maine. [LLNV.249/264]

COOPER, ISAAC, a servant of Craigie Wallace, a prisoner in Edinburgh Tolbooth, sent to Holland as a soldier in 1689. [RPCS.13.573]

CORBET, Captain WALTER, Governor of Blair Castle, Perthshire, papers 1690. [NRS.E95.13]

CORCORAN, WILLIAM, a militiaman in Colonel Colleton's Regiment in Barbados in 1680. [Hotten.2.127]

CORFOD, ANDREW, a prisoner in Edinburgh Tolbooth, sent to Holland as a soldier in 1689. [RPCS.XVI.55]

CORRIE, ALEXANDER, a Sergeant of Captain Bontein's Company, married Gerrbrech Gerrits from Haarlem, Holland, there on 14 December 1597. [Haarlem Marriage Register]

COUPAR, Sir JAMES, late Admiral of the Dutch East India Fleet around 1689. [NRS.GD26.Sec.7.275]

COUTTS, GEORGE, a Captain in Dutch Service in 1665. [JCP.I.136]

COUTTS, ..., a Lieutenant Colonel in Dutch Service in 1665. [JCP.I.136]

COWAN, JOHN, a prisoner of war who was captured at the Siege of Worcester on 2 September 1651, was transported via London to New England on the <u>John and Sarah of London</u> and landed in Boston on 13 February 1652. [Suffolk Deeds, 1/5-6]

COWE, ALESTER, a prisoner of war who was captured at the Siege of Worcester on 2 September 1651, was transported via London to New England on the <u>John and Sarah of London</u> and landed in Boston on 13 February 1652. [Suffolk Deeds, 1/5-6]

COWE, WILLIAM, from Prestonpans, Midlothian, a musketeer on board the Dutch ship <u>Sandenburch</u> in 1645. [ZA]

CRAFFORD, Major JAMES, in Ballyniskrean, County Londonderry, Ireland, in 1659. [C]

CRAIG, JAMES, a thief from Paisley, Renfrewshire, a prisoner who was released to go to Holland as a soldier under Captain Thomas Hamilton on 1 April 1684. [RPCS.8.694]

CRAIG, JOHN, a prisoner of war who was captured at the Siege of Worcester on 2 September 1651, was transported via London to New England on the <u>John and Sarah of London</u> and landed in Boston on 13 February 1652. [Suffolk Deeds, 1/5-6]

CRAIG, Colonel THOMAS, of Riccarton, with a Regiment of Horse in Leven's Army of 1643; with 2 Troops of Cavalry, fought at the Battle of Dunbar on 3 September 1650.

CRAIG, WILLIAM, a thief from Paisley, Renfrewshire, a prisoner who was released to go to Holland as a soldier under Captain Thomas Hamilton on 1 April 1684. [RPCS.VIII.694]

CRAIG, WILLIAM, a militiaman in Colonel Bate's Regiment in Barbados in 1679. [Hotten.2.181]

CRAIGEN, JOHN, a prisoner of war who was captured at the Siege of Worcester on 2 September 1651, was transported via London to New England on the <u>John and Sarah of London</u> and landed in Boston on 13 February 1652. [Suffolk Deeds, 1/5-6]

CRAMOND, WILLIAM, Captain of Colonel George Hamilton's Regiment of Foot, was admitted as a burgess of Ayr in 1699. [ABR]

CRANSTON, JAMES, Lieutenant of the Cameronian Regiment at the Siege of Dunkeld in August 1689. [BK.146]

CRANSTON, JAMES, Captain of Colonel James Ferguson's Regiment in Flanders, a deed, 1696. [NRS.RD2.79.838]

CRANSTON, JOHN, a servant to Captain Charters, a prisoner in Edinburgh Tolbooth who was released to go to Holland as a soldier in 1689. [RPCS.13.573]

CRANSTOUN, WILLIAM, Colonel of Cranstoun's Foot in 1644, at the Siege of Newcastle in 1644. [CA.128]

CRANSTOUN, Captain, fought at the Battle of Hochstadt, Germany, in 1704. [NRS.GD44.14.4.6]

CRAWFORD ALEXANDER, a soldier Quartermaster to the Scottish garrison at Gluckstadt in 1627-1628, via Denmark and Sweden to Moscow in 1628, later in Novgorod, Russia. [SSA.49][SAA.II.111]

CRAWFORD, Quartermaster ARCHIBALD, in Carrickfergus, Ireland, 1653. [OB83]

CRAWFORD, DAVID, a soldier of Captain James Douglas's Company in Breda, Brabant, having been found guilty of mutiny was sentenced to death on 2 July 1691. [NRS.E99.41.15]

CRAWFORD-LINDSAY, GEORGE Earl of, a General under Gustavus Adolphus in Germany, 1630. [SIG.282]

CRAWFORD, HUGH, Major of Argyll's Regiment in the Army of the Covenant in 1643. [CA.110]

CRAWFORD, HENRY, a soldier in Colonel Alexander Leslie's Company in Muscovite Service from 1630 to 1632. [STW.179]

CRAWFORD, JAMES, a Jacobite at the Battle of Killiecrankie, Perthshire, on 27 July 1689. [APS.IX.55]

CRAWFORD, JOCK, a Corporal in Colonel Alexander Leslie's Company in Muscovite Service from 1630 to 1632. [STW.179]

CRAWFORD, JOHN, a prisoner in Edinburgh Tolbooth, was released to go to Germany as a soldier under Colonel Sinclair in June 1628. [RPCS.II.333]

CRAWFORD, JOHN, Captain of the Earl of Glencairn's Regiment at Carrickfergus, Ireland, in 1642. [TNA.SP18.120]

CRAWFORD, Lieutenant JOHN, probate, 1661, Derry.

CRAWFORD, JOHN, from Otter, Argyll, a soldier in Argyll's Rebellion, a prisoner in Edinburgh, was transported via Leith to Jamaica on 12 December 1685. [RPCS.11.136][ETR.373]

CRAWFORD, JOHN, of the Stafford County Horse Militia, Virginia, in 1701. [TNA.CO5.1312/2]

CRAWFORD, Major General LAURENCE, Routemaster of Crawford's Troop of Horse in 1645, was killed at the Siege of Hereford in September 1645. [CA.128]

CRAWFORD, MALCOLM, Captain of the Earl of Glencairn's Regiment at Carrickfergus, Ireland, in 1642. [TNA.SP18.120]

CRAWFORD, PATRICK, a Scottish army officer sent to Ulster in 1608, Provost of Strabane, Ireland, in 1613, killed in 1614. [SBT.30]

CRAWFORD, ROBERT, a soldier of the Surry County Militia, Virginia, in 1701. [TNA.CO5.1312/2]

CRAWFORD, THOMAS, a militiaman in Colonel Stanfast's Regiment in Barbados in 1679. [Hotten.2.157]

CRAWFORD, WILLIAM, a Lieutenant of Captain Vintner's Troop of Horse Militia in Barbados in 1679. [Hotten.2.5/205]

CRAWFORD, WILLIAM, Sergeant of the Militia of Dundee in 1643. [DCW.13]

CRAWFORD, WILLIAM, of Ardmillan, a Jacobite at the Battle of Killiecrankie, Perthshire, on 27 July 1689. [APS.IX.55]

CRAWFORD, Lieutenant Colonel WILLIAM, of Fraser's Dragoons, in 1643, fought and was captured at the Battle of Dunbar in 1650.

CRICHTON, Cornet DAVID, of Livingstone's Regiment of Dragoons at the Battle of Cromdale, Strathspey, on 1 May 1690. [BK.177]

CRICHTON, GEORGE, a Lieutenant in Danish Service in 1628. [GAA.119]

CRICHTON, LEWIS, Viscount of Fendraught, Lieutenant Colonel of the Foot Guards, a Jacobite soldier in 1689. [APS.acc.ix.56]

CRICHTON, ROBERT, Ensign of the Cameronian Regiment at the Siege of Dunkeld, Perthshire, on 21 August 1689. [BK.146]

CRICHTON, WILLIAM, a soldier, who was banished from Leiden, Holland, for smuggling beer, on 21 September 1618. [Leiden Court Records.8.231]

CRICHTON, Captain WILLIAM, son of Reverend John Crichton in Dublin, Ireland, deeds, 1676, 1686. [NRS.RD3.41.524; RD4.59.592]

CROCKFORD, JAMES, a prisoner of war who was captured at the Siege of Worcester on 2 September 1651, was transported via London to New England on the John and Sarah of London and landed in Boston on 13 February 1652. [Suffolk Deeds, 1/5-6]

CROMB, JOHN, a prisoner of war who was captured at the Siege of Worcester on 2 September 1651, was transported via London to New England on the John and Sarah of London and landed in Boston on 13 February 1652. [Suffolk Deeds, 1/5-6]

CROOK, ALEXANDER. Colonel of a Regiment of Horse in 1643.

CROOKS, JAMES, from Garturk, a soldier who died at Darien in 1699, testament, 1707, Comm. Edinburgh. [NRS]

CROSSHONE, [?], PATRICK, a prisoner of war who was captured at the Siege of Worcester on 2 September 1651, was transported via London to New England on the John and Sarah of London and landed in Boston on 13 February 1652. [Suffolk Deeds, 1/5-6]

CUMINE, WILLIAM, a weaver, a thief, possibly from Paisley, Renfrewshire, a prisoner who was released to go to Holland as a soldier under Captain Thomas Hamilton on 1 April 1684. [RPCS.8.694]

CUMMING, ROBERT, from Dundee, a musketeer aboard the Dutch ship Vere in 1644. [ZA]

CUMMING, THOMAS, a militiaman in Colonel Bayley's Regiment in Barbados in 1679. [Hotten.2.143]

CUMMINS, ROBERT, a militiaman in Barbados in 1679. [Hotten.2.165]

CUNNINGHAM, A., a 'fourier' [assistant Ensign] of Cockburn's Regiment in Swedish Service in 1609. [SIS.216]

CUNNINGHAM, ADAM, a Lieutenant in the German Army, bound for Germany in September 1662. [RGS.XI.318]

CUNNINGHAM, ADAM, formerly in Carsegoe, a Captain in the service of the King of France, a sasine, 13 December 1677. [NRS.RS.Caithness.i.40]

CUNNINGHAM, ALBERT, a Corporal in Marpa's Company of Erskine's Regiment in Danish Service in 1628. [SAA.117]

CUNNINGHAM, ALEXANDER, a Captain of Dunbarton's Regiment, was admitted as a burgess of Dundee in 1585. [DBR]

CUNNINGHAM, ALEXANDER, Captain of the Earl of Glencairn's Regiment, in Carrickfergus, Ireland, in 1642. [TNA.SP18.120]

CUNNINGHAM, ALEXANDER, a Captain of Militia in Barbados in 1679. [Hotten.2.106]

CUNNINGHAM, DAVID, a prisoner in Edinburgh Tolbooth who was released to go to Holland as a soldier under Captain Cunningham on 14 April 1682. [ETR]

CUNNINGHAM, DAVID, a prisoner in Edinburgh Tolbooth who was released to go to Holland as a soldier under Captain James Douglas on 14 November 1682. [ETR]

CUNNINGHAM, FERDINAND, Captain of Balfour's Regiment at the Battle of Killiecrankie, Perthshire, on 27 July 1689. [BK.95]

CUNNINGHAM, Major HENRY, of a Scottish regiment in the Service of the King of France in 1688. [DSA.159]

CUNNINGHAM, Lieutenant Colonel JAMES, of the Earl of Glencairn's Foot, at the Siege of Newcastle in 1644, and the Battle of Kilsyth in 1645. [CA.143]

CUNNINGHAM, Major JAMES, of Aiket, returned to Edinburgh from Darien via America, was admitted as a burgess of Edinburgh on 17 May 1699. [EBR]

CUNNINGHAM, JOHN, a Lieutenant Colonel in Antrim, Ireland, in 1645. [Cal.SP.Ire.260/137]

CUNNINGHAM, JOHN, a militiaman in Colonel Lyne's Regiment in Barbados in 1679. [Hotten.2.101]

CUNNINGHAM, NICHOLAS, a prisoner in Edinburgh Tolbooth who was released to go to Holland as a soldier under Captain Hutcheon in 1689. [RPCS.XIII.573]

CUNNINGHAM, ROBERT, of the Scots Guards of France in the 1560s. [NRS.NRAS.0.143]

CUNNINGHAM, ROBERT, Military Governor of Demmin, Mecklenburg, in 1636. [MGIF]

CUNNINGHAM, R., was commissioned into the Russian Army in 1632. [SSA.48]

CUNNINGHAM, ROBERT, Captain of the Earl of Glencairn's Regiment at Carrickfergus, Ireland, in 1642. [TNA.SP18.120]

CUNNINGHAM, ROBERT, a soldier, sent to Carolina before 1703. [SPC.1703.615]

CUNNINGHAM, WILLIAM, Lieutenant Colonel of the Earl of Glencairn's Regiment at Carrickfergus, Ireland, in 1642. [TNA.SP18.120]; at the Siege of Newcastle in 1644, and the Battle of Kilsyth in 1645. [CA.143]

CUNNINGHAM, WILLIAM, Captain of the Earl of Glencairn's Regiment at Carrickfergus, Ireland, in 1642. [TNA.SP18.120]

CUNNINGHAM, WILLIAM, a militiaman in Colonel Bayley's Regiment in Barbados in 1679. [Hotten.2.132]

CUNNINGHAM, WILLIAM, a soldier of Major William Foster's Company of Militia in Barbados in 1679. [Hotten.2.134]

CUNNINGHAM, Captain, of Maxwell's Troop of Horse Militia in Barbados in 1679. [Hutten.2.211]

CURRIE, ADAM, Quartermaster of Douglas's Regiment of Horse in France, dead by 1653. [NRS.GD18.2401]

CURRY, ROBERT, a militiaman in Colonel Thornhill's Regiment in Barbados in 1679. [Hotten.2.156]

DAIKERS, DAVID, a Corporal of Lord Charles Murray's Regiment of Dragoons in 1686. [NRS.E99.35]

DALYELL, Captain JOHN, with his company, was mustered at Glasgow in 1682. [DSA.126]

DALYELL, Major JOHN, of a Scottish regiment in the Service of the King of France in 1688. [DSA.159]

DALYELL, Ensign ROBERT, of Captain Dalyell's Company, was mustered at Glasgow in 1682. [DSA.126]

DALYELL, ROBERT, a Corporal of Captain Dalyell's Company, was mustered at Glasgow in 1682. [DSA.126]

DALYELL, THOMAS, born 1615, son of Tam Dalzell of the Binns, possibly at the Siege of La Rochelle, France, in 1628; Captain of Major General Monro's Regiment at Carrickfergus, Ireland, in 1642. [TNA.SP18.120]; Colonel in Carrickfergus, Ireland, in 1649. [SRS.Binns.239]; fought at the Siege of Worcester in 1651, captured and imprisoned in the Tower of London, escaped and fled to Russia in 1654, a Lieutenant Colonel in Russian Service, returned to Scotland in 1665. [NRS.GD22.1.195], fought against the Covenanters at the Battle of Rullion Green on 28 November 1666, died in 1685.

DALZELL, CHARLES, Lieutenant of the Cameronian Regiment at the Siege of Dunkeld on 21 August 1689. [BK.146]

DANIELS, WILLIAM, a soldier from Glasgow, married ..... Willetson from Perth, in Delft, Holland, on 9 November 1605. [Delft Marriage Register]

DARLING, GEORGE, a prisoner of war who was captured at the Battle of Dunbar on 3 September 1650, transported via London to Boston on the Unity of Boston in November 1650, an indentured servant at Lyn Ironworks in 1650s. [Suffolk Deeds.1226][LLNV]

DAVID, HENRY, a soldier in Colonel Alexander Leslie's Company in Muscovite Service from 1630 to 1632. [STW.179]

DAVIDSON, ALEXANDER, a Captain of Militia in Dundee in 1651. [DCW.54][CBRD.174]

DAVIDSON, JAMES, from Musselburgh, Midlothian, a gunner aboard the Dutch ship Vere on 1 August 1644. [ZA]

DAVIDSON, JAMES, a soldier in the Earl of Mar's Regiment, was court-martialled in March 1680. [NRS.GD124.13.17]

DAVIDSON, MATTHEW, from Aberdeen, a gunner aboard the Dutch ship Middelburg in 1631. [ZA]

DAVIDSON, MICHAEL, a Jacobite soldier captured at the Battle of Cromdale, Strathspey, on 1 May 1690. [RPCS.XV.304]

DAVIDSON, NICHOLAS, a prisoner in Edinburgh Tolbooth who was released to go to Holland as a soldier under Captain Hutcheon in 1689. [RPCS.13.573]

DAVIDSON, ROBERT, a soldier from Cupar, Fife, married Adriaen Michiels in Breda, Brabant, in 1594. [Breda Marriage Register]

DAVIDSON, Lieutenant Colonel THOMAS, served in Kedainai Lithuania, around 1662. [SCL.159]

DEAS, HENRY, from Leith, a gunner aboard the Dutch ship White Lion in 1630. [ZA]

DELL, WILLIAM, a prisoner of war who was captured at the Siege of Worcester on 2 September 1651, was transported via London to New England on the John and Sarah of London and landed in Boston on 13 February 1652. [Suffolk Deeds, 1/5-6]

DENHOLME, JAMES, Captain of Leven's Regiment at the Battle of Killiecrankie, Perthshire, on 27 July 1689. [BK.96]

DENNY JOHN, a soldier of New Kent County Militia, in Virginia in 1701. [TNA.CO5.1312/2]

DENOON, ..., an Ensign of Mackay's Regiment in Swedish Service in 1629, promoted in Ruthven's Regiment. [TGSI.VIII.188]

DENNISON, ANDREW, Ensign of the Cameronian Regiment at the Siege of Dunkeld on 21 August 1689. [BK.146]

DEVENER, JAMES, a prisoner in Edinburgh Tolbooth who was released to go to Holland as a soldier under Captain William Douglas on 6 March 1683. [ETR]

DEWAR, JAMES, a soldier of Mackay's Regiment, was killed at the Battle of Killiecrankie, Perthshire, on 27 July 1689. [RPCS.XIV]

DEWAR, JOHN, a soldier under Colonel Murray, married Belijntgen Frederixdaughter from Utrecht, Holland, in Leiden, Holland, on 27 December 1597. [Leiden Marriage Register]

DEWAR, STEPHEN, a militiaman in Colonel Carter's Troop of Militia in Barbados in 1679. [Hotten.2.51]

DICHEN, EDWARD, a prisoner in Edinburgh Tolbooth who was released to go to Holland as a soldier under Captain John Maxwell in 1689. [RPCS.13.573]

DICK, PETER, a Scottish soldier married Else Rabe, in St Johann's, Memel, on 24 November 1630.

DIGNAN, JAMES, a prisoner in Canongate Tolbooth, was released to go to Holland as a soldier under Captain Robert Reid of Bonakettle on 18 June 1690. [RPCS.XV.713]

DIXON, Lieutenant Colonel JAMES, of Aytoun's Foot, 1644-1645, fought at the Siege of Newcastle. [CA.113]

DON, JOHN, a soldier, was buried in Greyfriars, Edinburgh in 1696.

DONALD, HUGH, a soldier of Captain Hamilton's Company, a medical certificate dated 1694. [NRS.E100.22.141]

DONALDSON, JAMES, a prisoner of war who was captured at the Battle of Dunbar on 3 September 1650, transported via London to Boston on the Unity of Boston in November 1650, an indentured servant at Lyn Ironworks in 1650s. [Suffolk Deeds.1226]

DONALDSON, JAMES, Captain of Kenmure's Regiment, fought at the Battle of Killiecrankie, Perthshire, on 27 July 1689, a prisoner of the Jacobites. [BK.95/121][NRS.GD124.16.76]

DONALDSON, ..., a prisoner in Edinburgh Tolbooth who was released to go to Holland as a soldier in 1689. [RPCS.13.548]

DOUGALL, ALEXANDER, a prisoner of war who was captured at the Battle of Dunbar on 3 September 1650, transported via London to

Boston on the Unity of Boston in November 1650, an indentured servant at Lyn Ironworks in 1650s. [Suffolk Deeds.1226][LLNV]

DOUGAL, ANDREW, from Wemyss, Fife, pilot of the Zeeland Admiralty warship Wapen van Zeelant in 1665. [ZA.Rekenkamer C6985]

DOUGALL, EDWARD, a prisoner of war who was captured at the Siege of Worcester on 2 September 1651, was transported via London to New England on the John and Sarah of London and landed in Boston on 13 February 1652. [Suffolk Deeds, 1/5-6]

DOUGALL, WILLIAM, a prisoner of war who was captured at the Siege of Worcester on 2 September 1651, was transported via London to New England on the John and Sarah of London and landed in Boston on 13 February 1652. [Suffolk Deeds, 1/5-6]

DOUGLAS, ALBERT, a soldier in Danzig, [Gdansk], married Susanna, daughter of Hans Notiges, in the Reformed Church of Peter and Paul in Danzig on 26 March 1658.

DOUGLAS, Captain ALEXANDER, of the Gluckstadt Garrison in 1627. [SAA.ii.112]

DOUGLAS, Captain ANDREW, of HMS Larke cruising off the western Highlands opposing the Jacobites in 1690. [BK.174]

DOUGLAS, Captain ARCHIBALD, in Danish Service in Gluckstadt and in Bremen n 1627, later died in Swedish Service in Frankfurt/Oder in 1631. [SAA.120]

DOUGLAS, Lord GEORGE, Colonel of a Scottish regiment in France during the 1560s. [NRS.NRAS.0.13]

DOUGLAS, Sir GEORGE, Military Governor of Creuznach from 1632 to 1635. [MGIF] [SIG.282]

DOUGLAS, Lord GEORGE, to raise officers and men in Scotland for service under the King of France, in 1656, [NRS.NRAS.2171.554];

Colonel of the Old Scots Regiment in France, a deed, 1665. [NRS.RD4.14.209]

DOUGLAS, GEORGE, Ruitmaster, his widow Catherine Grattuid of Wandougin, was buried in Greyfriars, Edinburgh, on 9 March 1673.

DOUGLAS, Ensign GEORGE, died at Darien, testament, 1707, Comm. Edinburgh. [NRS]

DOUGLAS, JAMES, born 1617 son of William Douglas the Earl of Angus, Colonel of the Scottish Regiment formerly commanded by Sir John Hepburn, was killed at Douai, France, on 21 October 1645. [SP.I.204]; was recruiting 300 men in Scotland for service in France in 1640. [NRS.GD109.1506]

DOUGLAS, JAMES, a Captain in Steinhoven, Germany, a sasine dated 27 October 1642. [NRS.RS24.40.473]

DOUGLAS, JAMES, Colonel of a Scottish regiment in Dutch Service in 1681. [NRS.GD26.Sec.9.213]

DOUGLAS, Colonel JAMES, Master General of HM Ordnance, 1686. [DSA.166]

DOUGLAS, Lieutenant General JAMES, in Limerick, Ireland, in 1690. [NRS.RH15.127.11]

DOUGLAS, JOHN, a soldier in the Company of Colonel Brock of the Rotterdam Garrison, married Marytgen Christiaesdaughter from Leiden, residing in Rotterdam, in Leiden, Holland, on 13 February 1629. [Leiden Marriage Register]

DOUGLAS, JOHN, an Ensign of the Earl of Dunfermline's Regiment in France, a deed, 1676. [NRS.RD4.39.200]

DOUGLAS, JOHN, Captain of Colonel Hugh Mackay's Regiment under the Prince of Orange, a charter party in 1678. [NRS.RD4.43.26]

DOUGLAS, JOHN, a soldier in Edinburgh Castle was buried at Greyfriars on 2 March 1689.

DOUGLAS, NATHAN, a soldier in Captain Burton's Company of Militia in Barbados in 1679. [Hotten.2.184]

DOUGLAS, PETER, Captain of a Scottish company of soldiers in Flanders, testament, 19 February 1583, Comm. Edinburgh. [NRS]

DOUGLAS, RICHARD, Major of the Earl of Callendar's Foot in 1644-1645. CA.119]

DOUGLAS, ROBERT, a soldier of the 1st company of Cockburn's Regiment in Swedish Service in 1609. [SIS.217]

DOUGLAS, ROBERT, General of the Swedish Army in Germany, son of Patrick Douglas of Standingstone and his wife Christina Lessels, in 1648. [RGS.IX.1995]; he commanded the left wing of Torstensohn's Army at Iankowitz, [Jankau], Bohemia on 5 March 1645, Military Governor of Schwaben, Schwabia, from 1648 to 1650. [MGIF][STW.285] [SIG.282]

DOUGLAS, Lieutenant ROBERT, was buried at Greyfriars, Edinburgh, on 30 June 1658.

DOUGLAS, ROBERT, a marine aboard Cornels Tromp's flagship <u>Gouden Leeuw</u> in 1673. [SCA.348]

DOUGLAS, Sir WILLIAM, of Kirkness, of Lumsden's Brigade, who fought and was captured at the Battle of Dunbar on 3 September 1650. [SR.37]

DOUGLAS, Sir WILLIAM, son of the Duke of Roxburgh, a Lieutenant of the Royal Scots Dragoons in 1689. [BK.71]

DOUGLAS, WILLIAM, a Captain of Balfour's Regiment, who was killed at the Battle of Killiecrankie, Perthshire, on 27 August 1689. [BK.207]

DOUGLAS, WILLIAM, a soldier in Captain Hackett's Company of Militia in Barbados in 1680. [Hotten.2.128]

DOUGLAS, Colonel, with his 'Regiment de Gardes', from Leith bound for Dieppe, France, in 1643. [NRS.GD18.2429]

DOUGLAS, Captain, a soldier in Memel in 1631. [JSM]

DOUGLAS, Sir WILLIAM, of Livingstone's Regiment of Dragoons at the Battle of Cromdale, Strathspey, on 1 May 1690. [BK.177] [NRS.GD77.189]

DOUHTON, ROBERT, a soldier from Kelso, Roxburghshire, married Elizabeth Black from Scotland, in Schiedam, Holland, on 25 April 1637. [Schiedam Marriage Register]

DOWART, ROBERT, a soldier of Kerr's Company at the Battle of Killiecrankie, Perthshire, on 27 July 1689, was captured by the Jacobites. [RPCS.XIV]

DRUMMOND, ALEXANDER, a soldier of the 2nd company of Cockburn's Regiment in Swedish Service in 1609. [SIS.217]

DRUMMOND, ALEXANDER, Captain of the Earl of Lothian's Regiment in Carrickfergus, Ireland, in 1642. [TNA.SP28.120]

DRUMMOND, ALEXANDER, of Balhaldy, a Jacobite soldier in 1689. [APS.app.ix.131]

DRUMMOND, Sir DAVID, born 1593, a Lieutenant of the Swedish Life Guards in 1617, he was enobled in Sweden in 1627, Commander of the Smaland Regiment in 1627, served in as Military Governor of Stettin, [Szczecin], Pomerania, from 1631 to 1634, Major General of the Swedish Army in 1634, died imprisoned at Spandau, buried in Stockholm. [SS.42] [SIG.282]

DRUMMOND, HENRY, routemaster of a Troop of Horse in 1644. [CA.131

DRUMMOND, JOHN, from Edinburgh, Ensign of a Scottish regiment in Swedish Service, bound from Leith via Cromarty for Stralsund in 1638. [RPCS.7.84]

DRUMMOND, JOHN, Captain of Sir Mungo Campbell of Lawers' Regiment in Temple Patrick, Ireland, in 1642. [TNA.SP28.120]

DRUMMOND, JOHN, Ensign of a Scottish Company in the United Provinces, a deed, 1677. [NRS.RD3.42.534]

DRUMMOND, Sir JOHN, of Machanie, Cornet in the Scottish Horse in 1674, Lieutenant in 1687, a Jacobite soldier in 1689. [APS.acc.ix.56]

DRUMMOND, ROBERT, Captain of the Earl of Lindsay's Regiment in Bangor, Ireland, in 1642. [TNA.SP28.120]

DRUMMOND, ROBERT, a Sergeant, was wounded at Darien on 6 February 1699. [DP.86]

DRUMMOND, ROBERT, a Cornet of Lord Jedburgh's Regiment, later Captain of the Caledonia at Darien, a decreet, 29 May 1702. [NRS.NRAS.0364.63]

DRUMMOND, Captain THOMAS, at Caledonia, Darien, in 1699. [SPAWI.1699.902][NRS.NRAS.859.21.5]

DRUMMOND, THOMAS, from Edinburgh, a soldier at Darien, testament, 1707, Comm. Edinburgh. [NRS]

DRUMMOND, WILLIAM, a soldier from Dundee, married Adriaenke Adriaens in Dordrecht, Holland, on 22 March 1587. [Dordrecht Marriage Register]

DRUMMOND, WILLIAM, Captain of Major General Monro's Regiment in Carrickfergus, Ireland, in 1642. [TNA.SP28.120]

DRUMMOND, WILLIAM, born 1617, son of Lord Madderty, an officer in the Service of King Charles II, was captured at the Siege of Worcester in 1651, escaped to Russia, entered the Service of the Czar of Russia, was Military Governor of Smolensk, returned to Scotland in 1666. [NRS.NRAS.NA.17364]

DRUMMOND, ..., Captain of Dragoons in the Militia of Accomack County, Virginia, on 16 March 1702. [TNA.CO5.1312/2]

DULEN, [?], EDWARD, a prisoner of war who was captured at the Siege of Worcester on 2 September 1651, was transported via London to New England on the John and Sarah of London and landed in Boston on 13 February 1652. [Suffolk Deeds, 1/5-6]

DUNBAR, DAVID, a Jacobite captured at the Battle of Cromdale, Strathspey, on 1 May 1690. [RPCS.XV.304]

DUNBAR, JAMES, Major of Mackay's Regiment, in Danish Service in 1626, in Swedish Service in 1629, was killed at Bredenburg. [TGSI.VIII.185]

DUNBAR, JAMES, Quartermaster of Mackay' Regiment in Danish Service, at Gluckstadt in 1620s. [GAA.119]

DUNBAR, JAMES or JOHN, a Captain in Bohemia in 1620. [STW.111]

DUNBAR, Major JAMES, Military Governor of Breitenburg, Schlesvig Holstein in 1627. [MGIF]

DUNBAR, JAMES, a soldier of Mackenzie's Company in Danish Service in 1628. [SAA.ii.124]

DUNBAR, PATRICK, Ensign of Mackay's Regiment, in Swedish Service in 1629. [TGSI.VIII.188]

DUNBAR, PATRICK, Captain of Kenmure's Regiment at the Battle of Killiecrankie, Perthshire, on 27 July 1689. [BK.96]

DUNBAR, ..., a Lieutenant of Mackay's Regiment, in Danish Service in 1626, in Swedish Service in 1629, was promoted in Ruthven's Regiment. [TGSI.VIII.187]

DUNBAR, Lieutenant Colonel, fought and was captured at the Battle of Dunbar on 3 September 1650.

DUNCAN, ANDREW, a soldier of Captain Dent's Company of Militia in Barbados in 1679. [H.2.6]

DUNCAN, JOHN, a Captain of Militia in Dundee, was killed at the Siege of Dundee in 1651. [DCW.54][CRBD.174]

DUNCAN, ROBERT, of the Stafford County Horse Militia, Virginia, in 1701. [TNA.CO5.1312/2]

DUNCAN, THOMAS, a soldier of Captain Burrow's Company of Militia in Barbados in 1679. [H.2.181]

DUNCAN, WILLIAM, a soldier of Captain Pinket's Company of Militia in Barbados in 1679. [H.2.109]

DUNCAN, WILLIAM, Sergeant of the Militia of Dundee in 1643. [DCW.13]

DUNCAN, ..., Captain of Mackay's Regiment, in Danish Service in 1626, in Swedish Service in 1629. [TGSI.VIII.186]

DUNDAS, WALTER, son of Robert Dundas in Harbiston, a soldier who died at Darien, testament, 1707, Comm. Edinburgh. [NRS]

DUNDAS, JOHN, a soldier, married Margaret Pringnir [?] a widow from Scotland, in Haarlem, Holland, on 8 March 1594. [Haarlem Marriage Register]

DUNDAS, LAURENCE, scrivener of the Angus Regiment at the Battle of Marston Moor, Yorkshire, on 2 July 1644. [DCW.78]

DUNDAS, Lieutenant Colonel, fought and was captured at the Battle of Dunbar on 3 September 1650.

DUNLOP, ..., an Ensign who was wounded at Darien on 6 February 1699. [DP.86]

DUNNING, MALCOLM, a prisoner of war who was captured at the Battle of Dunbar on 3 September 1650, transported via London to Boston on the Unity of Boston in November 1650, an indentured servant at Lyn Ironworks in 1650s [Suffolk Court Files.1226] [LLNV.240]

DUNSMORE, JAMES, a prisoner of war who was captured at the Battle of Dunbar on 3 September 1650, transported via London to Boston on the Unity of Boston in November 1650, an indentured servant at Lyn Ironworks in 1650s [Suffolk Court Files.1226]

DURHAM, ARCHIBALD, a soldier of Captain Thornhill's Company of Militia in Barbados in 1679. [H.2.151]

DURHAM, JAMES, Captain of Robert Home of the Heugh's Regiment in Carrickfergus, Ireland, in 1642. [TNA.SP28.120]

EATON, ALEXANDER, a prisoner of war who was captured at the Battle of Dunbar on 3 September 1650, transported via London to Boston on the Unity of Boston in November 1650, an indentured servant at Lyn Ironworks in 1650s [Suffolk Court Files.1226] [LLNV.247]

ECHLIN, ROBERT, born in County Down, Ireland, in 1657, son of Robert Echlin, was educated at Trinity College, Dublin, in 1675, later a Lieutenant General. [Alumni Dublinensis]

EDMONSTONE, JAMES, of Newton, a Jacobite soldier in 1689. [APS.app.ix.55]

EDMONSTONE, JOHN, a prisoner of war who was captured at the Siege of Worcester on 2 September 1651, was transported via London to New England on the John and Sarah of London and landed in Boston on 13 February 1652. [Suffolk Deeds, 1/5-6]

EDMONSTONE, Captain WILLIAM, was granted a permit by the Governor of Laggan, Ireland, to go to Scotland on 21 April 1651, [NRS.GD40.2.5.30]; in Carrickfergus, Ireland, in 1653. [OB.80]

EDWARD, WILLIAM, Quartermaster of Oliphant's Company in Danish Service in 1628. [SAAii.143]

ELLIOT, Captain JOHN, in St Thomas, Barbados, in 1679. [H2.58]

ELPHINSTONE, Captain GABRIEL, in Russia around 1580. [SSA.47]

ELPHINSTONE, H., Captain of the 1st company of Cockburn's Regiment in Swedish Service in 1609. [SIS.216]

ELPHINSTONE, MICHAEL, Captain of Robert Home of the Heugh's Regiment in Carrickfergus, Ireland, in 1642. [TNA.SP28.120]

ELPHINSTONE, Captain WILLIAM, a soldier in Cork, Ireland, in 1626. [CalSPIre.1626.497; 253.489]

ELPHINSTONE, WILLIAM, a Cornet of Fraser's Dragoons, in 1644. [TFD.47]

ERSKINE, ALEXANDER, born 31 October 1598, a General in Swedish Service, settled in Bremen, Germany, died 24 August 1656. [Bremen Cathedral ms]

ERSKINE, Sir ARTHUR, of Scotscraig, with 3 Troops of Cavalry, fought at the Battle of Dunbar on 3 September 1650.

ERSKINE Lieutenant CHARLES, of a Scottish regiment in the Service of the King of France in 1688. [DSA.159]

ERSKINE, CHARLES, Captain of Leven's Regiment at the Battle of Killiecrankie, Perthshire, on 27 July 1689. [BK.96]

ERSKINE, HENRY, Lord Cardross, a Captain in the Service of William of Orange on 29 March 1688. [NRS.GD103.2.224]

ERSKINE, JOHN, Captain of the Angus Regiment at the Battle of Marston Moor, Yorkshire, on 2 July 1644. [DCW.78]

ERSKINE, THOMAS, Captain of Balfour's Regiment at the Battle of Killiecrankie, Perthshire, on 27 July 1689. [BK.95]

ERSKINE, Captain WILLIAM, of Lumsden's Foot, in 1644. [CA.145]

ERSKINE, Sergeant, late in Newcastle, Delaware, 1667, his widow Jane, 1678. [New York Hist. Docs. Dutch.xx/xxi.28/367]

ERSKINE, LUIS, a Colonel in Dutch Service in 1665. [JCP.I.136]

ERSKINE, WILLIAM, Earl of Buchan, a Jacobite soldier in 1689. [APS.acc.ix.56]

ESPLIN, JOHN, a soldier, bound from Leith on the Unicorn to Darien on 14 July 1698, died there on 1 July 1700. [DP.352]

EVANS, GEORGE, from Dundee, a musketeer aboard the Dutch ship Zeeridder on 1 May 1647. [ZA]

EWART, JAMES, a soldier of Captain Burrow's Company of Militia in Barbados in 1679. [H.2.181]

FAIR, ROBERT, a soldier from Ireland, in Ayr in 1642. [NRS.CH2.751.2/374]

FAIRFOUL, HUGH, Cornet of Viscount Claneboy's Troop of Horse in Ireland in 1642. [CalSPIre.260.63]

FAIRLEY, GEORGE, a soldier aboard De Witte Swaen bound for the Dutch West Indies in 1638. [GAR.ONA.293.117.139]

FALCONER, GEORGE, in Angus, of the Earl of Airlie's Militia in 1670. [NRS.GD16.53.39]

FALCONER, JAMES, in Angus, of the Earl of Airlie's Militia in 1670. [NRS.GD16.53.39]

FALCONER, JOHN, a drummer of Major Whyte's company mustered in Glasgow in 1682. [DSA.128]

FARQUHAR, Sir ROBERT, of Mounie, Paymaster of Mackay's Regiment, sailed from Leith via Holland bound for Holstein, Germany, in March 1627. [TGSI.VIII.133]

FARQUHARSON, JAMES, a prisoner of war who was captured at the Siege of Worcester on 2 September 1651, was transported via London to New England on the John and Sarah of London and landed in Boston on 13 February 1652. [Suffolk Deeds, 1/5-6]

FEA, ALEXANDER, a prisoner in Edinburgh Tolbooth who was released to go as a soldier to France with Lieutenant John McCulloch on 4 February 1676. [RPCS.IV.668]

FEA, JOHN, a prisoner in Edinburgh Tolbooth who was released to go as a soldier to France with Lieutenant John McCulloch on 4 February 1676. [RPCS.IV.668]

FEA, ROBERT, a prisoner in Edinburgh Tolbooth who was released to go as a soldier to France with Lieutenant John McCulloch on 4 February 1676. [RPCS.IV.668]

FENTON, DAVID, in Angus, of the Earl of Airlie's Militia in 1670. [NRS.GD16.53.39]

FENTON, DONALD, in Angus, of the Earl of Airlie's Militia in 1670. [NRS.GD16.53.39]

FERGUSON, ALEXANDER, Captain of Fraser's Dragoons at the Battle of Marston Moor, Yorkshire, on 2 July 1644. [TFD.47]

FERGUSON, ALEXANDER, a soldier from Maybole, Ayrshire, died at Darien in 1699, testament, 1707, Comm. Edinburgh. [NRS]

FERGUSON, DANIEL, a prisoner of war, captured at the Battle of Dunbar on 3 September 1650, transported via London on the Unity bound for New England, settled in Kittery, Berwick, Maine. [CEB] [LLNV.253]

FERGUSON, FINDEN, a Sergeant Major in Antrim, Ireland, in 1645. [Cal.SPIre.260.137]

FERGUSON, HUGH, Ensign of the Cameronian Regiment at the Siege of Dunkeld, Perthshire, on 21 August 1689. [BK.146]

FERGUSON, Lieutenant JACOB, fought at the Battle of Killiecrankie, Perthshire, on 27 July 1689, was captured by the Jacobites. [BK.207]

FERGUSON, JAMES, a soldier of Cunningham's Company in Balfour's Regiment, was killed at the Battle of Killiecrankie, Perthshire, on 27 July 1689. [RPCS.XIV]

FERGUSON, JAMES, a soldier of the King and Queen County, Virginia, Militia, in 1701. [TNA.CO5.1312/2]

FERGUSON, JOHN, Lieutenant Colonel of Kenmure's Regiment, was killed at the Battle of Killiecrankie, Perthshire, on 27 July 1689. [BK.95/207][EUL.Laing.ii.89/338]

FERGUSON, Lieutenant ROBERT, at Six Mile Quarter, Ireland, in 1653. [OB.80]

FERGUSON, ROBERT, a Sergeant of Fraser's Dragoons in 1645. [TFD.220]

FERGUSON, WILLIAM, Captain of the Angus Regiment at the Battle of Marston Moor, Yorkshire, on 2 July 1644; Lieutenant of Militia in Dundee in 1643. [DCW.13/78]

FERGUSON, WILLIAM, a soldier of Captain Standfast's Company of Militia in Barbados in 1679. [H.2.158]

FERGUSON, WILLIAM, a Captain of Militia in Dundee in 1643. [DCW.1643]

FERGUSON, ..., a trooper in Insterburg, Prussia, in 1691.

FERRAR, Captain CONSTANCE, bound to Cape Breton, Canada, with Lord Ochiltree, landed there on 1 July 1629, captured by the French on 10 September 1629 and deported to England. [CSP.Col.1574-1660, fo.104]

FERRIER, A., in Angus, of the Earl of Airlie's Militia in 1670. [NRS.GD16.53.39]

FERSEY, JOHN, a soldier from Glasgow, married Aechtgen Toupronne in Schiedam, Holland, on 22 October 1639. [Schiedam Marriage Register]

FETHIE, JOHN, Sergeant of the Militia of Dundee in 1643. [DCW.13]

FIELDING, ANDREW, a Scottish soldier under Captain de la Nouville, married Lydia Jacobs from Norwich, England, in Leiden, Holland, on 1 December 1600. [Leiden Marriage Register]

FIFE, ALEXANDER, a soldier of Colonel Colleton's Company of Militia in Barbados in 1680. [H.2.119]

FIFE, WILLIAM, a soldier of Captain Davies's Company of Militia in Barbados in 1679. [H.2.166]

FINLAY, HANS, a Lieutenant of Colonel John Buchan's Regiment of Foot in Flanders, a deed, 1699. [NRS.RD4.83.771]

FINLAYSON, JAMES, a soldier of the 1st Company of Cockburn's Regiment in Swedish Service in 1609. [SIS.217]

FINLAYSON, THOMAS, a soldier from Brechin, Angus, who married Elizabeth Peters from Gorinchem, in Heusden, Flanders, on 24 August 1628. [Heusden Marriage Register]

FITCHET, JOHN, a soldier of Surry County Militia, Virginia, in 1701. [TNA.CO5.1312/2]

FLECK, ALEXANDER, a soldier in Colonel Alexander Leslie's Company in Muscovite Service from 1630 to 1632. [STW.179]

FLECK, …., a Sergeant in government service, was wounded at the Battle of Killiecrankie, Perthshire, on 27 July 1689. [RPCS.XV]

FLEMING, Sir ALEXANDER, son of the Earl of Wigton, an Ensign of a Scottish regiment in Holland, married Helena Neilson, in Schiedam, Holland, on 24 April 1637. [Schiedam Marriage Register]

FLEMING, Colonel HENRY, in Germany in the service of Gustavus Adolphus, around 1630. [SIG.282]

FLETCHER, Captain DANIEL, in Barbados, a deed, 1644. [NRS.RD1.553.406]

FLETCHER, LUDOVICK, in Angus, of the Earl of Airlie's Militia in 1670. [NRS.GD16.53.39]

FORATH, Captain ALEXANDER, from Dundee, a Swedish naval officer at Nygraden, Stockholm, from 1611 to 1627.

[NRS.GD334.114-116]; died in a sea battle with the Polish Navy in the Bay of Gdansk [Danzig] on28 November 1627. [HS.IX.3]

FORBES, ALEXANDER, a fire-worker in the English Train of Artillery in Flanders in 1597. [NRS.GD52.110]

FORBES, ALEXANDER, Lieutenant Colonel of Mackay's Regiment in Danish Service in 1626, died in Holstein. [TGSI.VIII.185]

FORBES, ALEXANDER, 10th Lord Forbes, a Lieutenant General under Gustavus Adolphus in Hamburg, Germany, ca.1630. [SIG.282]

FORBES, CHARLES, formerly a Captain of Hill's Regiment, died at Matanzas Bay, Cuba, in 1700 on a voyage from Darien bound for Scotland. [DD.225]

FORBES, DUNCAN, Captain of Mackay's Regiment in Danish Service in 1626, in Swedish Service in 1629, killed at Breitenburg, Schlesvig Holstein. [TGSI.VIII.186]

FORBES, HENRY, of Tolquhan, a soldier in Swedish Service, died in Kirkholm, Russia, in 1605. [SIS]

FORBES, Captain JAMES, was authorised to raise 2000 men in Scotland for service in Russia under Alexander Leslie, on 28 March 1633. [RPCS.V.79/548]

FORBES, JAMES, a drummer, was wounded at Darien on 6 February 1699. [DP.86]

FORBES, JOHN, of Tullich, Major of Mackay's Regiment in Danish Service in 1626, killed at the Battle of Nordlingen, Bavaria, on 6 September 1634. [TGSI.VIII.185][SAA.121]

FORBES, JOHN, Major of Mackay's Regiment in Swedish Service around 1630, later in Dutch Service. [TGSI.VIII.186]

FORBES, Captain JOHN, of Lumsden's Foot, from Aberdeen with sixty me bound for England in February 1644. [CA.144]

FORBES, JOHN, a Captain under Major Robert Hog, who died in the Service of the Emperor in 164..., son of Thomas Forbes, a baillie of Aberdeen, and his wife Marjorie Menzies, 12 June 1649. [ACA; APB]

FORBES, Colonel JOHN, of Leslie's Regiment, who fought at the Battle of Dunbar on 3 September 1650, and at the Battle of Inverkeithing, Fife, on 20 July 1651. [SR.37]

FORBES, JOHN, a prisoner in Edinburgh Tolbooth, released to go as a soldier to Holland under Lieutenant Colonel Blair in 1689. [RPCS.13.573]

FORBES, Captain JOHN, of Grant's Regiment of Infantry at the Battle of Cromdale, Strathspey, on 1 May 1690. [BK.177]

FORBES, MATTHEW, Military Governor of Osnabruck, Saxony, in 1635. [MGIF]

FORBES, ROBERT, Captain of Major General Monro's Regiment in Carrickfergus, Ireland, in 1642. [TNA.SP28.120]

FORBES, THOMAS, a Lieutenant of the Scots Guards of France in the 1560s. [NRS.NRAS.O.143]

FORBES, THOMAS, a Captain of Collingwood's Regiment, died in the West Indies in 1703, probate PCC. [TNA]

FORBES, WILLIAM, a chaplain of Mackay's Regiment in Swedish Service in 1629. [TGSI.VIII.189]

FORBES, WILLIAM, a prisoner of war, captured at the Battle of Dunbar on 3 September 1650, transported via London on the Unity bound for Boston on 11 November 1650, an indentured servant at Kittery Sawmills, Maine. [SG.34.4][LLNV.249]

FORBES, Colonel WILLIAM, Military Governor of Burg at Bremen Verden, Germany, from 1649 to 1657. [MGIF]

FORBES, Captain, a soldier, from Leith on the Unicorn to Darien on 14 July 1698, died at the Bay of Matanzas, Cuba, on 25 July 1699. [DP.196]

FORBES, Lord, a Colonel in Swedish Service, died in Hamburg around 1630. [SIG.282]

FOREMAN, THOMAS, a Sergeant of Colonel Philip Balfour's Company at Schiedam, Holland, in 1640. [GAR.ONA.328.293.3601]

FORRESTER, Lieutenant ANDREW, with Sir William Alexander to Nova Scotia, Commander of Port Royal in 1629, captured by the French and deported to England on the St Jean in February 1633. [DCB]

FORRESTER, JOHN, a Scottish soldier, married Agnes .... in Danzig, [Gdansk], on 9 September 1612. [St Marien Kirche register]

FORRESTER, JOHN, Captain of Fraser's Dragoons, at the Battle of Marston Moor, Yorkshire, on 2 July 1644. [TFD.47]

FORRESTER, JOHN, Lieutenant of the Cameronian Regiment at the Siege of Dunkeld on 21 August 1689. [BK.146]

FORSYTH, JAMES, was wounded at Darien on 6 February 1699. [DP.86]

FORTUNE, THOMAS, a soldier of Captain Thorburne's Company of Militia in Barbados in 1679. [H.2.140]

FOSTER, PETER, from Dundee, a gunner aboard the Dutch ship Arms of Zeeland in 1644. [ZA]

FOSSEM {?}, MATTHEW, a prisoner of war captured at the Siege of Worcester on 2 September 1651 who was transported via London on the John and Sarah of London to Boston in December 1651, landed there on 13 February 1652. [Suffolk Deeds.1/5-6]

FOSSEM [?] MICHAEL, a prisoner of war who was captured at the Siege of Worcester on 2 September 1651, was transported via London to New England on the John and Sarah of London in

December 1651 and landed in Boston on 13 February 1652. [Suffolk Deeds, 1/5-6]

FRAME, JACK, a soldier under Captain Nesbit, married Mayke Jans from Haarlem, Holland, there on 2 July 1596. [Haarlem Marriage Register]

FRASER, ALEXANDER, a soldier who died at Darien in 1699, testament, 1707, Comm. Edinburgh. [NRS]

FRASER, ANDREW, Sergeant of Oliphant's Regiment in Danish Service in 1628. [SAA.ii.143]

FRASER, ANDREW, a soldier in Tilsit, Lithuania, around 1675. [SIG.262]

FRASER, HUGH, Colonel of a Regiment of Dragoons, in Scotland, 1643; fought at the Battle of Marston Moor, Yorkshire, on 2 July 1644. [TFD]

FRASER, HEW, Lieutenant Colonel of Major General Monro's Regiment in Carrickfergus, Ireland, in 1642. [TNA.SP28.120]

FRASER, Captain JOHN, of Philorth's Regiment, taken prisoner at the Battle of Preston, Lancashire, on 18 August 1648.

FRASER, JOHN, a soldier of the James City County, Virginia, Militia, in 1701. [TNA.CO5.1312/2]

FRASER, THOMAS, a soldier from Dundee, married Lubberich Reyers in Harderwijk, Holland, on 15 February 1607. [Harderwijk Marriage Register]

FRASER, W., a soldier of the 2nd Company of Cockburn's Regiment in Swedish Service in 1609. [SIS.217]

FRASER, WILLIAM, of Foyers, Captain of Mar's Regiment of Foot in 1681, a Jacobite soldier in 1689. [APS.app.ix.148]

FRASER, Captain, at Darien in 1698. [DSP.93]

FRAZER, Captain, of James City County Militia, Virginia, in 1702. [TNA.CO5.1312/2]

FREW, WILLIAM, a Scottish soldier under Captain Halewijn, married Elizabeth Greig from Scotland, in Leiden, Holland, on 15 December 1608. [Leiden Marriage Register]

FRISELL, DANIEL, a soldier of Colonel Lewis's Company of Militia in Barbados in 1679. [H.2.101]

FRISSELL, EDWARD, a prisoner of war who was captured at the Siege of Worcester on 2 September 1651, was transported via London to New England on the John and Sarah of London and landed in Boston on 13 February 1652. [Suffolk Deeds, 1/5-6]

FRISSELL, GEORGE, a soldier under Captain Nesbit, married Janneken Willems a widow, in Haarlem, Holland, on 17 April 1594. [Haarlem Marriage Register]

FRISSELL, JOHN, a soldier of Colonel Pinket's Company of Militia in Barbados in 1680. [H.2.109]

FRISSEL, THOMAS, a soldier of the New Kent County Militia, Virginia, in 1701. [TNA.CO5.1312/2]

FRISSELL, WILLIAM, a prisoner of war who was captured at the Siege of Worcester on 2 September 1651, was transported via London to New England on the John and Sarah of London and landed in Boston on 13 February 1652. [Suffolk Deeds, 1/5-6]

FULLARTON, HUGH, Captain of Colonel Ferguson's Regiment in Flanders, a deed, 1697. [NRS.RD4.80.835]

FULLARTON, JOHN, of Dudwick, a Lieutenant Colonel under Colonel Alexander Erskine from 1640 to 1645, in France, later in Germany. [NRS.NRAS.O.107.8]

FULLARTON, JOHN, Captain of Leven's Regiment at the Battle of Killiecrankie, Perthshire, on 27 July 1689. [BK.96]

FULLARTON, Captain JOHN, in County Antrim, Ireland, a will, 1706, Derry.

FULLARTON, ..., of Fullarton, a Jacobite soldier in 1689. [APS.app.ix.159]

GALBRAITH, ANDREW, a Scottish soldier under Captain Robrecht Schotgen, married Katelijne Stepmans from Haarlem, Holland, in Leiden on 27 January 1604. [Leiden Marriage Register]

GALBRAITH, JAMES, a Sergeant Major in Antrim, Ireland, in 1645. [Cal.SPIre.260.137]

GALLOWAY, BRIAN, a soldier of Colonel Thorburn's Company of Militia in Barbados in 1680. [H.2.58]

GALLOWAY, JAMES, Lord Dunkeld, a Jacobite at the Battle of Killiecrankie, Perthshire, on 27 July 1689. [APS.IX.55]

GARDEN, ALEXANDER, Military Governor of Brux in 1646. [MGIF]

GARDEN, JEREMY, a soldier, via Denmark to Moscow in 1628. [SSA.49]

GARDEN, THOMAS, Ensign of the Angus Regiment in 1644. [DCW.78]

GARDEN, WILLIAM, a lance corporal in Forbes of Tullich's Company in Danish Service in 1628. [SAA.ii.121]

GARDINER, G., a soldier of the 2nd Company of Cockburn's Regiment in Swedish Service in 1609. [SIS.217]

GARDINER, Major JAMES, served in Radziwill's Militia in Lithuania between 1660 and 1673. [SCL.159]

GARDNER [?], JAMES, a prisoner of war who was captured at the Siege of Worcester on 2 September 1651, was transported via London to New England on the John and Sarah of London and landed in Boston on 13 February 1652. [Suffolk Deeds, 1/5-6]

GARDNER, Lieutenant PATRICK, of Colonel Stanley's Regiment of Foot in Ireland, a deed, 1699. [NRS.RD4.85.1000]

GARDNER, THOMAS, a Captain of Militia in Dundee in 1650. [CBRD.174]

GARDYNE, Captain GEORGE, in Germany in 1639, son of Alexander Gardyne of Banchory, Aberdeenshire, and his wife Janet Strachan. [ACA.APB]

GARDINE, ROBERT, the elder, Sergeant of the Militia of Dundee in 1643. [DCW.13]

GARDYNE, THOMAS, a Captain of Militia in Dundee in 1650. [CRBD.174]

GAY, JOHN, from Dysart, Fife, a gunner aboard the Lion of Zeeland in 1631. [ZA]

GAY, WILLIAM, Captain in Colonel Brudnell's Regiment of Foot in Flanders, deeds, 1696, in Ireland in 1702. [NRS.RD4.78.188; RD4.90.352]

GAY, WILLIAM, Adjutant to HM Royal Regiment in Ireland, was admitted as a burgess of Edinburgh in 1687. [EBR]

GEDDES, CHARLES, of the Scots Guards of France in the 1560s. [NRS.NRAS.O.143]

GEDDES, J., a soldier of the James City County, Virginia, Militia, in 1701. [TNA.CO5.1312/2]

GEDDES, Captain of James City County Militia, Virginia, in 1702. [TNA.CO5.1312/2]

GEDDIE, JOHN, from Kinkell, Fife, a soldier in Holland in 1640. [NRS.S/H]

GENTLEMAN, JOHN, in Angus, of the Earl of Airlie's Militia in 1670. [NRS.GD16.53.39]

GEORGE, WILLIAM, from Kirkwall, Orkney, a soldier of Captain Archibald Johnstone's Company of Militia in Barbados in 1679. [H.2.164]

GIBB, ROBERT, from Aberdeen, a musketeer aboard the Dutch ship Sandenburgh in 1645. [ZA]

GIBB, ROBERT, from Dundee, a gunner aboard the Dutch ship Neptunus on 1 May 1645. [ZA]

GIBSON, HENRY, Captain of Sir Mungo Campbell of Lawers's Regiment in Temple Patrick, Ireland, in 1642. [TNA.SP28.120]

GIBSON, JOHN, in Angus, of the Earl of Airlie's Militia in 1670. [NRS.GD16.53.39]

GIBSON, JOHN, a Captain of Balfour's Regiment, who was killed at the Battle of Killiecrankie, Perthshire, on 27 August 1689. [BK.207]

GIBSON, WILLIAM, from Kirkcaldy, Fife, a gunner aboard the Arms of Zeeland in 1644. [ZA]

GIFFARD, B., a soldier of the 3rd Company of Cockburn's Regiment in Swedish Service in 1609. [SIS.217]

GIFFORD, JOHN, a soldier from Orkney, married Janneken le Beston in Cadzand, the Netherlands, on 16 July 1629. [Calzan Marriage Register]

GILBERT, DAVID, a Captain in the Service of Boris Godunov in Moscow before 1613. [SSA.47]

GILBERT, THOMAS, a soldier of the 2nd Company of Cockburn's Regiment in Swedish Service in 1609. [SIS.217]

GILCHRIST, ANDREW, Lieutenant of the Cameronian Regiment at the Siege of Dunkeld on 21 August 1689. [BK.146]

GILCHRIST, JAMES, Captain of the Cameronian Regiment at the Siege of Dunkeld, Perthshire, on 21 August 1689. [BK.146]

GILLESPIE, WILLIAM, a Quartermaster of Fraser's Dragoons, in 1645. [TFD.47/220]

GILLON, G., a soldier in Moscow in 1630. [SSA.50]

GLASS, Lieutenant Colonel ALEXANDER, of the East Lothian Foot in 1647. [CA.131]

GLEDSTANES, JOHN, a prisoner in Edinburgh Tolbooth, released to go to Holland as a soldier under Captain Bruce on 8 May 1685. [ETR]

GORDON, ADAM, Captain of Mackay's Regiment in Danish Service in 1626, in Swedish Service in 1629. [TGSI.VIII.186]

GORDON, ADAM, son of Sir Adam Gordon of Pake, Captain of Colonel Leslie's Regiment in Germany in 1638. [NRS.RH15.16.27a/229]

GORDON, ADAM, a Lieutenant of the Polish Army who was killed by the Swedes at Marienburg, Prussia, in 1659. ['Diary of Patrick Gordon, p30']

GORDON, Captain ADAM, born 1611, from Cromarty to Hamburg in 1631, in Germany in the service of Gustavus Adolphus, died at the Battle of Nordlingen, Bavaria, on 6 September 1634. [HG.1637]

GORDON, ALEXANDER, a soldier in Russian Service, who fought at the Battle of Smolensk in 1634. [SCL.296]

GORDON, ALEXANDER, a Lieutenant Colonel in Russian Service in 1634. [HG.III.1656]

GORDON, Captain ALEXANDER, of Lumsden's Foot, in 1644. [CA.145]

GORDON, ALEXANDER, a prisoner of war captured at the Siege of Worcester on 2 September 1651, was transported to New England on Captain John Allen's ship in 1652, an indentured servant in Watertown, Massachusetts in 1652 and in Exeter, New Hampshire, in 1654, died in 1697, probate 1698, N.H.

GORDON, ALEXANDER, a prisoner in Edinburgh Tolbooth, released to go to Holland as a soldier in 1689. [RPCS.13.573]

GORDON, ALEXANDER, in Angus, of the Earl of Airlie's Militia in 1670. [NRS.GD16.53.39]

GORDON, ALEXANDER, Captain of Kenmure's Regiment, fought at the Battle of Killiecrankie, Perthshire, on 27 July 1689. [BK.95]

GORDON, ALEXANDER, a Captain of Herbert's Regiment in Ireland in 1691. [IWD]

GORDON, ALEXANDER, of Kinstair, a Lieutenant of the Earl of Angus's Regiment of Foot in Flanders, a burgess of Ayr in 1692. [ABR]

GORDON, ANDREW, a Captain of the Russian Army in 1691. [HG.111.418]

GORDON, DONALD, a prisoner of war who was captured at the Siege of Worcester on 2 September 1651, was transported via London to New England on the John and Sarah of London and landed in Boston on 13 February 1652. [Suffolk Deeds, 1/5-6]

GORDON, FRANCIS, son of Peter Gordon, an Ensign of the Rifles of the King of Poland around 1696, an officer of the Russian Army in 1700 [HG.III.427]

GORDON, Lord GEORGE, Captain in Chief of a Company of Men at Arms in the Service of King Louis XIII of France, on 13 March 1625. [NRS.RH1.2.447]

GORDON, GEORGE, Captain of the Earl of Leven's Regiment in Carrickfergus, Ireland, in 1642. [TNA.SP28.120]

GORDON, Lord GEORGE, Colonel of Gordon's Foot, 1643-1644; he died at the Battle of Alford on 2 July 1645 as a Royalist. [CA.142]

GORDON, Major GEORGE, was confirmed as a nobleman in Poland-Lithuania in 1673. [SCA.102][STW.211][BPL][SCL.160]

GORDON, Captain GEORGE, of the Banff Militia in 1688. [NRS.E99.38]

GORDON, Captain GEORGE, of Grant's Regiment of Infantry at the Battle of Cromdale, Strathspey, on 1 May 1690. [BK.177]

GORDON, GEORGE, son of William Gordon in Konigsberg, an officer of the Russian Army in 1697. [HG.III.431]

GORDON, Lord HENRY, a Colonel in Polish Service around 1660. [ACA. birth brief, 17.2.1672]; was naturalised and confirmed as a nobleman in Poland-Lithuania in 1658. [SCA.102][STW.211] [BPL]

GORDON, HENRY, a Captain of the Russian Army in 1691. [HG.III.434]

GORDON, HUGH, an officer of Mackay's Regiment in Danish Service in 1626, in Swedish Service in 1629. [TGSI.VIII.188]

GORDON, JAMES, a prisoner of war who was captured at the Battle of Dunbar on 3 September 1650, was transported via London to New England on the Unity of Boston in November 1650, an indentured servant at Lynn Ironworks, in 1650s. [Suffolk Court Deeds.1226][LLV.247]

GORDON, JAMES, a prisoner of war who was captured at the Siege of Worcester on 2 September 1651, was transported via London to New England on the John and Sarah of London and landed in Boston on 13 February 1652. [Suffolk Deeds, 1/5-6]

GORDON, JAMES, son of John Gordon of Auchleuchris, was educated in Danzig, [Gdansk], from 1685-1686, later an officer of the Russian Army. [HG.III.1736]

GORDON, JAMES, Captain of Kenmure's Regiment, fought at the Battle of Killiecrankie, Perthshire, on 27 July 1689. [BK.95]

GORDON, Captain JOHN, of Colonel Brock's Regiment, married Cecilia de Bosiss on 6 May 1615. [Aardenburg Marriage Register]

GORDON, JOHN, of Craichlaw, a soldier in Germany under Lord Spynie in 1631. [RPCS.IV.371]

GORDON, JOHN, Military Governor of Eger in 1632. [MGIF]

GORDON, JOHN, a soldier from Aberdeen, bound from the Netherlands on the New Amsterdam for India in 1641. [GAR.ONA.347.100.209]

GORDON, JOHN, an officer in the army of the Emperor of Austria, was captured by the Swedes at Nuremburg, Bavaria, in November 1631, died in Danzig in December 1648. [HG.1753]

GORDON, JOHN, a prisoner of war who was captured at the Siege of Worcester on 2 September 1651, was transported via London to New England on the John and Sarah of London and landed in Boston on 13 February 1652. [Suffolk Deeds, 1/5-6]

GORDON, JOHN, son of William Gordon of Cottoun, Aberdeenshire, a Captain in the Swedish Army, died in Cracow, Poland, around 1664. [ACA. Birth brief 4.6.1668]

GORDON, JOHN, from Sutherland, Scotland, a soldier bound from the Netherlands on the Eendracht bound for the East Indies in 1668. [GAR.ONA.239.11.22]

GORDON, JOHN, in Angus, of the Earl of Airlie's Militia in 1670. [NRS.GD16.53.39]

GORDON, JOHN, of Edinglassie, the younger, was killed in Venetian Service when fighting the Turks in 1688. [RPCS.16.160]

GORDON, JOHN, Major of a Scottish regiment in the Service of the King of France in 1688. [DSA.159]

GORDON, Captain JOHN JAMES, was enobled in Poland in 1689. [STW.211]

GORDON, Captain JOSEPH, died at the Royal Hospital in Dublin on 23 February 1752, aged between 90 and 100. 'He raised and maintained a company at his own expense at the Siege of Derry'. [SM.14.101]

GORDON, J., born 1627, a soldier in the Service of the Grand Duke of Hesse, died 1657. [HG.1750]

GORDON, LACHLAN, a prisoner of war who was captured at the Siege of Worcester on 2 September 1651, was transported via London to New England on the John and Sarah of London and landed in Boston on 13 February 1652. [Suffolk Deeds, 1/5-6]

GORDON, Colonel NATHANIEL, 'an active adherent of the Marquis of Montrose', died in 1645. [NRS.GD220.3.163-170]

GORDON, PATRICK, son of Robert Gordon of Gollachie, a Colonel of the Polish Army around 1657. [HG.111.453]

GORDON, PATRICK, from Auchleuchries, Aberdeenshire, to Danzig, [Gdansk], in 1651, later in Konigsberg, a General in Russia from 1661, fought against the Poles, he was admitted as a burgess of Aberdeen on 6 May 1670, [ACA.ABR]; a Major General in the Service of the Empress of Russia, a deed, 1680, died in 1699. [NRS.RD4.46.437] [SOP.25] [NS.1/1.58]

GORDON, PETER, a soldier of Captain Brown's Company of Militia in Barbados in 1680. [H.2.106]

GORDON, ROGER, of Fraser's Dragoons in 1645. [TFD.220]

GORDON, Captain THOMAS, a soldier in the Service of Duke Janusz Radziwill in Lithuania in the 1660s. [SGB.179] [SCL.160]

GORDON, WILLIAM, Lieutenant of Oliphant's Company in Danish Service, in 1628. [SAA.ii.143]

GORDON, WILLIAM, Captain of Kenmure's Regiment at the Battle of Killiecrankie, Perthshire, on 27 July 1689. [BK.96]

GORDON, WILLIAM, son of James Gordon of Rothiemay, a Captain of the Russian Army in 1691, died in Reval, Estonia, in 1692. [HG.111.469]

GORDON, WILLIAM, Captain of a Scottish regiment in Flanders, a deed, 1695. [NRS.RD2.79.9]

GORDON, Colonel, at Lubeck, Germany, testament, 1648. [NRS. Misc. Executry pp]

GOURLAY, N., in Angus, of the Earl of Airlie's Militia in 1670. [NRS.GD16.53.39]

GOURLAY, ROBERT, Captain of William Stewart of Houston's Regiment, died in the Service of Danzig, [Gdansk], was buried in the Marienkirche there in 1577. [STW.195]

GOWAN, WILLIAM, a prisoner of war captured at the Battle of Dunbar on 3 September 1650, was transported via London on the Unity to Boston in November 1650, settled in Kittery, Berwick, Maine. [CEB]

GOWRIE, RICHARD, in Colonel Christopher Lyne's Company of Militia in Barbados in 1679. [H2.100]

GRAEME, ..., an officer of Mackay's Regiment in Danish Service in 1626, in Swedish Service in 1629. [TGSI.VIII.188]

GRAHAM, ALEXANDER, a soldier in Argyll's Rebellion, was imprisoned in Edinburgh, then banished to the American Plantations on 30 July 1685, was transported via Leith to East New Jersey in August 1685. [RPCS.11.126/131/136/330]

GRAHAM, ALLISTER, a prisoner of war captured at the Battle of Dunbar on 3 September 1650, was transported via London on the Unity of Boston to Boston in November 1650, an indentured servant at Lynn Ironworks in 1650s. [Suffolk Court Files.1226][LLNV.247]

GRAHAM, Major ARTHUR, in Enniskillen, Ireland, 1667. [NRS.RH15.91.6]

GRAHAM, CHARLES, Captain of Mackay's Regiment at the Battle of Killiecrankie, Perthshire, on 27 July 1689. [BK.96]

GRAHAM, DAVID, Quartermaster of the King's Regiment of Horse in 1682, a Jacobite at the Battle of Killiecrankie, Perthshire, on 27 July 1689. [APS.IX.55]

GRAHAM, Major GAVIN, of a Scottish regiment in the Service of the King of France in 1688. [DSA.159]

GRAHAM, HARRY, Major of Colonel Lewis Gordon's Regiment in Holland, a deed, 1663, [NRS.RD2.9.74]; 1665, [JCP.I.136]

GRAHAM, HENRY, Colonel of a Scottish Regiment in the Service of the Prince of Orange, was admitted as a burgess of Dundee on 4 April 1676. [DBR]; Lieutenant Colonel of a Scottish regiment in the Service of the King of France in 1688. [DSA.159]

GRAHAM, IVOR, from Innerneil, Argyll, a soldier in Argyll's Rebellion, was transported via Leith to Jamaica in August 1685. [RPCS.11.329]

GRAHAM, JAMES, born 1612, died 1650, Marquis of Montrose, Colonel of the Angus Foot in the Army of the Covenant from 1639 to 1640, a Royalist from 1643, fought successfully at the battles of Tippermuir, Perthshire, on 1 September 1644, Inverlochy, Inverness-shire, on 2 February 1645, Auldearn, Nairn, on 9 May 1645, Alford, Aberdeenshire, on 2 July 1645, and Kilsyth, Stirlingshire, on 15 August 1645, but was defeated at Philiphaugh, Roxburghshire, on 13 September 1645, and at Carbisdale, Sutherland, in 1650, after which he was captured and executed in Edinburgh on 21 May 1650. [CA.108]

GRAHAM, JOHN, a soldier of Captain Brown's Company of Militia in Barbados in 1680. [H.2.107]

GRAHAM, JOHN, Sergeant of Major Whyte's company mustered in Glasgow in 1682. [DSA.128]

GRAHAM, JOHN, of Claverhouse, Viscount Dundee, born 1643, Jacobite leader who died at the Battle of Killiecrankie, Perthshire, on 27 July 1689. [NRS]

GRAHAM, JOHN, a soldier of Northumberland County Militia, in Virginia in 1701. [TNA.CO5.1312/2]

GRAHAM, MALCOLM, a soldier from Perth, married Jenneken Marith from England, in 's Hertogenbosch on 23 November 1631. [s'Hertogenbosch Marriage Register]

GRAHAM, THOMAS, an archer of the Scots Guards of France in the 1560s. [NRS.NRAS.O.143]

GRAHAM, Captain THOMAS, tenant of Glaneimullener in the barony of Bunratty, Ireland, in 1656. [Inchiquin mss 1538]

GRAHAM, Major THOMAS, in Ireland, 1652-1666. [IWD]

GRAHAM, WILLIAM, muster master for Leinster and Ulster in 1628. [CPR Ireland.i.365]

GRAHAM, Sergeant WILLIAM, of Captain Dalyell's Company, was mustered at Glasgow in 1682. [DSA.126]

GRAHAM, WILLIAM, a prisoner in Edinburgh Tolbooth, released to go to Holland as a soldier under Captain Bruce on 8 May 1685. [ETR]

GRAHAM, Major WILLIAM, of Boquoppol, a Jacobite soldier in 1689. [APS.acc.ix.56]

GRAHAM, Lieutenant, bound from Darien aboard the Rising Sun was shipwrecked on the bar of the Ashley River, Charleston, South Carolina, on 5 September 1699, settled in Charleston. ['New Voyage to Carolina', London, 1709]

GRAME, DUNCAN, a Jacobite soldier captured at the Battle of Cromdale, Strathspey, on 1 May 1690. [RPCS.XV.304]

GRANT, ALEXANDER, a prisoner of war captured at the Siege of Worcester on 2 September 1651, was transported via London on the John and Sarah of London to Boston in December 1651, landed there in February 1652. [Suffolk Deeds.1/5-6]

GRANT, Captain ALEXANDER, of Grant's Regiment of Infantry at the Battle of Cromdale, Strathspey, on 1 May 1690. [BK.177]

GRANT, DAVID, in Lieutenant Colonel Alexander Riddoch's Company of Militia in Barbados, 1679. [H2.159]

GRANT, DONALD, a prisoner of war captured at the Siege of Worcester on 2 September 1651, was transported via London on the John and Sarah of London to Boston in December 1651, landed there in February 1652. [Suffolk Deeds.1/5-6]

GRANT, HUGH, in Captain Stephen Brown's Company of Militia in Barbados, 1679. [H2.108]

GRANT, JAMES, a soldier from Elgin, Moray, married Ann Lindsay from Dundee, in Schiedam, Holland, on 19 December 1637. [Schiedam Marriage Register]

GRANT, JAMES, [1], a prisoner of war captured at the Siege of Worcester on 2 September 1651, was transported via London on the John and Sarah of London to Boston in December 1651, landed there in February 1652. [Suffolk Deeds.1/5-6][LLNV.249]

GRANT, JAMES, [2], a prisoner of war captured at the Siege of Worcester on 2 September 1651, was transported via London on the John and Sarah of London to Boston in December 1651, landed there in February 1652. [Suffolk Deeds.1/5-6][LLNV.249]

GRANT, JAMES, [3], a prisoner of war captured at the Siege of Worcester on 2 September 1651, was transported via London on the John and Sarah of London to Boston in December 1651, landed there in February 1652. [Suffolk Deeds.1/5-6]

GRANT, JOHN, [1], a prisoner of war captured at the Siege of Worcester on 2 September 1651, was transported via London on the John and Sarah of London to Boston in December 1651, landed there in February 1652. [Suffolk Deeds.1/5-6]

GRANT, JOHN, [2], a prisoner of war captured at the Siege of Worcester on 2 September 1651, was transported via London on the John and Sarah of London to Boston in December 1651, landed there in February 1652. [Suffolk Deeds.1/5-6]

GRANT, JOHN, [3], a prisoner of war captured at the Siege of Worcester on 2 September 1651, was transported via London on

the John and Sarah of London to Boston in December 1651, landed there in February 1652. [Suffolk Deeds.1/5-6]

GRANT, JOHN, in Colonel Lyne's Company of Militia in Barbados in 1679. [H2.99]

GRANT, JOHN, of Ballindalloch, a Jacobite at the Battle of Killiecrankie, Perthshire, on 27 July 1689. [APS.IX.55]

GRANT, JOHN, the elder, a soldier in Lieutenant Colonel Alexander Riddoch's Company of Militia in Barbados in 1679. [H2.159]

GRANT, Captain JOHN, of Grant's Regiment of Infantry at the Battle of Cromdale, Strathspey, on 1 May 1690. [BK.177]

GRANT, JONAS, a Lieutenant in Danish Service, at Gluckstadt in 1628. [SAA.112]

GRANT, PATRICK, a prisoner of war captured at the Siege of Worcester on 2 September 1651, was transported via London on the John and Sarah of London to Boston in December 1651, landed there in February 1652. [Suffolk Deeds.1/5-6]

GRANT, Lieutenant Colonel PATRICK, of Grant's Regiment of Infantry at the Battle of Cromdale, Strathspey, on 1 May 1690. [BK.177] [NRS.GD77.189]

GRANT, PETER, a prisoner of war captured at the Battle of Dunbar on 3 September 1650, was transported via London on the Unity of Boston to Boston in November 1650, an indentured servant at Lynn Ironworks in 1650s. [Suffolk Court Files.1226][LLNV.266]

GRANT Captain ROBERT, of Grant's Regiment of Infantry at the Battle of Cromdale, Strathspey, on 1 May 1690. [BK.177]

GRANT, THOMAS, a prisoner of war captured at the Siege of Worcester on 2 September 1651, was transported via London on the John and Sarah of London to Boston in December 1651, landed there in February 1652. [Suffolk Deeds.1/5-6][LLNV.249]

GRANT, WILLIAM, a prisoner of war captured at the Siege of Worcester on 2 September 1651, was transported via London on

the John and Sarah of London to Boston in December 1651, landed there in February 1652. [Suffolk Deeds.1/5-6]

GRANT, WILLIAM, a soldier in Lieutenant Colonel Carter's Company of Militia in Barbados in 1679. [H2.201]

GRANT, Captain, a Jacobite, who was killed at the Battle of Killiecrankie, Perthshire, on 27 July 1689. [APS.IX.55]

GRAY, ALEXANDER, Sergeant of the Militia of Dundee in 1643. [DCW.13]

GRAY, ALEXANDER, a soldier in the Earl of Mar's Regiment, was court-martialled in March 1680. [NRS.GD124.13.17]

GRAY, Colonel Sir ANDREW, sailed from Leith to Hamburg with 1500 recruits for service under the King of Bohemia in 1620, later under Mansfeld fought in Danish Service against Spinola in the Netherlands. [RPCS.XII.2][STW.111][SAA.113]

GRAY, D., an Ensign of the 1st Company of Cockburn's Regiment in Swedish Service in 1609. [SIS.216]

GRAY, GEORGE, a prisoner of war captured at the Battle of Dunbar on 3 September 1650, was transported via London on the Unity of Boston to Boston in November 1650, settled at Kittery, Berwick, Maine, in 1656. [CEB][LLNV.250/267]

GRAY, JAMES, a prisoner in Edinburgh Tolbooth, released to go to Holland as a soldier on 12 April 1681. [ETR]

GRAY, MUNGO, a Sergeant of Mackenzie's Company in Danish Service in 1628. [SAA.ii.124]

GRAY, Cornet PATRICK, of Livingstone's Regiment of Dragoons at the Battle of Cromdale, Strathspey, on 1 May 1690. [BK.177]

GRAY, WILLIAM, a soldier under Captain Phillippe la Lou, married Josijnta Jacobsdaughter from Nieuwpoort in Flanders, in Leiden, Holland, on 16 March 1606. [Leiden Marriage Register]

GRAY, WILLIAM, in Angus, of the Earl of Airlie's Militia in 1670. [NRS.GD16.53.39]

GRAY, WILLIAM, a prisoner in Edinburgh Tolbooth, released to go to Holland as a soldier under Captain Bruce on 8 May 1685. [ETR]

GREER, Lieutenant THOMAS, in Lecale, Ireland, 1653. [OB.83]

GRIEVE, FRANCIS, in Angus, of the Earl of Airlie's Militia in 1670. [NRS.GD16.53.39]

GRIEVE, WILLIAM, Captain of the Cameronian Regiment at the Siege of Dunkeld on 21 August 1689. [BK.146]

GRIM, GEORGE, a soldier from Crail, Fife, married J.Wauchop in Schiedam, Holland, in 1636. [Schiedam Marriage Register]

GRINTON, ALEXANDER, a soldier in Edinburgh Castle, deserted in 1691. [NRS.RH.49.2]

GUNN, DANIEL, a prisoner of war captured at the Siege of Worcester on 2 September 1651, was transported via London on the <u>John and Sarah of London</u> to Boston in December 1651, landed there in February 1652. [Suffolk Deeds.1/5-6]

GUNN, GEORGE, an officer of Mackay's Regiment, in Danish Service in 1626, in Swedish Service in 1629. [TGSI.VIII.188]

GUNN, JOHN, a soldier of the 2nd Company of Cockburn's Regiment in Swedish Service in 1609. [SIS.217]

GUNN, JOHN, born in October 1608, an officer of Mackay's Regiment, in Danish Service in 1626, in Swedish Service in 1629. [TGSI.VIII.188]; a Colonel in Germany in the service of Gustavus Adolphus, ca.1630, Military Governor of Ohlua, Silesia, from 1638 until his death on 9 April 1649, buried in the Evangelical church there. [SIG.283/316][MGIF]

GUNN, JOHN, a soldier, was granted a pass to travel to Bergen, Holland, in 1620. [TNA.E157.86]

GUNN, JOHN, in Lieutenant Colonel Alexander Riddoch's Company of Militia in Barbados in 1679. [H2.159]

GUNN, WILLIAM, born 1597, a soldier, was granted a pass to travel to Rotterdam in 1621. [TNA.E157.8]

GUNN, Sir WILLIAM, Captain of Mackay's Regiment, in Danish Service in 1626, in Swedish Service in 1629, later Colonel of a Dutch Regiment. [TGSI.VIII.186]; a Colonel in Germany in the service of Gustavus Adolphus, ca.1630, later a General of the Imperial Army. [SIG.282]

GUTHRIE, Major GEORGE, was naturalised and confirmed as a nobleman in Poland-Lithuania in 1673, [SCA.102][BPL] [STW.211]; a Lieutenant Colonel in Polish Service, married Anna Constantia Combier, in the Reformed Church of Peter and Paul in Danzig, [Gdansk], on 26 April 1678. ['The Guthrie Family, 1985]

GUTHRIE, JOHN, Lieutenant of the Angus Regiment in 1646. [DCW.78]

GUTHRIE, ROBERT, a prisoner of war, possibly captured at the Battle of Dunbar on 3 September 1650, transported via London to New England, an indentured servant, later in Block Island. [NWI.I.159][LLNV.250]

GUTHRIE, ROBERT, in Angus, of the Earl of Airlie's Militia in 1670. [NRS.GD16.53.39]

GUTHRIE, Captain WILLIAM, in Ireland, testament, 1649, Comm. Edinburgh. [NRS]

HADDEN, ..., Ensign of Mackay's Regiment, in Swedish Service in 1629, was killed at New Brandenburg in 1631. [TGSI.VIII.188]

HADDOCK, Lieutenant JAMES, died in Mallon, Ireland, on 18 December 1657. [Drumbeg gravestone, County Down]

HADDOW, THOMAS, a soldier under Sir Henry Balfour, married Jean Marshall from Scotland, in Aardenburg, Holland, on 19 July 1608. [Aardenburg Marriage Register]

HAGOMAN [?], JOHN, a prisoner of war who was captured at the Siege of Worcester on 2 September 1651, was transported via London on the <u>John and Sarah of London</u> to Boston in December 1651, landed there in February 1652. [Suffolk Deeds.1/5-6]

HAIG, JOHN, a soldier from Scotland, married Dorothea, daughter of Albrecht Moercke, a labourer, in Altstadt, Konigsberg, on 20 May 1621. [Altstadt Marriage Register]

HALDANE, Sir JOHN, of Gleneagles, of Lawers' Brigade, who was killed at the Battle of Dunbar on 3 September 1650. [SR.37]

HALDANE, JOHN, Captain of the Cameronian Regiment at the Siege of Dunkeld on 21 August 1689. [BK.146]

HALIBURTON, ALEXANDER, the younger, a Captain of Militia in Dundee in 1651. [DCW.54][CBRD.174]

HALIBURTON, Lieutenant ALEXANDER, a Jacobite captured at the Battle of Cromdale, Strathspey, on 1 May 1690. [RPCS.XV.304]

HALIBURTON, DAVID, a soldier who fought in Sweden, Russia, and Poland around 1657, Lieutenant of Dragoons in Kedainai, Lithuania, in 1660s, settled in Kedainai. [SCL.160/305]

HALIBURTON, DAVID, of Pitcur, a Jacobite at the Battle of Killiecrankie, Perthshire, on 27 July 1689. [APS.IX.55]

HALIBURTON, JAMES, of the Angus Regiment at the Battle of Marston Moor, Yorkshire, on 2 July 1644. [DCW.78]

HALIBURTON, Major THOMAS, Military Governor of Steinburg in 1658. [MGIF]

HALLYBURTON, WILLIAM, an Ensign who died at Darien on 6 December 1698, testament, 1707, Comm. Edinburgh. [NRS]

HALKETT, Sir JAMES, with 3 Troops of Cavalry, fought at the Battle of Dunbar on 3 September 1650. [BD]

HALKET, ROBERT, from Dysart, Fife, a gunner aboard the <u>Lion of Zeeland</u> in 1631. [ZA]

HALKETT, Colonel ROBERT, with 2 Troops of Cavalry, fought at the Battle of Dunbar on 3 September 1650.

HALLIDAY, RICHARD, a soldier of the 1st Company of Cockburn's Regiment in Swedish Service in 1609. [SIS.217]

HAMILTON, Captain ALEXANDER, born 1613, son of Patrick Hamilton of Innerwick, died in 1648. [Old Abbey gravestone, Bangor, Ireland]; Captain of Nithsdale's Regiment, raised a Company of men in Ireland which were shipped via Scotland to Germany in 1628. [RPCS.II.241]

HAMILTON, ALEXANDER, Military Governor of Hanau, Hesse, from 1631 to 1634. [MGIF]

HAMILTON, ALEXANDER, a soldier in Halberstadt, Germany, a letter dated 1632. [NRS.GD406.1.1336]

HAMILTON, Sir ALEXANDER, of Redhouse, a Colonel in Swedish Service, cannon maker at Urbowe, Sweden, in 1630, General of Artillery in 1640; fought in the Wars of the Covenant in Scotland, was killed by an explosion at the Siege of Dunglass Castle. [TGSI.VIII.160][CA.112]

HAMILTON, ALEXANDER, a Quartermaster of Fraser's Dragoons, in 1646. [TFD.47]

HAMILTON, ALEXANDER, a Lieutenant Colonel in the Service of the Czar of Muscovy, a birth brief, 1670, [RPCS.3.143]; a deed, 1700. [NRS.RD3.94-95]

HAMILTON, Captain CHARLES, father of Reinhold who was baptised in the Reformed Church in Tilsit, Lithuania, on 3 May 1665.

HAMILTON, CLAUD, Captain of the Earl of Lindsay's Regiment in Bangor, Ireland, in 1642. [TNA.SP28.120]; Lieutenant Colonel of the East Lothian Foot from 1644 to 1647. [CA.131]

HAMILTON, DAVID, a prisoner of war captured at the Siege of Worcester on 2 September 1651, was transported via London on

the John and Sarah of London to Boston in December 1651, landed there in February 1652. [Suffolk Deeds.1/5-6]

HAMILTON, FREDERICK, Standard Bearer to Augustus of Norway, General of the Elector of Brandenburg in 1665. [EUL.Laing Charters.2589]

HAMILTON, Sir FREDERICK, an Ulster Scot, brought the Ulster Horse over in 1644, at the Siege of Newark in 1646. [CA.147]

HAMILTON, HANS, Lieutenant of Viscount Claneboy's Regiment on Bangor, Ireland, in 1642. [CalSPIre.260.63]

HAMILTON, HUGH, Military Governor of Greifswald, Mecklenburg, in 1646. [MGIF]

HAMILTON, JAMES, a prisoner, guilty of murder, opted to go to Flanders as a soldier in 1596. [RPCS.VIII.799]

HAMILTON, JAMES, Marquis of Hamilton, a General under Gustavus Adolphus in Germany, 1630. [SIG.282]

HAMILTON, JAMES, a prisoner of war captured at the Siege of Worcester on 2 September 1651, was transported via London on the John and Sarah of London to Boston in December 1651, landed there in February 1652. [Suffolk Deeds.1/5-6]

HAMILTON, Captain JAMES, son of William Hamilton, was killed at the Battle of Blenburb, Ireland, on 5 June 1646. [Blenburb monument]

HAMILTON, Lieutenant Colonel JAMES, of Forthills, County Meath, Ireland, an assignation, 1709. [NRS.GD10.508]

HAMILTON, JOHN, an archer of the Scots Guards of France in 1560. [NRS.NRAS.O.143]

HAMILTON, Colonel JOHN, was licenced by King James VI to 'strek drummes and mak proclamatioun in all burghs to recruit four companies for Flanders' in 1596. [NRS.GD86.D162.18]

HAMILTON, JOHN, in an Irish muster roll of 1618.
[CalSPIre.1618.501][BM.Add.ms.18735]

HAMILTON, JOHN, Captain of the Earl of Eglinton's Regiment on Bangor, Ireland, in 1642. [TNA.SP28.120]

HAMILTON, JOHN, Lieutenant Colonel of the Earl of Lindsay's Regiment on Bangor, Ireland, in 1642. [TNA.SP28.120]

HAMILTON, JOHN, from Hamilton, a soldier in Dutch Service, bound from Amsterdam to the New Netherlands on De Bonte Koe on 15 April 1660. [New York Colonial ms.XIII.fo.88]

HAMILTON, Sir JOHN, Captain of Belhaven's Troop of Horse at the Battle of Killiecrankie, Perthshire, on 27 July 1689. [BK.96]

HAMILTON, Sir J., a Colonel in Germany in the service of Gustavus Adolphus, around 1630. [SIG.282]

HAMILTON, Ensign MALCOLM, in Carrickfergus, Ireland, in 1708. [PRONI.D162.18]

HAMILTON, NICHOLAS, a soldier, guilty of assault, was banished from Leiden, Holland, on 28 January 1593. [Leiden Court Records.3.17]

HAMILTON, PATRICK, Commandant of the Fortress of Klaipeda, Lithuania, from 1668 to 1684. [SCL]

HAMILTON, ROBERT, Captain of the Earl of Lindsay's Regiment on Bangor, Ireland, in 1642. [TNA.SP28.120]

HAMILTON, ROBERT, Lieutenant Colonel of Aytoun's Foot from 1645 to 1647, in the Army of the Covenant. [CA.113]

HAMILTON, Sir ROBERT, Captain of Leven's Regiment at the Battle of Killiecrankie, Perthshire, on 27 July 1689. [BK.95] [NRS.GD77.189]

HAMILTON, ROBERT, a Sergeant in Tilsit, Lithuania, 1681.[SCL]

HAMILTON, ROBERT, Captain of Colonel John Buchan's Regiment of Foot in Flanders, a deed, 1696. [NRS.RD2.79.878]

HAMILTON, RORY, a prisoner of war captured at the Siege of Worcester on 2 September 1651, was transported via London on the John and Sarah of London to Boston in December 1651, landed there in February 1652. [Suffolk Deeds.1/5-6]

HAMILTON, THOMAS, Lieutenant Colonel of the Train of Artillery in the Army of the Covenant in 1643. [CA.112]

HAMILTON, Captain THOMAS, with recruits, bound for Holland in 1684. [RPCS.VIII]

HAMILTON, THOMAS, from Bathgate, West Lothian, formerly a Captain of Sir John Hill's Regiment, an overseer in Darien, testament, 1707, Comm. Edinburgh. [NRS]

HAMILTON, Lieutenant Colonel WALTER, fought and was captured at the Battle of Dunbar on 3 September 1650.

HAMILTON, Colonel WALTER, on Nevis, West Indies, in 1699. [SPAWI.1699.714]

HAMILTON, WILLIAM, at muster rolls in County Cavan, Ireland, in 1618-1619. [CalSPIre.1618.501][Carew.ms211/3]

HAMILTON, WILLIAM, Captain of Sir Mungo Campbell of Lawers' Regiment in Temple Patrick, Ireland, in 1642. [TNA.SP28.120]

HAMILTON, Captain WILLIAM, of Lochcurran, County Tyrone, Ireland, a sasine, 1663. [NRS.RS42.II.67]

HAMILTON, WILLIAM, a soldier of Captain Allamby's Company of Militia in Barbados in 1679. [H2.155]

HAMILTON, WILLIAM, Lieutenant of Belhaven's Troop of Horse at the Battle of Killiecrankie, Perthshire, on 27 July 1689. [BK.96]

HAMILTON, WILLIAM, an Ensign who died at Darien in 1698. [NLS.RY2B8/19]

HAMILTON, Lieutenant Colonel, in the Service of the Empress of Russia, a birth brief dated 1670. [RPCS.1.40.326]

HANNA, ALEXANDER, Captain of the Scottish Company, in Memel in 1629. [St Johann's Marriage Register]

HANTON, JOHN, recruited for Danish Service in 1627, possibly died in Gluckstadt. [RPCS.IV.343][SAA.113]

HARKNESS, ADAM, Lieutenant of the Cameronian Regiment at the Siege of Dunkeld on 21 August 1689. [BK.146]

HARPER, JAMES, a soldier in Tilsit, Lithuania, in 1697. [SIG.262]

HARRISON, Lieutenant, at the Battle of Killiecrankie, Perthshire, on 27 July 1689. [BK.123][NRS.GD406.1.3647]

HAY, ALEXANDER, Captain of Mackay's Regiment, in Danish Service in 1626, in Swedish Service in 1629, a Lieutenant Colonel of Dragoons in the Swedish Army. [SHR.IX.270][TGSI.VIII.186]

HAY, ANDREW, a soldier under Captain de Fort, married Cathelijne Gisens from Brugge, [Bruges], Flanders, in Leiden, Holland, on 15 June 1603. [Leiden Marriage Register]

HAY, DAVID, a soldier who died in Darien, testament, 1707, Comm. Edinburgh. [NRS]

HAY, GEORGE, Ensign of Oliphant's Company in Danish Service, in 1628. [SAA.ii.143]

HAY, HENRY, Military Governor of Cobronskance in 1682, and of Kokenhusen from 1680 to 1695. [MGIF]

HAY, JAMES, born 1597, a soldier, was granted a pass to travel to Rotterdam in 1622. [TNA.E157.11]

HAY, JOHN, son of the Marquis of Tullibardine, a Lieutenant of the Royal Scots Dragoons, fought at the Battle of Killiecrankie, Perthshire, on 27 July 1689, was captured by the Jacobites. [BK.121][NRS.GD124.16.76; GD77.189]

HAY, JOHN, a soldier of Captain Liston's Company of Militia in Barbados in 1679. [H2.143]

HAY, JOHN, Ensign of the Cameronian Regiment at the Siege of Dunkeld on 21 August 1689. [BK.146]

HAY, JOHN, a prisoner in Canongate, was released to go to Holland as a soldier under Captain Robert Reid of Bonakettle on 18 June 1690. [RPCS.XV.713]

HAY, Lieutenant JOHN, died on the voyage to Darien on 28 October1698, testament, 1707, Comm. Edinburgh. [NRS]

HAY, PATRICK, from Edinburgh, formerly a Lieutenant of Lord Lindsay's Regiment of Foot, an overseer at Darien, testament, 1707, Comm. Edinburgh. [NRSa]

HAY, PETER, a carpenter with the Ducal Artillery, married Catherina a widow, in the Schlosskirche, Konigsberg, on 12 November 1691.

HAY, THEODORE, Lieutenant of Lord George Hamilton's Regiment in Flanders, a deed, 1697. [NRS.RD2.81/1.202]

HAY, WILLIAM, a soldier of Captain Cleaver's Company of Militia in Barbados in 1679. [H2.127]

HAY, Captain WILLIAM, of the Cameronian Regiment at the Siege of Dunkeld on 21 August 1689. [BK.146]

HEATLEY, GEORGE, a Captain of Mackay's Regiment, in Danish Service in 1626, in Swedish Service in 1629, was killed at Oberlin. [TGSI.VIII.186]; a Captain in Germany in the service of Gustavus Adolphus, ca.1630.

HEDDERICK, WILLIAM, a prisoner of war captured at the Siege of Worcester on 2 September 1651, was transported via London on the John and Sarah of London to Boston in December 1651, landed there in February 1652. [Suffolk Deeds.1/5-6]

HENDERSON, Captain ARCHIBALD, in Antigua in 1660s. [SPAWI.1672.806]

HENDERSON, BLAIS, a soldier, was granted a pass to travel to Tiel, Holland, in 1621. [TNA.E157.16]

HENDERSON, Major JAMES, of the Cameronian Regiment at the Siege of Dunkeld on 21 August 1689. [BK.146]

HENDERSON, JOHN, from Glasgow, a gunner aboard the <u>Arms of Zeeland</u> in 1644. [ZA]

HENDERSON, JOHN, a soldier of Lieutenant Colonel Tidcom's Company of Militia in Barbados in 1679. [H2.133]

HENDERSON, Sir JOHN, Colonel of a regiment in Holland, testament, 16 October 1693, Comm. Edinburgh. [NRS]

HENDERSON, MATTHEW, a soldier of Captain Ely's Company of Militia in Barbados in 1679. [H2.179]

HENDERSON, RICHARD, a soldier of Colonel Thornhill's Company of Militia in Barbados in 1679. [H2.146]

HENDERSON, Sir ROBERT, of Tenegask, Colonel of a Scottish regiment in the Low Countries, was admitted as a burgess and guilds-brother of Edinburgh on 27 June 1617. [EBR]

HENDERSON, Captain WILLIAM, from Edinburgh, formerly of McGill's Regiment, an overseer at Darien, died there in 1699, testament, 1707, Comm. Edinburgh. [NRS]

HENDERSON, JOHN, a soldier of Lieutenant Colonel Tidcom's Company of Militia in Barbados in 1679. [H2.133]

HENDERSON, WILLIAM, born 1590, a soldier, was granted a pass to travel to Den Haag, [The Hague], Holland, in 1624. [TNA.E157.12]

HENDRY, GEORGE, a soldier of Captain Lewgar's Company of Militia in Barbados in 1679. [H2.145]

HENDRY, HENDRY, a soldier from Orkney, married Grietge Williams from Ireland, in Rotterdam on 26 March 1606. [Rotterdam Marriage Register]

HENRYSON, JAMES, was admitted as a burgess of Stirling, having served in the burgh's company of soldiers, on 31 May 1644. [SBR]

HEPBURN, Sir ADAM, treasurer and commissary general of the Earl of Leven's Army in 1640; Colonel of the East Lothian Foot from 1645 to 1647. [CA.132]

HEPBURN, Captain DAVID, in Belfast, a deed, 1680. [NRS.RD4.47.866]

HEPBURN, JAMES, of the Angus Regiment at the Battle of Marston Moor, Yorkshire, on 2 July 1644. [D,CW.78]

HEPBURN, Sir JOHN, born 1598, second son of George Hepburn of Athelstaneford, East Lothian, was educated at Marischal College in Aberdeen, was in the Service of Frederick of Bohemia from 1620 to 1623, a Colonel of the Swedish Army from 1625 to 1632, Military Governor of Rugenwalde in 1630, Military Governor of Landshut 1631-1632, in French Service, a Marechal de France, entered the Service of Bernard of Weimar in 1635, died at the Siege of Saverne, France, on 8 July 1636, [MGIF] [SHR.IX.49]; testament, 1 June 1638, Comm. Edinburgh. [NRS] [SIG.282]

HEPBURN, Sir PATRICK, of Waughton, Colonel of the East Lothian Foot from 1643 to 1645, fought at the Siege of York and the Battle of Marston Moor. [CA.131]

HEPBURN, PATRICK, Major of East Lothian's Foot from 1644 to 1645, was killed at the Siege of Newcastle on 19 October 1645. [CA.132]

HEPBURN, PATRICK, a soldier of Major Foster's Company of Militia in Barbados in 1679. [H2.134]

HEPBURN, ROBERT, Captain of Robert Home of the Heugh's Regiment in Carrickfergus, Ireland, in 1642. [TNA.SP28.120]

HEPBURN, Sir ROBERT, Major of the Scots Army in Ireland, testament, 1647, Comm. Edinburgh. [NRS]

HERIOT, Captain ARCHIBALD, in Ireland, testament, 1667, Comm. Edinburgh. [NRS]

HERRIES, WALTER, a surgeon from Dunbarton, late of the Royal Navy, to Darien in 1698. [DD]

HERRIES, WILLIAM, Captain of the Cameronian Regiment at the Siege of Dunkeld on 21 August 1689. [BK.146]

HERRON, PATRICK, a prisoner of war captured at the Siege of Worcester on 2 September 1651, was transported via London on the John and Sarah of London to Boston in December 1651, landed there in February 1652. [Suffolk Deeds.1/5-6]

HERWICH, [Harvie?], JOHN, a Scottish soldier, father of Maria who was baptised in the Polish church in Steindamm, Prussia, on 4 December 1635.

HIGHEN, ROBERT, a prisoner of war captured at the Siege of Worcester on 2 September 1651, was transported via London on the John and Sarah of London to Boston in December 1651, landed there in February 1652. [Suffolk Deeds.1/5-6]

HILL, Colonel JOHN, Governor of Fort William, Inverness-shire, a letter, 1691. [NRS.E99.41.10]

HILL, THOMAS, Captain of Stewart's Regiment of Foot in Ireland, 1710. [IWD]

HILL, WILLIAM, Captain of Leven's Regiment at the Battle of Killiecrankie, Perthshire, on 27 July 1689. [BK.96]

HISLOP, FRANCIS, Ensign of the Cameronian Regiment at the Siege of Dunkeld, Perthshire, on 21 August 1689. [BK.146]

HOGG, DANIEL, a prisoner of war captured at the Siege of Worcester on 2 September 1651, was transported via London on the John and Sarah of London to Boston in December 1651, landed there in February 1652. [Suffolk Deeds.1/5-6]

HOGG, INGRAM, a soldier, was granted a pass to travel to Flanders in 1631. [TNA.E157.15]

HOGG, JOHN [1], a prisoner of war captured at the Siege of Worcester on 2 September 1651, was transported via London on the John and Sarah of London to Boston in December 1651, landed there in February 1652. [Suffolk Deeds.1/5-6]

HOGG, JOHN [2], a prisoner of war captured at the Siege of Worcester on 2 September 1651, was transported via London on the John and Sarah of London to Boston in December 1651, landed there in February 1652. [Suffolk Deeds.1/5-6]

HOGG, JOHN [3], a prisoner of war captured at the Siege of Worcester on 2 September 1651, was transported via London on the John and Sarah of London to Boston in December 1651, landed there in February 1652. [Suffolk Deeds.1/5-6]

HOGG, NEIL, a prisoner of war captured at the Siege of Worcester on 2 September 1651, was transported via London on the John and Sarah of London to Boston in December 1651, landed there in February 1652. [Suffolk Deeds.1/5-6]

HOLBOURNE, Major General JAMES, a Brigade commander who fought at the Battle of Dunbar on 3 September 1650. [SR.37]

HOME, ALEXANDER, Colonel of a Regiment of Horse in 1643.

HOME, Sir ALEXANDER, of Manderston, Captain of a Company of Foot in Dutch Service, testament, 22 January 1702, Comm. Edinburgh. [NRS]

HOME, Sir DAVID, of Wedderburn, an infantry officer who fought at the Battle of Dunbar on 3 September 1650. [SR.37]

HOME, GEORGE, Ensign of the Angus Regiment in 1645. [DCW.78]

HOME, GEORGE, a prisoner of war captured at the Siege of Worcester on 2 September 1651, was transported via London on the John and Sarah of London to Boston in December 1651, landed there in February 1652. [Suffolk Deeds.1/5-6]

HOME, HENRY, of the Scots Guards of France in 1560s. [NRS.NRAS.O.143]

HOME, JOHN, Major of the Earl of Leven's Regiment in Carrickfergus, Ireland, in 1642. [TNA.SP28.120]

HOME, Sir JOHN, of Aytoun, Colonel of Aytoun's Regiment of Foot Army of the Covenant in 1644. [CA.113]

HOME, Colonel ROBERT, in Carrickfergus, Ireland, in 1642. [TNA.SP28.120]

HOME, ROBERT, Captain of the Lifeguards of Foot in Donaghadee, Ireland, in 1642. [TNA.SP16.539.1/105]

HOME, THOMAS, a prisoner of war captured at the Battle of Dunbar on 3 September 1650, transported via London probably on the Unity of Boston in November 1650, settled in Kittery, Berwick, Maine, by 1656. [CEB][LLNV.250]

HOME, Lieutenant Colonel WILLIAM, of the East Lothian Foot from 1643 to 1644, he was killed at the Siege of Newcastle on 19 November 1644. [CA.132]

HOOD, ALEXANDER, a Scottish soldier under Captain Hay, married Neeltgen Gijsenbaert from Diksmuide in Flanders, in Leiden, Holland, on 23 February 1580. [Leiden Marriage Register]

HOOD, ANDREW, from Dundee, a soldier in the Service of the Dutch West India Company in Brazil in 1644. [GAA.NA.629.1095]

HOOD, MARTIN, a soldier from Burntisland, Fife, married Annette Antonis in Briellele, the Netherlands, in 1681. [Briellele Marriage Register]

HOPE, THOMAS, son of Alexander Hope of Kerse, a soldier bound from Leith on the Unicorn to Darien on 14 July 1698, died in Jamaica, testament, 1707, Comm. Edinburgh. [NRS]

HOUSTOUN, Captain ALEXANDER, was killed at Aulra in 1643. [Synod of Lothians and Tweedale, 1640-1649, p.143]

HOUSTOUN, JOHN, Captain of the Earl of Glencairn's Regiment in Carrickfergus, Ireland, in 1642. [TNA.SP28.120]

HOUSTOUN, Lieutenant, at Six Mile Quarter, Ireland in 1653. [OB.80/83]

HOW, DANIEL, a prisoner of war captured at the Siege of Worcester on 2 September 1651, was transported via London on the John and Sarah of London to Boston in December 1651, landed there in February 1652. [Suffolk Deeds.1/5-6]

HUDSON, DANIEL, a prisoner of war captured at the Siege of Worcester on 2 September 1651, was transported via London on the John and Sarah of London to Boston in December 1651, landed there in February 1652. [Suffolk Deeds.1/5-6]

HUDSON, JOHN, a prisoner of war captured at the Siege of Worcester on 2 September 1651, was transported via London on the John and Sarah of London to Boston in December 1651, landed there in February 1652. [Suffolk Deeds.1/5-6]

HUME, ALESTER, a prisoner of war captured at the Siege of Worcester on 2 September 1651, was transported via London on the John and Sarah of London to Boston in December 1651, landed there in February 1652. [Suffolk Deeds.1/5-6]

HUME, DAVID, [1], a prisoner of war captured at the Siege of Worcester on 2 September 1651, was transported via London on the John and Sarah of London to Boston in December 1651, landed there in February 1652. [Suffolk Deeds.1/5-6]

HUME, DAVID, [2], a prisoner of war captured at the Siege of Worcester on 2 September 1651, was transported via London on the John and Sarah of London to Boston in December 1651, landed there in February 1652. [Suffolk Deeds.1/5-6]

HUME, JOHN, a prisoner of war captured at the Siege of Worcester on 2 September 1651, was transported via London on the John and Sarah of London to Boston in December 1651, landed there in February 1652. [Suffolk Deeds.1/5-6]

HUME, PATRICK, Lieutenant Colonel of Lord Jedburgh's Dragoons, was admitted as a burgess of Ayr in 1699. [ABR]

HUME, ROBERT, a Captain of Mackay's Regiment in Danish Service in 1626, in Swedish Service in 1629. [TGSI.VIII.186]; a Captain in Germany in the service of Gustavus Adolphus, ca.1630. [SIG.282]

HUME, THOMAS, a prisoner of war captured at the Battle of Dunbar on 3 September 1650, transported from London on the Unity of Boston to Boston in November 1650, an indentured servant in York, New England. [York County Records.2.7.1672]

HUME, WILLIAM, from Glasgow, a gunner aboard the Dutch ship Neptunus on 1 May 1645. [ZA]

HUNTER, JOHN, a Corporal of Fraser's Dragoons in 1645. [TFD.219]

SHUNTER, JOHN, a soldier of Captain Walley's Company of Militia in Barbados in 1679. [H2.80]

HUNTER, WILLIAM, a soldier of Captain Adam's Company of Militia in Barbados in 1679. [H2.115]

INGLIS, ALEXANDER, from Dunblane [?], a drummer under Captain George Hume, married Emmeken Clerclx from Moerebeecke in Flanders, in Arnemuiden, Zeeland, on 2 June 1612. [Arnemuiden Marriage Register]

INGLIS, Lieutenant Colonel, ALEXANDER, fought and was captured at the Battle of Dunbar on 3 September 1650.

INGLIS, DENIS, was released from prison in Edinburgh to go as a soldier to Flanders in the Earl of Leven's Regiment in 1692. [NRS.GD26.7.74]

INGLIS, JAMES, a prisoner of war captured at the Siege of Worcester on 2 September 1651, was transported via London on the John and Sarah of London to Boston in December 1651, landed there in February 1652. [Suffolk Deeds.1/5-6]

INGLIS, Lieutenant JAMES, died 3 November 1698 on the voyage to Darien. [WP.88][DD.157]

INGLIS, Captain JOHN, in Angus, of the Earl of Airlie's Militia in 1670. [NRS.GD16.53.39]

INGLIS, PATRICK, a prisoner of war captured at the Siege of Worcester on 2 September 1651, was transported via London on the John and Sarah of London to Boston in December 1651, landed there in February 1652. [Suffolk Deeds.1/5-6]

INGLIS, THOMAS, a soldier in Edinburgh Castle, was to be discharged on 31 July 1700. [NRS.GD26.9.68]

INGLIS, Major WILLIAM, in Slutsk, Lithuania, in 1657. [SCL.160]

INNES, ALEXANDER, a prisoner of war captured at the Battle of Dunbar on 3 September 1650, transported from London on the Unity of Boston to Boston in November 1650, an indentured servant at the Lynn Ironworks in the 1650s. [Suffolk Court Files.1226][LLNV.247]

INNES, ALEXANDER, was appointed as chaplain to the garrison at New York on 20 April 1686. [SPAWI.1686.896]

INNES, ALEXANDER, from West Lothian, a gunner's boy on the St Andrew bound from Leith to Darien on 14 July 1698, testament, 1707, Comm. Edinburgh. [NRS]

INNES, Captain ANDREW, was enobled in Poland in 1662. [STW.211][BPL]

INNES, Captain GEORGE, of Lumsden's Foot, in 1644. [CA.145]

INNES, Sir JOHN, a Colonel in Germany in the Service of Gustavus Adolphus, ca.1630; a Brigade commander, who fought at the Battle of Dunbar on 3 September 1650. [SR.37] [SIG.282]

INNES, JOHN, son of William Innes of Sandside, an officer of Mackay's Regiment, in Danish Service in 1626, a Captain in

Swedish Service in 1629, was killed at Stralsund, Germany. [TGSI.VIII.188] [SIG.282]

INNES, Lieutenant Colonel JOHN, of Dalhousie's Foot, 1643, fought at the Siege of Newcastle and the Battle of Marston Moor in 1644, also at the Battle of Philiphaugh in 1645. [CA.129]

INNES, JOHN, a soldier of Captain Thornhill's Company of Militia in Barbados in 1679. [H2.151]

INNES, PATRICK, a Captain of Mackay's Regiment in Danish Service in 1626, a Captain in Swedish Service in 1629, was killed at Nurnberg, Bavaria, in 1632. [TGSI.VIII.186] [SIG.282]

INNES, ROBERT, a Captain of Mackay's Regiment in Danish Service in 1626, in Swedish Service in 1629. [TGSI.VIII.186]

INNES, WILLIAM, Captain of Lord Sinclair's Regiment in Newry, Ireland, in 1642. [TNA.SP28.120]

INNES, WILLIAM, in Angus, of the Earl of Airlie's Militia in 1670. [NRS.GD16.53.39]

INNES, WILLIAM, a soldier of Captain Affleck's Company of Militia in Barbados in 1679. [H2.148]

IRVING, ALEXANDER, Military Governor of Regensburg, Bavaria, in 1633. [MGIF]

IRVING, Colonel ALEXANDER, Military Governor of Stade, Saxony, from 1654 -1656. [MGIF]

IRVING, Captain JAMES, of Colonel Alexander Leslie's Company in Muscovite Service from 1630 to 1632. [STW.179]

IRVING, ROBERT, Captain of Livingstone's Regiment of Dragoons at the Battle of Cromdale, Strathspey, on 1 May 1690. [BK.177]

IRVING, Captain ROBERT, of the King of France's Guards on 7 March 1656. [RGS.X.525]

ISLAY, Captain JOHN, of Livingstone's Regiment of Dragoons at the Battle of Cromdale, Strathspey, on 1 May 1690. [BK.177]

JACK, GEORGE, from Leith, a gunner aboard the Dutch ship Zeeridder on 1 May 1647. [ZA]

JACK, JAMES, a smith, late of Colonel Ferguson's Regiment in Holland, a burgess of Ayr in 1699. [ABR]

JACK, WILLIAM, from Prestonpans, Midlothian, a musketeer aboard the Dutch ship Sandenburch in 1645. [ZA]

JACKSON, JAMES, a prisoner of war captured at the Siege of Worcester on 2 September 1651, was transported via London on the John and Sarah of London to Boston in December 1651, landed there in February 1652. [Suffolk Deeds.1/5-6]

JACKSON, PATRICK, a prisoner of war captured at the Siege of Worcester on 2 September 1651, was transported via London on the John and Sarah of London to Boston in December 1651, landed there in February 1652. [Suffolk Deeds.1/5-6]

JACKSON, RICHARD, a prisoner of war captured at the Siege of Worcester on 2 September 1651, was transported via London on the John and Sarah of London to Boston in December 1651, landed there in February 1652. [Suffolk Deeds.1/5-6]

JACKSON, WALTER, a prisoner of war captured at the Siege of Worcester on 2 September 1651, was transported via London on the John and Sarah of London to Boston in December 1651, landed there in February 1652. [Suffolk Deeds.1/5-6]

JAMES, Captain, a Scottish soldier long in the Service of Muscovy, 1591. [CSP.X.584]

JAMIESON, DAVID, a prisoner of war captured at the Siege of Worcester on 2 September 1651, was transported via London on the John and Sarah of London to Boston in December 1651, landed there in February 1652. [Suffolk Deeds.1/5-6]

JAMIESON, NEIL, a prisoner of war captured at the Siege of Worcester on 2 September 1651, was transported via London on the John and Sarah of London to Boston in December 1651, landed there in February 1652. [Suffolk Deeds.1/5-6]

JAMIESON, PATRICK, a prisoner of war captured at the Siege of Worcester on 2 September 1651, was transported via London on the John and Sarah of London to Boston in December 1651, landed there in February 1652. [Suffolk Deeds.1/5-6]

JARDINE, WILLIAM, a prisoner of war captured at the Battle of Dunbar on 3 September 1650, transported from London on the Unity of Boston to Boston in November 1650, an indentured servant at the Lynn Ironworks in the 1650s. [Suffolk Court Files.1226][LLNV.247]

JOHNSON, ALEXANDER, a soldier from St Andrews, Fife, married Aechtge Willems in Rotterdam in 1588. [Rotterdam Marriage Register]

JOHNSON, Colonel FRANCIS, in Narva, Estonia, in 1639, [SSNE]; in Riga, Latvia, in 1663. [GAA.NA.2157.54]

JOHNSON, JAMES, master of the Dutch West India warship Golden Lion of Walcheren off the coast of Guinea in the 1660s. [SCA.333]

JOHNSON, NEIL, a prisoner of war captured at the Siege of Worcester on 2 September 1651, was transported via London on the John and Sarah of London to Boston in December 1651, landed there in February 1652. [Suffolk Deeds.1/5-6]

JOHNSON, THOMAS, from Edinburgh, a mariner on the Dutch warship Waaenaer, testament, 1666. [GAA.ONA.224.10.34]

JOHNSTONE, ALEXANDER, a soldier in Kerr's Company at the Battle of Killiecrankie, Perthshire, on 27 July 1689, was captured by the Jacobites. [RPCS.XIV]

JOHNSTONE, ALEXANDER, a soldier who died at Darien in 1699, testament, 1707, Comm. Edinburgh. [NRS]

SCOTTISH SOLDIERS IN EUROPE AND AMERICA, 1600-1700.

JOHNSTONE, ARCHIBALD, Captain of a Company of Militia in Barbados in 1679. [H2.164]

JOHNSTONE, Sergeant ARCHIBALD, of Captain Dalyell's Company, was mustered at Glasgow in 1682. [DSA.126]

JOHNSTON, FRANCIS, Military Governor of Narva, Estonia, in 1639. [MGIF]

JOHNSTON, JAMES, Military Governor of Koporic in 1640. [MGIF]

JOHNSTONE, Sir JAMES, of Elphinstone, a Captain of the Army of the Duke of Lunenburg in 1677. [NRS.GD190.3.195]

JOHNSTON, JOHN, son of a maltman in Culross, a prisoner in Edinburgh Tolbooth, released to go to Holland as a soldier with Captain Thomas Hamilton on 11 March 1684. [RPCS.8.403/683]

JOHNSTON, Sir JOHN, Major of a Scottish regiment in the Service of the King of France in 1688. [DSA.159]

JOHNSTONE, JOHN, Captain of Annandale's Troop of Horse at the Battle of Killiecrankie, Perthshire, on 27 July 1689. [BK.96]

JOHNSTON, Ensign ROBERT, in County Fermanagh, Ireland, in 1659. [C]

JOHNSTONE, Captain ROBERT, of the Stirling Militia in 1677. [NRS.B66.25.381]

JOHNSTON, THOMAS, Ensign of Forbes of Tullich's Company in Danish Service in 1628. [SAA.ii.121]

JOHNSTONE, WILLIAM, of Blacklaws, second son of James Johnstone the Marquis of Annandale and his wife Margaret Douglas, Lieutenant Colonel of the Douglas Regiment in French Service, died at Newbie in 1656. [SP.I.258]

JOHNSTON, WILLIAM, in Angus, of the Earl of Airlie's Militia in 1670. [NRS.GD16.53.39]

JOHNSTONE, WILLIAM, Ensign of Colonel Stanfast's Regiment of Militia in Barbados in 1679. [H2.157]

JOHNSTONE,....., an officer of Mackay's Regiment in Danish Service in 1626, in Swedish Service in 1629. [TGSI.VIII.188]

JONES, JOHN, a Scottish soldier under Captain Phillippe le Lou, married Christijna Wuaqebuyrs in Leiden, Holland, on 1 March 1606. [Leiden Marriage Register]

JONES, PATRICK, a prisoner of war captured at the Siege of Worcester on 2 September 1651, was transported via London on the John and Sarah of London to Boston in December 1651, landed there in February 1652. [Suffolk Deeds.1/5-6]

JORDAN, DAVID, Lieutenant Colonel of Dragoons in Lithuania, 1651-1658. [SCL.160]

JOYNER, DAVID, born 1664, a government soldier, wounded at the Battle of Killiecrankie, Perthshire, on 27 July 1689. [RPCS.XIV]

KEIR, JOHN, a soldier, father of William who was baptised in Lobenicht, Prussia, on 11 April 1625.

KEIR, M. in Angus, of the Earl of Airlie's Militia in 1670. [NRS.GD16.53.39]

KEITH, Captain GEORGE, of Aden, Aberdeenshire, of the Earl Marischal's Regiment in the Army of the Covenant, fought at the Siege of Newcastle in 1644, also at Hereford and Newark in England in 1644.

KEITH, GEORGE, a Sergeant Major in Antrim, Ireland, in 1645. [Cal.SPIre.260.137]

KEITH, GEORGE, of Colonel Keith's Regiment, fought at the Battle of Preston, Lancashire, where he was captured in 1648, and later fought at the Siege of Worcester in 1651.

KEITH, GEORGE, a Lieutenant Colonel in Ireland, later in Muscovy, where he died in 16... [ACA.APB.8.7.1662]

KEITH, THOMAS, a soldier of Captain Bowcher's Company of Militia in Barbados in 1679. [H2.9]

KEITH, WILLIAM, a Major of Mackay's Regiment in Danish Service in 1626, in Swedish Service in 1629. [TGSI.VIII.186]

KEITH, ..., a Lieutenant of Mackay's Regiment in Danish Service in 1626, in Swedish Service in 1629, was killed at New Brandenburg. [TGSI.VIII.187]

KELLO, JOHN, a prisoner in Edinburgh Tolbooth, was released to go to Holland as a soldier in 1691. [RPCS.XVI]

KELLY, TIMOTHY, a prisoner in Canongate Tolbooth was released to go to Holland as a soldier under Captain Robert Reid of Bonakettle on 18 June 1690. [RPCS.XV.713]

KELSO, ANDREW, from Wemyss, Fife, a musketeer aboard the Dutch ship Sandenburch in 1645. [ZA]

KELTON, THOMAS, a prisoner of war captured at the Battle of Dunbar on 3 September 1650, transported from London on the Unity of Boston to Boston in November 1650, an indentured servant at the Lynn Ironworks in the 1650s. [Suffolk Court Files.1226][LLNV.247]

KEMPER, DANIEL, a prisoner of war captured at the Siege of Worcester on 2 September 1651, was transported via London on the John and Sarah of London to Boston in December 1651, landed there in February 1652. [Suffolk Deeds.1/5-6]

KENNEDY, Sir ARCHIBALD, of Culzean, a Jacobite at the Battle of Killiecrankie, Perthshire, on 27 July 1689. [APS.IX.55]

KENNEDY, CORNELIUS, a Colonel in Dutch Service in 1709. [NRS.GD27.3.1-50]

KENNEDY, DANIEL, a soldier of Captain Thorburn's Company of Militia in Barbados in 1679. [H2.140]

KENNEDY, HUMPHREY, a soldier of Captain Thorburn's Company of Militia in Barbados in 1679. [H2.41]

KENNEDY, JAMES, a soldier of Captain Lewgar's Company of Militia in Barbados in 1679. [H2.138]

KENNEDY, JOHN, a soldier of Captain Lyne's Company of Militia in Barbados in 1679. [H2.138]

KENNEDY, JOHN, a defaulter from Captain Lyne's Company of Militia in Barbados in 1679. [H2.156]

KENNEDY, JOHN, a trooper of Captain John Leslie's Troop of Militia in Barbados in 1679. [H2.208]

KENNEDY, RICHARD, a soldier of Lieutenant Colonel Affleck's Company of Militia in Barbados in 1679. [H2.148]

KENNEDY, ROBERT, Captain of Robert Home of the Heugh's Regiment in Carrickfergus, Ireland, in 1642. [TNA.SP28.120]

KENNEDY, THOMAS, a soldier of Captain Ely's Company of Militia in Barbados in 1679. [H2.177]

KENNEDY, THOMAS, Captain of Kenmure's Regiment at the Battle of Killiecrankie, Perthshire, on 27 July 1689. [BK.96]

KENNEDY, WILLIAM, a soldier of Captain Merrell's Company of Militia in Barbados in 1679. [H2.153]

KENNEDY, WILLIAM, a soldier of Captain Adam's Company of Militia in Barbados in 1679. [H2.115]

KENNEDY, ..., a soldier in Flanders in 1696, possibly from Ayr. [NRS.CH2.751.8/139]

KERR, ANDREW, a Cornet of Fraser's Dragoons, in 1643 [TFD.47]

KER, Sir ANDREW, of Greenhead, an infantry officer who fought at the Battle of Dunbar on 3 September 1650. [SR.37]

KERR, DANIEL, of Kerrsland, a Major of the Earl of Angus's Regiment of Foot [the Cameronian Regiment], at the Siege of Dunkeld on 21 August 1689. [BK.146], later in Flanders, a burgess of Ayr in 1692. [ABR]

KER, GILBERT, with his Regiment of Horse, fought at the Battle of Dunbar on 3 September 1650.

KERR, JOHN, a prisoner in Edinburgh Tolbooth, was released to go to Holland as a soldier with Captain Sharp on 12 July 1689. [RPCS.XIII.585]

KERR, ROBERT, Quartermaster of the Scottish regiments which returned from England, was quartered in Linlithgow, West Lothian, in 1645. [NRS.GD76.237]

KER, Major General THOMAS, killed at Leipzig, Saxony, in the service of Gustavus Adolphus, ca.1630. [SIG.282]

KERR, THOMAS, an engineer, late from Flanders, to Darien in 1699, died in the West Indies, testament, 1707, Comm. Edinburgh. [NRS]

KERR, WILLIAM, a Captain of Mackay's Regiment in Danish Service in 1626, in Swedish Service in 1629. [TGSI.VIII.186]

KER, WILLIAM, Sergeant of Forbes of Tullich's Company in Danish Service in 1628. [SAA.ii.121]

KERR, WILLIAM, Captain of the Earl of Lothian's Regiment in Carrickfergus, Ireland, in 1642. [TNA.SP28.120]

KEY, JOHN, a prisoner of war captured at the Battle of Dunbar on 3 September 1650, transported from London on the <u>Unity of Boston</u> to Boston in November 1650. [Suffolk Court Files.1226]

KIDD, JAMES, Lieutenant of Militia in Dundee in 1643. [DCW.13]

KIDD, JAMES, a soldier of Captain Hall's Company of Militia in Barbados in 1679. [H2.136]

KIDD, ROBERT, a soldier from Edinburgh, married Trijnntge Pieters from Hamburg, in Schiedam, Holland, on 25 January 1634. [Schiedam Marriage Register]

KIDD, WILLIAM, a soldier of Captain Woodward's Company of Militia in Barbados in 1680. [H2.156]

KILPATRICK, Captain, an officer in Dutch Service in 1684. [RPCS.VIII.392]

KINCAID, EDWARD, an army chaplain under General Baner, was buried in St Elisabeth's, Danzig, [Gdansk], in 1641. [CRD]

KINCAID, Captain ROBERT, at Island Magee, Ireland, in 1653. [OB.80]

KING, Sir JAMES, of Dudwick, born 1589, son of David King, moved to Sweden in 1609, a General under Gustavus Adolphus, Military Governor of Vlotho, returned to Scotland in 1639, fought for King Charles I at Marston Moor, Yorkshire, on 2 July 1644, died in Stockholm on 9 June 1652. [AUR.34.119][SHR.IX.40][SS.39][SIG.282]

KINNAIRD, JAMES, of Culbin, Quartermaster of the King's Regiment of Horse, a Jacobite soldier in 1689. [APS.app.xi.161]

KINNAIRD, JOHN, was commissioned into the Russian Army in 1632. [SSA.48]

KINNAIRD, Ensign, son of the laird of Culbin, died at Darien in 1700. [DD.325]

KINNENMONT, Lieutenant JOHN, married Janneken Jans van den Bossche from Gelderland, in Aardenburg, Holland, on 27 September 1609. [Aardenburg Marriage Register]

KINNEMOND, JOHN, Military Governor of Noteborg [Nettenburg, Russia?] from 1633 to 1634. [MGIF][RPCS.1.37.173]

KINNEMOND, PATRICK, Military Governor of Anklam in 1638. [MGIF]

KINNEMOND, THOMAS, Military Governor of Augsberg in 1632, later of Koporic in 1637, and of Dunamonde from 1640 to 1650. [MGIF]

KINNAMONTH, DAVID, at a muster roll in Dungannon, County Tyrone, Ireland, in 1618. [CalSPIre.1618.601][BM.Add.ms18735]

KIRKCALDY, DAVID, a soldier from St Andrews, Fife, married Adriaenken van Baerdsen from Geertruidenberg, in Dordrecht, Holland, on 24 December 1589. [Dordrecht Marriage Register]

KIRKLAND, JOHN, Ensign of the Cameronian Regiment at the Siege of Dunkeld, Perthshire, on 21 August 1689. [BK.146]

KIRKPATRICK, JOHN, a Colonel in Dutch Service in 1665. [JCP.I.136]

KIRKPATRICK, JOHN, a Major in Dutch Service in 1665. [JCP.I.136]

KIRKPATRICK, JOHN, formerly of the Earl of Argyll's Regiment, a Lieutenant at Darien in 1699, testament, 1707, Comm. Edinburgh. [NRS]

KNOX, ANDREW, a soldier in Lyck, Eastern Prussia, in 1687.

KNOX, WILLIAM. Captain of the Earl of Glencairn's Regiment in Carrickfergus, Ireland, in 1642. [TNA.SP28.120]

KYLE, NINIAN, in Potter Row, Edinburgh, a militiaman in 1688. [NRS.GD1.399.49]

LAING, D., a soldier of the 1st Company of Cockburn's Regiment in Swedish Service in 1609. [SIS.217]

LAING, WILLIAM, a prisoner of war captured at the Siege of Worcester on 2 September 1651, was transported via London on the John and Sarah of London to Boston in December 1651, landed there in February 1652. [Suffolk Deeds.1/5-6]

LAMB, ALEXANDER, from Dundee, a gunner aboard the Arms of Zeeland in 1644. [ZA]

LAMB, Captain Lieutenant JOHN, of the Perth Militia in 1680. [NRS.B59.32.8]

LAMONT, WALTER, from Strathlachlan, Argyll, son of John Og Lamont, a soldier who died at Darien in 1700. [LamontClan.263]

LAMY, ALEXANDER, a Captain of Mackay's Regiment, who was killed at the Battle of Killiecrankie, on 27 August 1689. [BK.207]

LAMMIE, ..., a Lieutenant of Lammie's Regiment, who was captured by the Jacobites at the Battle of Killiecrankie, Perthshire, on 27 August 1689. [BK.207]

LANG, JOHN, Ensign of the Cameronian Regiment at the Siege of Dunkeld, Perthshire, on 21 August 1689. [BK.146]

LAUDER, GEORGE, a Lieutenant in Dutch Service in 1665, [JCP.I.136]; a Lieutenant Colonel under the States of Holland, testament, 22 July 1671, Comm. Edinburgh. [NRS]

LAUDER, GEORGE, Major of Balfour's Regiment at the Battle of Killiecrankie, Perthshire, on 27 July 1689. [BK.95]

LAUDER, Colonel GEORGE, of Ravelrig, married Elizabet Willemina van Ghent in Gelderland in April 1682, they divorced in Edinburgh on 27 February 1692. [NRS.Consistorial Court Records]

LAUDER, Lieutenant LEWIS, of Livingstone's Regiment of Dragoons at the Battle of Cromdale, Strathspey, on 1 May 1690. [BK.177]

LAUGHTON, PATRICK, from Kirkwall, Orkney, a gunner's mate on the St Andrew on 14 July 1698, testament, 1707, Comm. Edinburgh. [NRS]

LAUSON, GEORGE, a Sergeant of Beest's Company, was killed at the Battle of Killiecrankie, Perthshire, on 27 July 1689. [RPCS.XIV]

LAWSON, ANDREW, a Scottish soldier, married JannekeWillems van het Tolhuys, in Leiden, Holland, on 18 April 1603. [Leiden Marriage Register]

LAUSON, JOHN, a, Artillery Lieutenant from Forfar, Angus, who was confirmed as a nobleman in Poland-Lithuania in 1685. [SCA.102]

LAWSON, Captain RICHARD, a burgess of Glasgow in 1650, moved to Ireland in 1655. [GBR]

LAWSON, WILLIAM, from Edinburgh, an Ensign who died at Darien in 1699, testament, 1707, Comm. Edinburgh. [NRS]

LEARMONTH, CHARLES, son of Robert Learmonth in Edinburgh, a Lieutenant at Darien, died 1699, testament, 1744, Comm. Edinburgh. [NRS]

LEARMONTH, Captain DAVID, was authorised to raise soldiers for service in Bohemia in 1627, later he was garrisoned in Gluckstadt. [SAA.114]

LEARMONTH, GEORGE, a soldier in Polish Service, then in Muscovite Service from 1613. [STW.201]

LEARMONTH, G, a Captain in Swedish Service who was killed at Boitzenburg in July 1627. [SIG.282]

LEARMONTH, JACK, Corporal of Captain Nesbit's Company, married Neelkiij Allaerts from Haarlem, Holland, there on 30 December 1597. [Haarlem Marriage Register]

LEARMONTH, JOHN, brother of Lord Balcomie, a Captain of Mackay's Regiment in Danish Service in 1626, a Captain in in Germany in the service of Gustavus Adolphus, was killed at Boitzenberg in July 1627. [TGSI.VIII.186]

LEARMONTH, JOHN, in Danish Military Service at Gelnckstadt on 1 August 1628. [NRS.RH15.43.36]

LEARMONTH, PETER, Commandant of the Polish forces in Smolesk and Viazma, later fought in the Polish Army against Moscow from 1617 to 1621. [STW.200/206]

LEARMONTH, Captain PATRICK, in Danzig, [Gdansk], in 1617. [RPCS.11.174]

LEARMONTH, WILLIAM, a soldier of Captain Alleyne's Company of Militia in Barbados in 1680. [H2.163]

LEARMONTH, WILLIAM, a soldier of Captain Merrell's Company of Militia in Barbados in 1679. [H2.152]

LEES, HENRY, from Kirkcaldy, Fife, a gunner aboard the Lion of Zeeland in 1631. [ZA]

LEGGE, Major General WILLIAM, Military Governor of Bremen, Germany, 1633, in the service of Gustavus Adolphus. [MGIF] [SIG.282]

LENNOX, JAMES, Captain of Sir Mungo Campbell of Lawers' Regiment in Temple Patrick, Ireland, in 1642. [TNA.SP28.120]

LENNOX, ROBERT, a soldier, papers from 1683 to 1686. [NRS.GD10.244]

LESLIE, Sir ALEXANDER, later Earl of Leven, born 1582 son of George Leslie, a Captain in the Dutch-Spanish War in 1605, a Swedish Army officer from 1608 to 1638, fought in Russia, Colonel of a Swedish Regiment from 1623 to 1629, Major General and Military Governor of Stralsund, Germany, from 1629 to 1632, Colonel of a Company in Muscovite Service from 1630 to 1632, letter from Brandenburg dated 1631, Major General in Lower Saxony in 1635, Field Marshal under Gustavus Adolphus, Governor of the Baltic Provinces, returned to Scotland to lead the Covenanter Army into England in 1639, died in Balgonie, Fife, in 1661. [STW.179] [MGIF] [SIG.282] [NRS.GD26.3.215/221; GD406.1.234] [SHR.IX.40] [SS.41]

LESLIE, Lieutenant Colonel ANDREW, of Colonel Robert Montgomerie's Regiment, in Linlithgow, West Lothian, in 1646. [NRS.GD76.241]

LESLIE, ANDREW, a Lieutenant of Captain Cleaver's Company of Militia in Barbados in 1680. [H2.126]

LESLIE, DAVID, a soldier under Captain Hay, was witness to a marriage in Leiden, Holland, on 23 February 1580. [Leiden Marriage Register]

LESLIE, DAVID, a Swedish Army officer under Gustavus Adolphus. [SHR.IX.40]; Major General of Horse in 1640; Lieutenant General

David Leslie, a Cavalry officer, with 3 Troops of Cavalry, fought at the Battle of Dunbar on 3 September 1650. [BD]

LESLIE, GEORGE, a drummer of Colonel Alexander Leslie's Company in Muscovite Service from 1630 to 1632. [STW.179]

LESLIE, GEORGE, from Aberdeen, a Corporal aboard the Zeelandia on 1 November 1646. [ZA]

LESLIE, GEORGE, a Captain in Danish Service in Gluckstadt in 1628, [GAA.114]; Colonel of a regiment in Germany in 1636. [NRS.RH15.16.22]; a Colonel in Germany in the service of Gustavus Adolphus, ca.1630, Military Governor of Vechna in Oldenburg, Saxony, died in 1638. [SIG.283][MGIF][NRS.RH15.16.22]

LESLIE, GEORGE, from Logiedurno, Aberdeenshire, Adjutant General of His Imperial Majesty's Army, was issued a birth brief in 1661. [ACA.APB]

LESLIE, JOHN, a Major General in Germany in the service of Gustavus Adolphus, Military Governor of Frankfurt in 1631. [MGIF] [SIG.282]

LESLIE, JOHN, a soldier from Kirkcaldy, Fife, married Belijtgie van Maaseyck in Schiedam, Holland, in 1632. [Schiedam Marriage Register]

LESLIE, JOHN, Captain of the Earl of Leven's Regiment in Carrickfergus, Ireland, in 1642. [TNA.SP28.120]

LESLIE, JOHN, Captain of Major General Monro's Regiment in Carrickfergus, Ireland, in 1642. [TNA.SP28.120]

LESLIE, JOHN, a soldier of Colonel Colleton's Company of Militia in Barbados in 1680. [H2.119]

LESLIE, JOHN, Captain of a Troop of Militia in Barbados in 1680. [H2.208]

LESLIE, Colonel LUDOVICK, in Germany in the service of Gustavus Adolphus, ca.1630. [SIG.282][SAA.114]; Quartermaster General of the Earl of Leven's Army in 1640; Quartermaster of Aytoun's Regiment of Foot in the Army of the Covenant from 1645 to 1647. [CA.113]S

LESLIE, PATRICK, General Adjutant of Lord Sinclair's Regiment in Newry, Ireland, in 1642. [TNA.SP28.120]

LESLIE, ROBERT, son of Andrew Leslie portioner of Logiedurno and his wife Isobel Stewart, Adjutant General to His Imperial Majesty's Army, 16... [ACA.APB.25.1.1661]

LESLIE, WALTER, son of John Leslie of Balqhan and his wife Jean Erskine, Aberdeenshire, a Colonel in Hungary by 1637. [RGS.IX.648]

LESLIE, WALTER, a soldier of Captain Morris's Company of Militia in Barbados in 1679. [H2.119]

LESLIE, WALTER, a Sergeant of Captain Thornhill's Company of Militia in Barbados in 1680. [H2.179]

LESLIE, Captain, of Fraser of Philorth's Regiment, taken prisoner at the Battle of Preston, Lancashire, on 18 August 1648. [SR.45]

LESLIE, Lieutenant Colonel, fought and was captured at the Battle of Dunbar on 3 September 1650.

LETHAM, DUNCAN, a soldier under Captain Robert Scott, married Hester Giellens of Leiden, Holland, there on 8 January 1604. [Leiden Marriage Register]

LICHTOUN, JOHN, Lieutenant Colonel to General Stolhouse in Sweden, was admitted as a burgess of Aberdeen in 1634. [ABR]

LICHTON, ROBERT, Governor of Reval, Estonia, from 1681 to 1685. [MGIF]

LIDDERDALE, JAMES, Captain of Major General Monro's Regiment in Carrickfergus, Ireland, in 1642. [TNA.SP28.120]

LIDDLE, JAMES, a prisoner of war captured at the Battle of Dunbar on 3 September 1650, transported from London on the Unity of Boston to Boston in November 1650. [Suffolk Court Files.1226] [LLNV.247]

LIDDLE, JOHN, a soldier from Edinburgh, married Grietken Hendricx from Diepenheim, in Dordrecht, Holland, on 7 May 1595. [Dordrecht Marriage Register]

LIDDLE, JOHN, from Leith, a musketeer aboard the Dutch ship Vere on 1 May 1646. [ZA]

LIDDLE, WILLIAM, a trooper under Captain Edmund, married Catelyn de Greim in Nijmegen, Gelderland on 23 September 1599. [Nijmegen Marriage Register]

LINDSAY, Colonel ALEXANDER, in Germany in the service of Gustavus Adolphus, around 1630. [SIg.282]

LINDSAY, ALEXANDER, Captain of the Earl of Lothian's Regiment in Carrickfergus, Ireland, in 1642. [TNA.SP28.120]

LINDSAY, BERNARD, at a muster at Dungannon, County Tyrone, Ireland, in 1618. [CalSPIre.1618.501][BM.Add.ms18735]

LINDSAY, DANIEL, a soldier of Captain Lillington's Company of Militia in Barbados in 1679. [H2.154]

LINDSAY, Colonel G., was killed at Neu Brandenburg, Germany, in the service of Gustavus Adolphus, ca.1630. [SIG.282]

LINDSAY, HENRY, an officer of Mackay's Regiment, in Danish Service in 1626, in Swedish Service in 1629, later Lieutenant Colonel of Leslie's Regiment. [TGSI.VIII.188]

LINDSAY, Colonel HENRY, in Hamburg, Germany, in the Service of Gustavus Adolphus, ca.1630; in Anclam, Pomerania, on 8 June 1638, and at Lutzen, Saxony, on 16 November 1632. [UStA.Hay of Leyes ms 684/685], died in Hamburg. [SIG.282]

LINDSAY, Captain JAMES, of the Cameronian Regiment at the Siege of Dunkeld, Perthshire, on 21 August 1689. [BK.146]

LINDSAY, JAMES, a prisoner in Canongate Tolbooth, was released to go to Holland as a soldier under Captain Robert Reid of Bonakettle on 18 June 1690. [RPCS.XV.713]

LINDSAY, JOHN, of Bainshaw, born 1603, Lieutenant Colonel of Lord Reay's Highlanders in Swedish Service, was killed at the Siege of New Brandenburg in 1631. [TGSI.VIII.185][SHR.IX.50]

LINDSAY, JOHN, from Edinburgh, a gunner aboard the Dutch ship Neptunus on 1 May 1645. [ZA]

LINDSAY, Colonel JOHN, of Edzell, Angus, an infantry officer who fought at the Battle of Dunbar on 3 September 1650. [SR.37]

LINDSAY, Major JOHN, from Greenock to Caledonia, Darien, in 1699, was killed at Darien on 30 March 1700. [NRS.GD406/1][DD.317]

LINDSAY, Colonel J., was killed in Neumark, Brandenburg, in the service of Gustavus Adolphus, ca.1630. [SIG.282]

LINDSAY, Lieutenant, of Captain Robert Adair's Troop, to be cashiered in 1646. [Cal.SPIre.261.41]

LINDSAY, WALTER, Major of Clydesdale's Foot in 1644. [CA.122]

LINDSAY, WILLIAM, Lieutenant Colonel of the Clydesdale Foot in 1644. [CA.122]

LISTON, CHARLES, a prisoner of war captured at the Siege of Worcester on 2 September 1651, was transported via London on the John and Sarah of London to Boston in December 1651, landed there in February 1652. [Suffolk Deeds.1/5-6]

LITTLEJOHN, JOHN, a soldier under Captain Hay, was witness to a marriage in Leiden, Holland, on 23 February 1580. [Leiden Marriage Register]

LIVINGSTONE, JAMES, an officer of the Dutch Army before 1633, Colonel of Callendar's Foot in 1644 in the Army of the Covenant. [CA119]

LIVINGSTONE, Sir THOMAS, a Major of Colonel John Kirkpatrick's Regiment in Holland in 1661; a Lieutenant Colonel under the States of Holland, deeds, 1670. [NRS.RD2.2.326; RD2.27.139; RD2.26.44]; in 1665, [JCP.I.136]; Lieutenant Colonel of Balfour's Regiment at the Battle of Killiecrankie, Perthshire, on 27 July 1689. [BK.95]; Colonel of Livingstone's Dragoons of Grant's Regiment of Infantry at the Battle of Cromdale, Strathspey, on 1 May 1690. [BK.177]

LOCKHART, Sir JAMES, Captain of the Earl of Lothian's Regiment in Carrickfergus, Ireland, in 1642. [TNA.SP28.120]

LOCKHART, JAMES, Captain of the Nansemond County Militia, Virginia, in 1702. [TNA.CO5.1312/2]

LOCKHART, WILLIAM, Lieutenant of Annandale's Troop of Horse at the Battle of Killiecrankie, Perthshire, on 27 July 1689. [BK.96]

LOGAN, ANDREW, a Sergeant at Darien in 1699. [DD.262]

LOGAN, JACK, from Ayr, a soldier under Captain Brog, married Mariken Crichton from Sanquhar, Dumfries-shire, in Dordrecht, Holland, on 5 August 1590. [Dordrecht Marriage Register]

LOGAN, ROBERT, Major of the Edinburgh Foot from 1645 to 1647. [CA.133]

LOGAN, THOMAS, Major of the Edinburgh Foot from 1643 to 1645. [CA.133]

LOGIE, THOMAS, from Leith, a gunner aboard the Dutch ship Neptunus on 1 May 1645. [ZA]

LOTHIAN, ABRAHAM, from Renfrew, a soldier at Darien, died there in 1699, testament, 1707, Comm. Edinburgh. [NRS]

LOTHIAN, ANDREW, born 1660, a government soldier, wounded at the Battle of Killiecrankie, Perthshire, on 27 July 1689. [RPCS.XIV]

LOVELL, GEORGE, a soldier from Dundee, married Janneker Claes, in Bergen-op-Zoom, Holland, on 26 October 1602. [Bergen-op-Zoom Marriage Register]

LOUGHLAN, DENIS, a defaulter from Captain Woodward's Company of Militia in Barbados in 1679. [H2.156]

LOUGHLAN, EDWARD, a soldier of Lieutenant Colonel Affleck's Company of Militia in Barbados in 1680. [H2.148]

LOWE, ALISTAIR, a prisoner of war captured at the Siege of Worcester on 2 September 1651, was transported via London on the John and Sarah of London to Boston in December 1651, landed there in February 1652. [Suffolk Deeds.1/5-6]

LOWSON, JOHN, the younger, Sergeant of the Militia of Dundee in 1643. [DCW.13]

LUMSDEN, DAVID, Captain of Fraser's Dragoons, at the Battle of Marston Moor, Yorkshire, on 2 July 1644. [TFD.47]

LUMSDEN, J., a 'fourier', [assistant Ensign], of the 1st Company of Cockburn's Regiment in Swedish Service in 1609. [SIS.217]

LUMSDEN, Sir JAMES, of Innergellie in Fife, Lieutenant Colonel under Gustavus Adolphus in Germany, Military Governor of Osnabruck, Saxony, from 1633 to 1639, a sasine, 1635. [NRS.RS.XI.273]; Colonel of Lord Gordon's Foot in 1643-1647, at the Sieges of Newcastle and York, also at the Battle of Marston Moor in 1644, Governor of Newcastle in 1645; a Brigade Commander, who fought and was taken prisoner at the Battle of Dunbar on 3 September 1650. [SR.37][MGIF] [SIG.282][CA.144]

LUMSDEN, ROBERT, of Balwhinnie, an officer of Mackay's Regiment, in Danish Service in 1626, in Swedish Service in 1629. [TGSI.VIII.188]; returned to Scotland in 1639 to serve in the

Covenanters Army, was appointed Military Governor of Dundee, was killed at the Siege of Dundee in 1650. [DCW][SAA.ii.131]

LUMSDEN, WILLIAM, Captain of Mackay's Regiment, in Danish Service in 1626, 'sole survivor of the Massacre of Bredenburg'., Schlesvig Holstein. [TGSI.VIII.186]

LUNDY, D., was commissioned into the Russian Army in 1632. [SSA.48]

LUNDIE, Lieutenant Colonel JAMES, commander of Bremervorde, Saxony, from 1649 to 1657. [MGIF]

LUNDIE, JAMES, Captain of Leven's Regiment at the Battle of Killiecrankie, Perthshire, on 27 July 1689. [BK.96]

LUNDY, JAMES, Sergeant of Militia of Charles City County, Virginia, in 1701. [TNA,CO5.1312/2]

LUNDY, Colonel ROBERT, born in Dunbarton, an officer of the Earl of Dunbarton's Regiment [later the Royal Scots] in France, to Tangiers with the Royal Scots Regiment from 1678 to 1680, later a Lieutenant Colonel of an Irish regiment, Governor of Londonderry, Ireland, in 1688. [NRS.GD26.7.37]; in Londonderry, a deed, 1693. [NRS.RD4.72.338]; an officer in Portuguese Service from 1706 to 1712.

LYELL, JAMES, Lieutenant of Mackay's Regiment, in Danish Service in 1626, in Swedish Service in 1629, later a Captain of Ruthven's Regiment, was murdered in Westphalia. [TGSI.VIII.187]

LYELL, WILLIAM, Ensign of the Angus Regiment at the Battle of Marston Moor, Yorkshire, on 2 July 1644. [DCW.78]

LYON, Major JOHN, returned from Germany in 1650, [RPCS.XVI.526]; in Angus, of the Earl of Airlie's Militia in 1670. [NRS.GD16.53.39]

MCADAM, ARCHIBALD, a soldier in Argyll's Rebellion, a prisoner in Edinburgh, transported from Leith on William Arbuckle's ship bound for New England in July 1685. [RPCS.11.94]

MCALISTER, ALEXANDER, of Loupe, Argyll, a Jacobite soldier in 1689. [APS.app.ix.154]

MACALLISTER, ALISTER, a prisoner of war captured at the Siege of Worcester on 2 September 1651, was transported via London on the John and Sarah of London to Boston in December 1651, landed there in February 1652. [Suffolk Deeds.1/5-6]

MACALLISTER, DANIEL, a prisoner of war captured at the Siege of Worcester on 2 September 1651, was transported via London on the John and Sarah of London to Boston in December 1651, landed there in February 1652. [Suffolk Deeds.1/5-6]

MACALLISTER, JOHN, a prisoner of war captured at the Siege of Worcester on 2 September 1651, was transported via London on the John and Sarah of London to Boston in December 1651, landed there in February 1652. [Suffolk Deeds.1/5-6]

MCALLISTER, THOMAS, from Inverness, a soldier of Captain Walley's Company of Militia in Barbados in 1680. [H2.137]

MCANDREW, WILLIAM, a prisoner of war captured at the Siege of Worcester on 2 September 1651, was transported via London on the John and Sarah of London to Boston in December 1651, landed there in February 1652. [Suffolk Deeds.1/5-6]

MCARTHUR, Major JOHN, born 1648, Deputy Governor of St Kitts, died 4 April 1704. [SPAWI.1699.282/658][ActsPCCol.1699]

MACAULAY, ALEXANDER, Captain of the Marquis of Argyll's Regiment in Ballycastle, Ireland, in 1642. [TNA.SP28.120]

MACAULAY, HUGH, a prisoner in Edinburgh Tolbooth, was released to go as a soldier to Holland with Major Gordon in 1689. [RPCS.XIII.573]

MCBANE, DONALD, born 1664, formerly an apprentice tobacco spinner in Inverness, enlisted in Captain McKenzie's Company in1687, fought at the Battle of Killiecrankie, Perthshire, on 27 July 1689. [TNA.WO116.1]

MCBEAN, ANGUS, a soldier of Colonel Hill's Regiment at Inverlochy, Inverness-shire, married Isobel, daughter of William Macintosh in Corryburgh in 1687, a process of divorce on 7 March 1696. [NRS.CS8.6.65]

MCCASKELL, ALLAN, a soldier of Captain Davies's Company of Militia in Barbados in 1679. [H2.166]

MCCALL, DANIEL, a soldier of Colonel Lyne's Company of Militia in Barbados in 1679. [H2.109]

MCCALL, JAMES, a prisoner of war captured at the Battle of Dunbar on 3 September 1650, transported from London on the Unity of Boston to Boston in November 1650, an indentured servant at the Lynn Ironworks in the 1650s. [Suffolk Court Files.1226][LLNV.247]

MCCALL, WILLIAM, a soldier of Captain Allemby's Company of Militia in Barbados in 1679. [H2.155]

MCCALLEY, DOUGALL, was wounded at Darien on 6 February 1699. [DP.86]

MCCALLUM, ARCHIBALD, a soldier in Argyll's Rebellion, was transported via Leith to Jamaica in August 1685. [RPCS.11.136]

MCCALLUM, DUNCAN, a farmer at Otter in Argyll, a soldier in Argyll's Rebellion, a prisoner in Edinburgh, banished to the American Plantations on 24 July 1685, transported from Leith on William Arbuckle's ship bound for New England in July 1685. [RPCS.11.129/136/329]

MCCALLUM, JOHN, from Argyll, a soldier in Argyll's Rebellion, a prisoner in Edinburgh, banished to the American Plantations on 31 July 1685, transported from Leith on the Henry and Francis of Newcastle bound for East New Jersey on 5 September 1685. [RPCS.11.126/131]

MACCALLUM, MALCOLM, a prisoner of war captured at the Battle of Dunbar on 3 September 1650, transported from London on the Unity of Boston to Boston in November 1650, an indentured servant at the Lynn Ironworks in the 1650s. [Suffolk Court Files.1226] [LLNV.247]

MCCALLUM, NEIL, a soldier in Argyll's Rebellion, was transported via Leith to Jamaica in August 1685. [RPCS.11.330]

MACCANN, DONALD, a prisoner of war captured at the Siege of Worcester on 2 September 1651, was transported via London on the John and Sarah of London to Boston in December 1651, landed there in February 1652. [Suffolk Deeds.1/5-6]

MACCAULLY, JAMES, a prisoner of war captured at the Siege of Worcester on 2 September 1651, was transported via London on the John and Sarah of London to Boston in December 1651, landed there in February 1652. [Suffolk Deeds.1/5-6]

MCCAWLER, DUNCAN, a soldier of Kerr's Company at the Battle of Killiecrankie, Perthshire, on 27 July 1689, was captured by the Jacobites. [RPCS.XIV]

MCCHARLATIE, JOHN, a soldier in Argyll's Rebellion, was transported via Leith to Jamaica in August 1685. [RPCS.11.136]

MCCLELLAN, THOMAS, a Highland soldier, was accused of torturing two witches in North Berwick in 1652. [NRS.GD17.546]

MCCLELLAN, WILLIAM, Captain of the Earl of Leven's Regiment in Carrickfergus, Ireland, in 1642. [TNA.SP28.120]

MCCLELLAND, Sir ROBERT, to Ireland with a troop of 50 horse and 100 foot in 1626; 1629. [CPR Ireland.i.181/506]

MCCLELLANE, ..., Captain of the Marquis of Argyll's Regiment in Dunluce, Ireland, in 1642. [TNA.SP28.120]

MCCOLIN, ALEXANDER, a soldier of Colonel Colleton's Company of Militia in Barbados in 1680. [H2.119]

MCCOMBE, DAVID, a prisoner of war captured at the Siege of Worcester on 2 September 1651, was transported via London on the John and Sarah of London to Boston in December 1651, landed there in February 1652. [Suffolk Deeds.1/5-6]

MCCOMBE, JOHN, a prisoner of war captured at the Siege of Worcester on 2 September 1651, was transported via London on the John and Sarah of London to Boston in December 1651, landed there in February 1652. [Suffolk Deeds.1/5-6]

MCCOMBIE, JAMES, Captain of the Earl of Eglinton's Regiment in Bangor, Ireland, in 1642. [TNA.SP28.120]

MCCOMBUS, ALEXANDER, a soldier of Captain Jack's Company of Militia in Barbados in 1680. [H2.123]

MCCONACHIE, DUGALL, a servant of Craiginterve in Argyll, a soldier in Argyll's Rebellion, captured in Dunbarton, banished to the American Plantations on 30 July 1684, transported there in August 1685. [PRCS.11.126/311]

MCCONACHIE, NEIL, a soldier in Argyll's Rebellion, was transported via Leith to Jamaica in August 1685. [RPCS.11.136]

MCCONN, FINLAY, a prisoner of war captured at the Siege of Worcester on 2 September 1651, was transported via London on the John and Sarah of London to Boston in December 1651, landed there in February 1652. [Suffolk Deeds.1/5-6]

MCCONNELL, ALEXANDER, a prisoner of war captured at the Siege of Worcester on 2 September 1651, was transported via London on the John and Sarah of London to Boston in December 1651, landed there in February 1652. [Suffolk Deeds.1/5-6]

MCCONNELL, CANA, a prisoner of war captured at the Siege of Worcester on 2 September 1651, was transported via London on the John and Sarah of London to Boston in December 1651, landed there in February 1652. [Suffolk Deeds.1/5-6]

MCCONNELL, DONALD, [1], a prisoner of war captured at the Siege of Worcester on 2 September 1651, was transported via London on the John and Sarah of London to Boston in December 1651, landed there in February 1652. [Suffolk Deeds.1/5-6]

MCCONNELL, DONALD, [2], a prisoner of war captured at the Siege of Worcester on 2 September 1651, was transported via

London on the John and Sarah of London to Boston in December 1651, landed there in February 1652. [Suffolk Deeds.1/5-6]

MCCONNELL, WILLIAM, a prisoner of war captured at the Siege of Worcester on 2 September 1651, was transported via London on the John and Sarah of London to Boston in December 1651, landed there in February 1652. [Suffolk Deeds.1/5-6]

MCCORKADALE, ARCHIBALD, a soldier in Argyll's Rebellion, was transported via Leith to Jamaica in August 1685. [RPCS.11.136]

MCCORMACK, Corporal THOMAS, in Belfast, Ireland, in 1653. [OB.80]

MCCORMACK, Ensign, in Antrim, Ireland, in 1653. [OB.80]

MCCORMACK, WILLIAM, a drummer of Major Whyte's company mustered in Glasgow in 1682. [DSA.128]

MCCOWAN, NEIL, a prisoner of war captured at the Siege of Worcester on 2 September 1651, was transported via London on the John and Sarah of London to Boston in December 1651, landed there in February 1652. [Suffolk Deeds.1/5-6]

MCCOY, HUGH, a prisoner of war captured at the Siege of Worcester on 2 September 1651, was transported via London on the John and Sarah of London to Boston in December 1651, landed there in February 1652. [Suffolk Deeds.1/5-6]

MCCRAITH, JAMES, a prisoner of war captured at the Siege of Worcester on 2 September 1651, was transported via London on the John and Sarah of London to Boston in December 1651, landed there in February 1652. [Suffolk Deeds.1/5-6]

MCCRAITH, PATRICK, a prisoner of war captured at the Siege of Worcester on 2 September 1651, was transported via London on the John and Sarah of London to Boston in December 1651, landed there in February 1652. [Suffolk Deeds.1/5-6]

MCCRORY, ALISTER, a prisoner of war captured at the Siege of Worcester on 2 September 1651, was transported via London on the <u>John and Sarah of London</u> to Boston in December 1651, landed there in February 1652. [Suffolk Deeds.1/5-6]

MCCULLOCH, DAVID, Corporal of Major Whyte's company mustered in Glasgow in 1682. [DSA.128]

MCCULLOUGH, Captain JAMES, on Island Magee, Ireland, in 1653. [OB.80]

MCCULLOCH, JOHN, Captain of Kenmure's Regiment at the Battle of Killiecrankie, Perthshire, on 27 July 1689. [BK.96]

MCCULLOCH, Lieutenant JOHN, bound for France in February 1676. [RPCS.IV.668]

MCCULLOCH, ... , Ensign of the Cameronian Regiment at the Siege of , Perthshire, on 21 August 1689. [BK.146]

MCCUREITH, ARCHIBALD, a soldier in Argyll's Rebellion, was captured and transported via Leith to Jamaica in August 1685. [RPCS.11.330]

MCCURRIE, DONALD, a soldier in Argyll's Rebellion, was captured and transported via Leith to Jamaica in August 1685. [RPCS.11.330]

MACDONALD, ALASTAIR, of Appin, a Jacobite at the Battle of Killiecrankie, Perthshire, on 27 July 1689. [APS.IX.55]

MACDONALD, ALEXANDER, of Glengarry, Inverness-shire, a Jacobite at the Battle of Killiecrankie, Perthshire, on 27 July 1689. [APS.IX.55]

MACDONALD, Sir DONALD, of Sleat, Inverness-shire, a Jacobite officer at the Battle of Killiecrankie, Perthshire, on 27 July 1689. [BK.95]

MACDONALD, DUNCAN, a Jacobite soldier captured at the Battle of Cromdale, Strathspey, on 1 May 1690. [RPCS.XV.304]

MCDONALD, RONALD, of Keppoch, Inverness-shire, a Jacobite soldier in 1689. [APS.app.ix.55]

MCDONALD, ..., of Auchterawe, a Jacobite soldier in 1689. [APS.app.ix.55]

MACDONELL, JOHN, a prisoner of war captured at the Siege of Worcester on 2 September 1651, was transported via London on the John and Sarah of London to Boston in December 1651, landed there in February 1652. [Suffolk Deeds.1/5-6]

MCDOUGALL, DUNCAN, a soldier in Argyll's Rebellion, was captured and transported via Leith to Jamaica in August 1685. [RPCS.11.136]

MACDOUGALL, Colonel JAMES, in Germany in the service of Gustavus Adolphus, ca.1630, fought at Landsberg, Schweinfurt, and Liegnitz, Military Governor of Stralsund in 1630, of Frankfurt in 1631, and of Silesia in 1632. [MGIF] [SIG.282]

MCDOUGALL, Cornet JOHN, of Livingstone's Regiment of Dragoons at the Battle of Cromdale, Strathspey, on 1 May 1690. [BK.177]

MCDOUGALL, ..., commander of Brandenburg troops in 1633. [NRS.GD246.26.5.21]

MCDOUGALL, ROBERT, Commander of Sir John Ogle's fleet at Wexford, Ireland, in 1626. [CalSPIre.242.355]

MCDOUNIE, JOHN, a soldier in Argyll's Rebellion, was captured and transported via Leith to Jamaica in August 1685. [RPCS.11.330]

MACDOWELL, ALEXANDER, a prisoner of war captured at the Siege of Worcester on 2 September 1651, was transported via London on the John and Sarah of London to Boston in December 1651, landed there in February 1652. [Suffolk Deeds.1/5-6]

MCDOWALL, JOHN, clerk of Captain Woodward's Company of Militia in Barbados in 1679. [H2.156]

MCDOWALL, WILLIAM, born in 1678 near Stranraer, Galloway, a Colonel of Militia in St Kitts. [HS.X.3]

MACEACHERN, PATRICK, a prisoner of war captured at the Siege of Worcester on 2 September 1651, was transported via London on the <u>John and Sarah of London</u> to Boston in December 1651, landed there in February 1652. [Suffolk Deeds.1/5-6]

MCEAN-VCALLAN, JOHN BAN, a soldier at Duart, Argyll, in 1685. [NRS.SC54.17.2.12.52]

MCEWAN, ARCHIBALD, a soldier in Argyll's Rebellion, was captured and transported via Leith to Jamaica in August 1685. [RPCS.11.136]

MCEWAN, DONALD, a soldier in Argyll's Rebellion, imprisoned in Edinburgh Tolbooth, was transported via Leith to Jamaica in August 1685. [RPCS.11.136][ETR]

MCFARLANE, ARCHIBALD, a soldier of Captain Mason's Company of the Surry County Militia, Virginia, in 1701. [TNACO5.1312/2]

MCFARLANE, JOHN, a soldier of Colonel Bayley's Company of Militia in Barbados in 1679. [H2.131]

MCFINDLAY, CHARLES, born 1630, died in Tipperary, Ireland, in June 1773. 'he was a Captain in the reign of King Charles I, and went with Oliver Cromwell into Ireland. [SM.35.335]

MACGHIE, Lieutenant ALEXANDER, sent from Darien as an emissary to the Spanish in Carthagena in 1699. [DD.195]

MCGIBBON, ARCHIBALD, a soldier in Argyll's Rebellion, was transported via Leith to Jamaica in August 1685. [RPCS.11.329]

MCGIBBON, HECTOR, a soldier in Argyll's Rebellion, was transported via Leith to Jamaica in August 1685. [RPCS.11.329]

MCGIBBON, JOHN, from Glen Ochil, a soldier in Argyll's Rebellion, was transported via Leith to Jamaica in August 1685. [RPCS.11.329]

MCGILL, GEORGE, Captain of Robert Home of the Heugh's Regiment in Carrickfergus, Ireland, in 1642. [TNA.SP28.120]

MACGILL, JOHN, a prisoner of war captured at the Siege of Worcester on 2 September 1651, was transported via London on the John and Sarah of London to Boston in December 1651, landed there in February 152. [Suffolk Deeds.1/5-6]

MCGILLICH, JOHN, a soldier in Argyll's Rebellion, was transported via Leith to Jamaica in August 1685. [RPCS.11.329]

MACGILLIN, DANIEL, a prisoner of war captured at the Siege of Worcester on 2 September 1651, was transported via London on the John and Sarah of London to Boston in December 1651, landed there in February 1652. [Suffolk Deeds.1/5-6]

MACGILLIN, JOHN, a prisoner of war captured at the Siege of Worcester on 2 September 1651, was transported via London on the John and Sarah of London to Boston in December 1651, landed there in February 1652. [Suffolk Deeds.1/5-6]

MCGOUNE, JOHN, a Sergeant of the Earl of Angus's Regiment of Foot in Flanders, a burgess of Ayr in 1692. [ABR]

MCGOWAN, JOHN, a soldier in Argyll's Rebellion, was transported via Leith to Jamaica in August 1685. [RPCS.11.136]

MCGREGOR, JOHN, a soldier of Captain Bowcher's Company of Militia in Barbados in 1679. [H2.112]

MCGREGORIE, Colonel PATRICK, from Scotland to America in 1684, settled in Orange County, New York, Muster Master General of Militia in New York in 1686, died in New York in March 1691. [New York Documents.3.395][SPAWI.1686/867; 1699/524, 1154; 1691/1380]

MCHATTON, NEIL, a tenant farmer in Kilhall, Argyll, a soldier of Argyll's Rebellion, a prisoner in Edinburgh, transported from Leith on William Arbuckle's ship to New England in July 1685. [RPCS.11.94/312]

MCHEART, ANDREW, of Fraser's Dragoons in 1644. [TFD.220]

MACHENRY, Lieutenant WILLIAM, of the British Regiment of Fusiliers commanded by Colonel Lallo of Ghent, Flanders, in 1709. [NRS.GD30.1759]

MCICHAN, JOHN, from Baranazare, Lorne, a soldier in Argyll's Rebellion, was transported from Leith to Jamaica in August 1685. [RPCS.11.329]

MCILBRYDE, DUNCAN, a soldier in Argyll's Rebellion, was transported from Leith to Jamaica in August 1685. [RPCS.11.136]

MCILMOON, DONALD, a soldier in Argyll's Rebellion, was transported from Leith to Jamaica in August 1685. [RPCS.11.329]

MCILROY, GILBERT, a soldier in Argyll's Rebellion, in Edinburgh Tolbooth, was transported from Leith to Jamaica in August 1685. [ETR.369]

MCILROY, WILLIAM, a soldier in Argyll's Rebellion, was transported from Leith to Jamaica in August 1685. [RPCS.11.329]

MCILSHALLUM, JOHN, a soldier in Argyll's Rebellion, was transported from Leith to Jamaica in August 1685. [RPCS.11.330]

MCILVAIN, ARCHIBALD, from Glendaruel, Argyll, a soldier in Argyll's Rebellion, was transported from Leith to Jamaica in August 1685. [RPCS.11.329]

MCILVERRAN, DONALD, a soldier in Argyll's Rebellion, was transported from Leith to Jamaica in August 1685. [RPCS.11.136]

MCILVORY, DUNCAN, a soldier in Argyll's Rebellion, was transported from Leith to Jamaica in August 1685. [RPCS.11.136]

MCILVORY, JOHN, from Cragintyrie, a soldier in Argyll's Rebellion, was transported from Leith to Jamaica in August 1685. [RPCS.11.126]

MCINLAY, NEIL, a soldier in Argyll's Rebellion, was transported from Leith to Jamaica in August 1685. [RPCS.11.136]

MCINNES, ..., a soldier in Captain Allemby's Company of Militia in Barbados in 1679. [H2.155]

MACINTOSH, DONALD, a prisoner of war captured at the Siege of Worcester on 2 September 1651, was transported via London on the John and Sarah of London to Boston in December 1651, landed there in February 1652. [Suffolk Deeds.1/5-6]

MCINTOSH, LACHLAN, Sergeant Major of Oliphant's Company in Danish Service, in 1628. [SAA.ii.143]

MACINTOSH, THOMAS, from Kellochie, Inverness-shire, formerly a Lieutenant of the Earl of Tullibardine's Regiment, died at Darien in 1699, testament, 1707, Comm. Edinburgh. [NRS]

MACINTOSH, WILLIAM, a Captain in Danish Service in 1620s. [GAA.114]

MACINTOSH, WILLIAM, a prisoner of war captured at the Siege of Worcester on 2 September 1651, was transported via London on the John and Sarah of London to Boston in December 1651, landed there in February 1652. [Suffolk Deeds.1/5-6]

MCINTYRE, ARCHIBALD, from Glendaruel, Argyll, a soldier in Argyll's Rebellion, was transported from Leith to Jamaica in August 1685. [RPCS.11.329]

MCINTYRE, MALCOLM, a prisoner of war captured at the Battle of Dunbar on 3 September 1650, transported via London probably on the Unity of Boston in November 1650, probate 2 October 1705, Maine. [LLNV.250]

MCINTYRE, MALCOLM, a prisoner of war captured at the Siege of Worcester on 2 September 1651, was transported via London on the John and Sarah of London to Boston in December 1651, settled in York, Maine, in 1668.

MACINTYRE, ROBERT, a prisoner of war captured at the Battle of Dunbar on 3 September 1650, transported via London probably on the Unity of Boston in November 1650, an indentured servant at Lynn Ironworks in 1650s. [Suffolk Court Files.1226][LLNV.247]

MCISAAC, MURDOCH, from Machrimore in Kintyre, Argyll, a soldier in Argyll's Rebellion, imprisoned in Dunbarton Tolbooth, was transported via Leith on William Arbuckle's ship bound for New England in July 1685. [RPCS.11.94/310]

MCIVAR, ANGUS, from Glassary, Argyll, a soldier in Argyll's Rebellion, was imprisoned in Edinburgh then transported via Leith on William Arbuckle's ship bound for New England in July 1685. [RPCS.11.94]

MCIVAR, DONALD, a soldier in Argyll's Rebellion, was transported from Leith to Jamaica in August 1685. [RPCS.11.136]

MCIVAR, DUNCAN, a soldier in Argyll's Rebellion, was transported from Leith to Jamaica in August 1685. [RPCS.11.136]

MCIVAR, JOHN, from Tullich in Argyll, a soldier in Argyll's Rebellion, was transported from Leith to Jamaica in August 1685. [RPCS.11.136]

MCIVAR, MALCOLM, from Glassary in Argyll, a soldier in Argyll's Rebellion, was transported from Leith to Jamaica in August 1685. [RPCS.11.136]

MACKAIL, ALESTAR, a prisoner of war captured at the Siege of Worcester on 2 September 1651, was transported via London on the John and Sarah of London to Boston in December 1651, landed there in February 1652. [Suffolk Deeds.1/5-6]

MACKAIL, JAMES, a prisoner of war captured at the Siege of Worcester on 2 September 1651, was transported via London on the John and Sarah of London to Boston in December 1651, landed there in February 1652. [Suffolk Deeds.1/5-6]

MACKAIL, JAMES, a prisoner of war captured at the Siege of Worcester on 2 September 1651, was transported via London on the John and Sarah of London to Boston in December 1651, landed there in February 1652. [Suffolk Deeds.1/5-6]

MCKAIRNE, NEIL, from Argyll, a soldier in Argyll's Rebellion, was transported from Leith to Jamaica in August 1685. [RPCS.11.136]

MACKAY, Major AENEAS, of a Scottish regiment in the Service of the King of France in 1688. [DSA.159]

MACKAY, Major AENEAS, of Livingstone's Regiment of Dragoons at the Battle of Cromdale, Strathspey, on 1 May 1690. [BK.177]

MACKAY, AENEAS, son of Lord Reay, an officer of the Scots Brigade in Dutch Service, married Margaret von Puckler in 1692, and died in 1697. [SP.VII.171]

MACKAY, ALEXANDER, a prisoner of war captured at the Siege of Worcester on 2 September 1651, was transported via London on the John and Sarah of London to Boston in December 1651, landed there in February 1652. [Suffolk Deeds.1/5-6]

MACKAY, ANGUS, Captain of Mackay's Regiment at the Battle of Killiecrankie, Perthshire, was killed on 27 July 1689. [BK.96/207]

MACKAY, Sir DONALD, born 1591, Lord Reay, Colonel of Mackay's Regiment in Danish Service in 1626, in Swedish Service in 1629, [TGSI.VIII.1228]; in Amsterdam on 23 December 1629. [NRS.GD84.2.177]; was appointed Colonel of a regiment of 3000 Scots raised for service in Bohemia and who were to be shipped to Gluckstadt in 1626; was commissioned by Gustavus Adolphus to recruit 2000 soldiers in Scotland in 1630; died in 1649. [NRS.GD84.sec.2.149/180] [SIG.282][SAA.118]

MACKAY, HUGH, son of William Mackay of Bighouse, an officer of Mackay's Regiment, in Danish Service in 1626, in Swedish Service in 1629. [TGSI.VIII.188][SAA.ii.124]

MACKAY, HUGH, 3rd son of Mackay of Scourie, Sutherland, an officer of the Scots Brigade in the Netherlands, later of Dunbarton's Regiment in the Service of Louis XIV, King of France, Army Commander in Scotland, fought at the Battle of Killiecrankie, Perthshire, on 27 July 1689, and at the Siege of Dunkeld on 21

August 1689, was killed at the Battle of Steenkirk, Flanders, on 3 August 1692.

MACKAY, HUGH, a prisoner of war captured at the Siege of Worcester on 2 September 1651, was transported via London on the John and Sarah of London to Boston in December 1651, landed there in February 1652. [Suffolk Deeds.1/5-6]

MACKAY, Major HUGH, of Grant's Regiment of Infantry at the Battle of Cromdale, Strathspey, on 1 May 1690. [BK.177]

MACKAY, Captain HUGH, Commander at Ruthven Castle in 1691. [NRS.E99.41.14]

MACKAY, Captain HUGH, of Borlay, in St Kitts in 1700. [NRS.GD21.1.1700; GD84.sec.1/22/9B]

MACKAY, IYE, son of William Mackay of Bighouse, Captain of Mackay's Regiment, in Danish Service in 1626, in Swedish Service in 1629. [TGSI.VIII.187]

MACKAY, JAMES, Lieutenant Colonel of Mackay's Regiment at the Battle of Killiecrankie, was killed on 27 July 1689. [BK.95/207] [NRS.GD406.1.3595]

MACKAY, JAMES, a Major of Ramsay's Regiment, who was killed at the Battle of Killiecrankie, Perthshire, on 27 August 1689. [BK.207]

MACKAY, JOHN, a prisoner of war captured at the Siege of Worcester on 2 September 1651, was transported via London on the John and Sarah of London to Boston in December 1651, landed there in February 1652. [Suffolk Deeds.1/5-6]

MCKAY, MARTIN, a soldier in Argyll's Rebellion, was transported from Leith to Jamaica in August 1685. [RPCS.11.136]

MACKAY, NEIL, a prisoner of war captured at the Siege of Worcester on 2 September 1651, was transported via London on

the John and Sarah of London to Boston in December 1651, landed there in February 1652. [Suffolk Deeds.1/5-6]

MACKAY, Sir PATRICK, of Lairg, Sutherland, Captain of Mackay's Regiment, in Danish Service in 1626, died of wounds received at Oldenburg, Saxony, in October 1627. [TGSI.VIII.186]

MACKAY, ROBERT, a soldier of the 1st Company of Cockburn's Regiment in Swedish Service in 1609. [SIS.217]

MACKAY, ROBERT, Captain of Mackay's Regiment at the Battle of Killiecrankie, Perthshire, was wounded on 27 July 1689. [BK.96/207]

MACKAY, RORY, a prisoner of war captured at the Siege of Worcester on 2 September 1651, was transported via London on the John and Sarah of London to Boston in December 1651, landed there in February 1652. [Suffolk Deeds.1/5-6]

MACKAY, WILLIAM, son of Donald Mackay of Scourie, Sutherland, Captain of Mackay's Regiment in Danish Service in 1626, in Swedish Service in 1629, later Lieutenant Colonel of the Swedish Army, was killed at the Battle of Lutzen on 16 November 1632. [TGSI.VIII.187] [SIG.282]

MACKAY, WILLIAM, Captain of Mackay's Regiment in Danish Service in 1626, in Swedish Service in 1629. [TGSI.VIII.187]

MACKAY, ..., Lieutenant of Mackay's Regiment in Danish Service in 1626, in Swedish Service in 1629, later in Ruthven's Regiment. [TGSI.VIII.187]

MACKEAN, ALESTER, a prisoner of war captured at the Siege of Worcester on 2 September 1651, was transported via London on the John and Sarah of London to Boston in December 1651, landed there in February 1652. [Suffolk Deeds.1/5-6]

MACKEAN, DANIEL, [1], a prisoner of war captured at the Siege of Worcester on 2 September 1651, was transported via London on the John and Sarah of London to Boston in December 1651, landed there in February 1652. [Suffolk Deeds.1/5-6]

MACKEAN, DANIEL, [2], a prisoner of war captured at the Siege of Worcester on 2 September 1651, was transported via London on the John and Sarah of London to Boston in December 1651, landed there in February 1652. [Suffolk Deeds.1/5-6]

MACKEAN, JOHN, [1], a prisoner of war captured at the Siege of Worcester on 2 September 1651, was transported via London on the John and Sarah of London to Boston in December 1651, landed there in February 1652. [Suffolk Deeds.1/5-6]

MACKEAN, JOHN, [2], a prisoner of war captured at the Siege of Worcester on 2 September 1651, was transported via London on the John and Sarah of London to Boston in December 1651, landed there in February 1652. [Suffolk Deeds.1/5-6]

MACKEAN, NEIL, [1], a prisoner of war captured at the Siege of Worcester on 2 September 1651, was transported via London on the John and Sarah of London to Boston in December 1651, landed there in February 1652. [Suffolk Deeds.1/5-6]

MACKEAN, NEIL, [2], a prisoner of war captured at the Siege of Worcester on 2 September 1651, was transported via London on the John and Sarah of London to Boston in December 1651, landed there in February 1652. [Suffolk Deeds.1/5-6]

MACKEAN, PATRICK, a prisoner of war captured at the Siege of Worcester on 2 September 1651, was transported via London on the John and Sarah of London to Boston in December 1651, landed there in February 1652. [Suffolk Deeds.1/5-6]

MACKEAN, ROBERT, a prisoner of war captured at the Siege of Worcester on 2 September 1651, was transported via London on the John and Sarah of London to Boston in December 1651, landed there in February 1652. [Suffolk Deeds.1/5-6]

MACKEAN, SAMUEL, a prisoner of war captured at the Siege of Worcester on 2 September 1651, was transported via London on the John and Sarah of London to Boston in December 1651, landed there in February 1652. [Suffolk Deeds.1/5-6]

MACKEAN, WILLIAM, [1], a prisoner of war captured at the Siege of Worcester on 2 September 1651, was transported via London on the John and Sarah of London to Boston in December 1651, landed there in February 1652. [Suffolk Deeds.1/5-6]

MACKEAN, WILLIAM, [2], a prisoner of war captured at the Siege of Worcester on 2 September 1651, was transported via London on the John and Sarah of London to Boston in December 1651, landed there in February 1652. [Suffolk Deeds.1/5-6]

MACKEE, DANIEL, a prisoner of war captured at the Siege of Worcester on 2 September 1651, was transported via London on the John and Sarah of London to Boston in December 1651, landed there in February 1652. [Suffolk Deeds.1/5-6]

MCKEICHAN, NEIL, from Baranazare in Lorne, a soldier in Argyll's Rebellion, was transported from Leith to Jamaica in August 1685. [RPCS.11.136]

MACKEITH, DAVID, a prisoner of war captured at the Siege of Worcester on 2 September 1651, was transported via London on the John and Sarah of London to Boston in December 1651, landed there in February 1652. [Suffolk Deeds.1/5-6]

MCLEAN, Sir ALEXANDER, a Jacobite soldier in 1689. [APS.acc.ix.56]

MACLELLAN, J., a soldier in Tilsit, Lithuania, in 1680. [SIG]

MCKELLAR, ANGUS, from Argyll, a soldier in Argyll's Rebellion, a prisoner in Edinburgh, was transported via Leith on William Arbuckle's ship bound for New England in July 1685. [RPCS.11.94]

MCKELLO, DONALD, a soldier in Argyll's Rebellion, was transported from Leith to Jamaica in August 1685. [RPCS.11.136]

MCKELLO, DUGALD, a soldier in Argyll's Rebellion, was transported from Leith to Jamaica in August 1685. [RPCS.11.136]

MCKELLO, JOHN, a soldier in Argyll's Rebellion, was transported from Leith to Jamaica in August 1685. [RPCS.11.136]

MACKELSEMER, [?], JOHN, from Edinburgh, a Corporal of Captain Johnston's Company, married Licile Berberkelen in Breda, Brabant, on 17 October 1602. [Breda Marriage Register]

MACKEN, WILLIAM, a prisoner of war captured at the Siege of Worcester on 2 September 1651, was transported via London on the John and Sarah of London to Boston in December 1651, landed there in February 1652. [Suffolk Deeds.1/5-6]

MACKENECHOW, JOHN, a prisoner of war captured at the Siege of Worcester on 2 September 1651, was transported via London on the John and Sarah of London to Boston in December 1651, landed there in February 1652. [Suffolk Deeds.1/5-6]

MCKENNY, ALISTER, a soldier in Captain Woodward's Company of Militia in Barbados in 1679. [H2.156]

MCKENZIE, ALEXANDER, a soldier in Darien, died in the West Indies, testament, 1707, Comm. Edinburgh. [NRS]

MCKENZIE, COLIN, Captain of Mar's Regiment of Foot in 1685, a Jacobite at the Battle of Killiecrankie, Perthshire, on 27 July 1689. [APS.IX.55]

MACKENZIE, GEORGE, muster master of Mackenzie's Company in Danish Service in 1628. [SAA.ii.124]

MCKENZIE, Captain GEORGE, in New York on 15 August 1689. [New York Documents.3.614][SPAWI.1689.352/360]

MCKENZIE, JOHN, a gunner on the Caledonia from Leith to Darien on 14 July 1698, testament, 1707, Comm. Edinburgh. [NRS]

MCKENZIE, KENNETH, of Dalemore, a Jacobite soldier in 1689. [APS.acc.ix.56]

MCKENZIE, MURDOCH, graduated MA from Marischal College in Aberdeen in 1622, a chaplain to Mackay's Regiment, in Danish Service in 1626, in Swedish Service in 1629, served under

Gustavus Adolphus before 1645, later minister of Suddie in Ross-shire. [TGSI.VIII.189][F.7.17]

MCKENZIE, THOMAS, brother of the Earl of Seaforth, Captain of Mackay's Regiment, in Danish Service in 1626, in Swedish Service in 1629. [TGSI.VIII.187]; wounded at Eckernfijord and at Stralsund in 1628. [SAA.ii.124]

MACKENZIE, ..., Captain of Mackay's Regiment at the Battle of Killiecrankie, Perthshire, was killed on 27 July 1689. [BK.96/207]

MCKERNESS, JACOB, a soldier in Colonel Coddrington's Company of Militia in Barbados in 1679. [H2.174]

MACKETH, NEIL, a prisoner of war captured at the Siege of Worcester on 2 September 1651, was transported via London on the John and Sarah of London to Boston in December 1651, landed there in February 1652. [Suffolk Deeds.1/5-6]

MACKIE, HILL [?], a prisoner of war captured at the Siege of Worcester on 2 September 1651, was transported via London on the John and Sarah of London to Boston in December 1651, landed there in February 1652. [Suffolk Deeds.1/5-6]

MACKIE, RORY, a prisoner of war captured at the Siege of Worcester on 2 September 1651, was transported via London on the John and Sarah of London to Boston in December 1651, landed there in February 1652. [Suffolk Deeds.1/5-6]

MCKILLON, DONALD, from Glendaruel, Argyll, a soldier in Argyll's Rebellion, was transported from Leith to Jamaica in August 1685. [RPCS.11.136]

MCKINLAY, JONAS, a soldier under Captain Robert Scott, married Judith van Tore from Norwich, England, in Leiden, Holland, on 17 November 1604. [Leiden Marriage Register]

MCKINLAY, NEIL, a soldier in Argyll's Rebellion, was transported from Leith to Jamaica in August 1685. [RPCS.11.136]

MACKINNON, JOHN a prisoner of war captured at the Siege of Worcester on 2 September 1651, was transported via London on the John and Sarah of London to Boston in December 1651, landed there in February 1652. [SG.35.3.136]

MCKINNON, JOHN, from Duppen in Kintyre, Argyll, a soldier in Argyll's Rebellion, was transported from Leith to Jamaica in August 1685. [RPCS.11.136]

MCKIRRECH, ARCHIBALD, a soldier in Argyll's Rebellion, was transported from Leith to Jamaica in August 1685. [RPCS.11.136]

MCLACHLAN, ARCHIBALD, a farmer in Craigintervie, Argyll, a soldier in Argyll's Rebellion, was transported from Leith to Jamaica in August 1685. [RPCS.11.136]

MCLACHLAN, DONALD, from Argyll, a soldier in Argyll's Rebellion, was transported from Leith to Jamaica in August 1685. [RPCS.11.136]

MCLACHLAN, JOHN DOW, from Achahouse in Argyll, a soldier in Argyll's Rebellion, was transported from Leith to Jamaica in August 1685. [RPCS.11.329]

MCLAUCHLAN, GEORGE, a prisoner in Dundee Tolbooth was released to go to Holland as a prisoner with Lieutenant Alexander Murray of Skirling on 13 September 1689. [RPCS.XIV.619]

MCLAUCHLAN, JOHN, [1], a prisoner in Dundee Tolbooth was released to go to Holland as a prisoner with Lieutenant Alexander Murray of Skirling on 13 September 1689. [RPCS.XIV.619]

MCLAUCHLAN, JOHN, [2], a prisoner in Dundee Tolbooth was released to go to Holland as a prisoner with Lieutenant Alexander Murray of Skirling on 13 September 1689. [RPCS.XIV.619]

MCLAUGHLIN, WALTER, a government soldier, was wounded at the Battle of Killiecrankie, Perthshire, on 27 July 1689. [RPCS.XIV

MCLAUCHLAN, WILLIAM, a prisoner in Dundee Tolbooth was released to go to Holland as a prisoner with Lieutenant Alexander Murray of Skirling on 13 September 1689. [RPCS.XIV.619]

MCLAUCHLANE, ..., a soldier of Mackay's Regiment, at the Battle of Killiecrankie, Perthshire, on 27 July 1689. [RPCS.XIV][TNA.WO116.1]

MCLEAN, Captain ALLAN, a Jacobite captured at the Battle of Cromdale, Strathspey, on 1 May 1690. [RPCS.XV.304]

MCLEAN, ANDREW, from Argyll, a soldier in Argyll's Rebellion, was transported from Leith to Jamaica in August 1685. [RPCS.11.330]

MCLEAN, DONALD, a Jacobite soldier captured at the Battle of Cromdale, Strathspey, on 1 May 1690. [RPCS.XV.304]

MCLEAN, HECTOR, of Lochbuie, Mull, a Jacobite soldier in 1689. [APS.app.ix.55]

MCLEAN, HUGH, from Argyll, a soldier in Argyll's Rebellion, was transported from Leith to Jamaica in August 1685. [RPCS.11.330]

MACLEAN, Sir JOHN, born 1670, a Jacobite officer at the Battle of Killiecrankie, Perthshire, on 27 July 1689. [RPCS.XIV]; was captured at the Battle of Cromdale, Strathspey, on 1 May 1690. [RPCS.XV.304]

MCLEAN, Lieutenant ALLAN, a Jacobite captured at the Battle of Cromdale, Strathspey, on 1 May 1690. [RPCS.XV.304]

MCLEAN, JOHN, from Portindryan, Argyll, a soldier in Argyll's Rebellion, was transported from Leith to Jamaica in August 1685. [RPCS.11.330]

MCLEAN, Ensign JOHN, a Jacobite captured at the Battle of Cromdale, Strathspey, on 1 May 1690. [RPCS.XV.304]

MACLEAN, JOHN, born 1661, died in Orange County, New York, in August 1770. 'he was a drummer in King William's army in Ireland'. [SM.32.630]

MCLEAN, LACHLAN, an officer at Darien, who sailed via Jamaica to Bristol in 1700. [DD.297]

MCLEAN, PETER, Military Governor of Stralsund, from 1679 to 1697. [MGIF]

MCLEAN, …., a prisoner of war captured at the Siege of Worcester on 2 September 1651, was transported via London on the John and Sarah of London to Boston in December 1651, landed there in February 1652. [Suffolk Deeds.1/5-6]

MCLEAN, Captain, Governor of Crab Island, one of the Leewards, in 1698. [DSP.78]

MCLELLAN, J, a soldier in Tilsit, Lithuania, in 1680. [SIG.262]

MCKELLAR, DUNCAN, a soldier in Lawers' Company in 1680. [NRS.SC54.17.2.10.6]

MCLEOD, DANIEL, a soldier in Captain Masson's Company of Militia in Barbados in 1679. [H2.193]

MCLEOD, DONALD, Captain of Colonel Aeneas Mackay's Regiment in Flanders, a sasine, 1696. [NRS.RS36.VI.167/463]

MCLEOD, JOHN, a prisoner of war captured at the Siege of Worcester on 2 September 1651, was transported via London on the John and Sarah of London to Boston in December 1651, landed there in February 1652. [Suffolk Deeds.1/5-6]

MCLEOD, 'MURTLE', a prisoner of war captured at the Siege of Worcester on 2 September 1651, was transported via London on the John and Sarah of London to Boston in December 1651, landed there in February 1652. [Suffolk Deeds.1/5-6]

MCLEOD, ….., son of Neil McLeod, a Sergeant of Mackenzie's Company in Danish Service, was killed at Keil in 1628. [SAA.ii.124]

MACLEY, Ensign DAVID, on Broadisland, Ireland, 1653. [OB.80]

MCLINE, ALEXANDER, from Argyll, a soldier in Argyll's Rebellion, was transported via Leith to Jamaica in August 1685. [RPCS.11.136]

MCMATH, JOHN, Muster Major in Tangiers, was admitted as a burgess of Edinburgh on 10 October 1691, [EBR]; testament, 9 January 1695, Comm. Edinburgh. [NRS]

MCMICHAEL, DUNCAN, from Islay, Argyll, a soldier in Argyll's Rebellion, was transported via Leith to Jamaica in August 1685. [RPCS.11.136]

MCMIALL, JOHN, a soldier of the Isle of Wight County, Virginia, Militia, in 1701. [TNA.CO5.1312/2]

MCMICHAEL, ROGER, a soldier in Argyll's Rebellion, was transported via Leith to Jamaica in August 1685. [RPCS.11.136]

MCMILLAN, ADAM, in Danish Service at Gluckstadt around 1627-1628. [SAA.114]

MCMILLAN, ALISTER, born 1631, a prisoner of war, was transported to Boston, an indentured servant at the Lynn Ironworks, settled in Salem, Massachusetts, by 1661. [Essex County Quarterly Court Files, vol.7.38][LLNV.247]

MCMILLAN, DUNCAN, from Carradale in Kintyre, Argyll, a soldier in Argyll's Rebellion, was transported via Leith to Jamaica in August 1685. [RPCS.11.329]

MCMILLAN, JOHN, a prisoner of war captured at the Battle of Dunbar on 3 September 1650, transported via London probably on the Unity of Boston in November 1650, an indentured servant at the Lynn Ironworks during the 1650s. [Suffolk Court Files.1226][LLNV.247]

MCMILLAN, JOHN, from Argyll, a soldier in Argyll's Rebellion, was imprisoned in Edinburgh and transported from Leith to New England in July 1685. [RPCS.11 94]

MCNAB, JAMES, a prisoner of war captured at the Siege of Worcester on 2 September 1651, was transported via London on the John and Sarah of London to Boston in December 1651, landed there in February 1652. [Suffolk Deeds.1/5-6]

MCNAB, Captain WILLIAM, of Lumsden's Foot, from Aberdeen with sixty men bound for England in February 1644. [CA.144]

MCNAUGHTON, ALLASTER, a prisoner in Dundee Tolbooth was released to go to Holland as a prisoner with Lieutenant Alexander Murray of Skirling on 13 September 1689. [RPCS.XIV.619

MCNAUGHTON, JOHN, born 1667, a government soldier, wounded at the Battle of Killiecrankie on 27 July 1689. [RPCS.XIV]

MCNAUGHTON, JOHN, a Jacobite soldier in 1689. [APS.acc.ix.56]

MCNAUGHTON, Ensign JOHN, a Jacobite captured at the Battle of Cromdale, Strathspey, on 1 May 1690. [RPCS.XV.304]

MCNAUGHTON, JOHN, a prisoner in Dundee Tolbooth was released to go to Holland as a prisoner with Lieutenant Alexander Murray of Skirling on 13 September 1689. [RPCS.XIV.619]

MCNAUGHTON, PETER, a soldier of Captain Mason's Company of the Surry County Militia, Virginia, in 1701. [TNA.CO5.1312/2]

MCNEIL, ALASTAIR, a prisoner of war captured at the Siege of Worcester on 2 September 1651, was transported via London on the John and Sarah of London to Boston in December 1651, landed there in February 1652. [Suffolk Deeds.1/5-6]

MCNEIL, ARCHIBALD, from Argyll, a soldier in Argyll's Rebellion, was transported via Leith to Jamaica in August 1685. [RPCS.11.136]

MCNEIL, DONALD, a prisoner of war captured at the Siege of Worcester on 2 September 1651, was transported via London on the John and Sarah of London to Boston in December 1651, landed there in February 1652. [Suffolk Deeds.1/5-6]

MCNEIL, HECTOR, from Argyll, a soldier in Argyll's Rebellion, was transported via Leith to Jamaica in August 1685. [RPCS.11.136]

MCNEIL, JAMES, a prisoner of war captured at the Siege of Worcester on 2 September 1651, was transported via London on the John and Sarah of London to Boston in December 1651, landed there in February 1652. [Suffolk Deeds.1/5-6]

MCNEIL, JOHN, a soldier in Argyll's Rebellion, was transported via Leith to Jamaica in August 1685. [RPCS.11.136]

MCNEIL, PATRICK, a prisoner of war captured at the Siege of Worcester on 2 September 1651, was transported via London on the John and Sarah of London to Boston in December 1651, landed there in February 1652. [Suffolk Deeds.1/5-6]

MCNEISH, DONALD, [1], a prisoner of war captured at the Siege of Worcester on 2 September 1651, was transported via London on the John and Sarah of London to Boston in December 1651, landed there in February 1652. [Suffolk Deeds.1/5-6]

MCNEISH, DONALD, [2], a prisoner of war captured at the Siege of Worcester on 2 September 1651, was transported via London on the John and Sarah of London to Boston in December 1651, landed there in February 1652. [Suffolk Deeds.1/5-6]

MCNEISH, PATRICK, a prisoner of war captured at the Siege of Worcester on 2 September 1651, was transported via London on the John and Sarah of London to Boston in December 1651, landed there in February 1652. [Suffolk Deeds.1/5-6]

MACNESTER, ALASTAIR, a prisoner of war captured at the Siege of Worcester on 2 September 1651, was transported via London on the John and Sarah of London to Boston in December 1651, landed there in February 1652. [Suffolk Deeds.1/5-6]

MCNESKAIR, DONALD ROY, possibly in Breadalbane to serve as a soldier, a bond dated 28 November 1699. [NRS.GD112.17.18/24]

MACOLEN, DUNCAN, a prisoner in Dundee Tolbooth was released to go to Holland as a prisoner with Lieutenant Alexander Murray of Skirling on 13 September 1689. [RPCS.XIV.619]

MACOLEN, GEORGE, a prisoner in Dundee Tolbooth was released to go to Holland as a prisoner with Lieutenant Alexander Murray of Skirling on 13 September 1689. [RPCS.XIV.619]

MCPHERSON, JOHN, [Jan MacFasse], a soldier in Amsterdam, and Mary Duncanson, [Maria Donckes.] born 1615 in Scotland, were married in Amsterdam in 1640. [NYGBR.125,125.1/6]

MCPHERSON, JOHN, a prisoner of war captured at the Siege of Worcester on 2 September 1651, was transported via London on the John and Sarah of London to Boston in December 1651, landed there in February 1652. [Suffolk Deeds.1/5-6]

MCPHERSON, 'ORIGLAIS', a prisoner of war captured at the Siege of Worcester on 2 September 1651, was transported via London on the John and Sarah of London to Boston in December 1651, landed there in February 1652. [Suffolk Deeds.1/5-6]

MACPHERSON, ROBERT, a prisoner of war captured at the Siege of Worcester on 2 September 1651, was transported via London on the John and Sarah of London to Boston in December 1651, landed there in February 1652. [Suffolk Deeds.1/5-6]

MCQUEEN, 'AMOS', a prisoner of war captured at the Siege of Worcester on 2 September 1651, was transported via London on the John and Sarah of London to Boston in December 1651, landed there in February 1652. [Suffolk Deeds.1/5-6]

MACQUEEN, ARCHIBALD, a soldier in Captain Scott's Company of Militia in Barbados in 1679. [H.2.191]

MCQUEEN, DUNCAN, a soldier in Argyll's Rebellion, was transported via Leith to Jamaica in August 1685. [RPCS.11.136]

MCQUEEN, GEORGE, a prisoner of war captured at the Siege of Worcester on 2 September 1651, was transported via London on

the John and Sarah of London to Boston in December 1651, landed there in February 1652. [Suffolk Deeds.1/5-6]

MCQUEEN, HUGH, a soldier in Argyll's Rebellion, was transported via Leith to Jamaica in August 1685. [RPCS.11.136]

MCQUILLAN, DONALD, a prisoner of war captured at the Siege of Worcester on 2 September 1651, was transported via London on the John and Sarah of London to Boston in December 1651, landed there in February 1652. [Suffolk Deeds.1/5-6]

MCQUILLAN, JOHN, a prisoner of war captured at the Siege of Worcester on 2 September 1651, was transported via London on the John and Sarah of London to Boston in December 1651, landed there in February 1652. [Suffolk Deeds.1/5-6]

MCRERY, ALEXANDER, a soldier of Lieutenant Colonel Jelly' Regiment, was buried in St Michael's, Barbados, in 1679. [H.438]

MACRORRY, J., a soldier of 1st Company of Cockburn's Regiment in Swedish Service in 1609. [SIS.217]

MCRUDDERY, W., a soldier of 2nd Company of Cockburn's Regiment in Swedish Service in 1609. [SIS.217]

MCSHANE, [McSween?], JOHN, a prisoner of war captured at the Siege of Worcester on 2 September 1651, was transported via London on the John and Sarah of London to Boston in December 1651, landed there in February 1652. [Suffolk Deeds.1/5-6] [LLNV.247]

MCTHOMAS, ALISTER, a prisoner of war captured at the Siege of Worcester on 2 September 1651, was transported via London on the John and Sarah of London to Boston in December 1651, landed there in February 1652. [Suffolk Deeds.1/5-6]

MCURICH, ARCHIBALD, a herd on McLay's land in Argyll, a soldier in Argyll's Rebellion, imprisoned in Edinburgh, then transported via Leith to New England in July 1685. [RPCS.11.312/330]

MCVERRAN, DONALD, a soldier in Argyll's Rebellion, was transported via Leith to Jamaica in August 1685. [RPCS.11.136]

MCVICAR, DONALD, a tenant in Inveraray, Argyll, a soldier in Argyll's Rebellion, was captured on the Muir of Kilpatrick, imprisoned in Glasgow and in Edinburgh, then transported via Leith to New England on William Arbuckle's ship in July 1685. [RPCS.11.94/312]

MCVICAR, DUNCAN, born 1668, son of baillie McVicar of Campbeltown, Argyll, a soldier in Argyll's Rebellion, imprisoned in Edinburgh, then transported via Leith to New England on William Arbuckle's ship in July 1685. [RPCS.11.94/317]

MCVIG, DUNCAN, a soldier in Argyll's Rebellion, was transported via Leith to Jamaica in August 1685. [RPCS.11.139]

MCWALTER, THOMAS, a prisoner of war captured at the Battle of Dunbar on 3 September 1650, transported from London on the Unity of Boston to Boston in November 1650, an indentured servant at the Lynn Ironworks in the 1650s. [Suffolk Court Files.1226]

MCWALTER, WILLIAM, a prisoner of war captured at the Battle of Dunbar on 3 September 1650, transported from London on the Unity of Boston to Boston in November 1650, an indentured servant at the Lynn Ironworks in the 1650s. [Suffolk Court Files.1226][LLNV.247]

MCWHIDDIE, ALLAN, a soldier in Argyll's Rebellion, was transported via Leith to Jamaica in August 1685. [RPCS.11.136]

MCWILLIAM, ['Monwilliam'], DANIEL, a prisoner of war captured at the Siege of Worcester on 2 September 1651, was transported via London on the John and Sarah of London to Boston in December 1651, landed there in February 1652. [Suffolk Deeds.1/5-6]

MCWILLIAM, ['Monwilliam'], DAVID, a prisoner of war captured at the Siege of Worcester on 2 September 1651, was transported via

London on the John and Sarah of London to Boston in December 1651, landed there in February 1652. [Suffolk Deeds.1/5-6]

MCWILLIAM, 'GELLUST, a prisoner of war captured at the Siege of Worcester on 2 September 1651, was transported via London on the John and Sarah of London to Boston in December 1651, landed there in February 1652. [Suffolk Deeds.1/5-6]

MCWILLIE, JOHN, a soldier in Argyll's Rebellion, a prisoner in Edinburgh Tolbooth, was transported via Leith to Jamaica in August 1685. [RPCS.11.136][ETR]

MAIN, GEORGE, a soldier from St Andrews, Fife, married Margaret Brand from Aberdeen, in Geertruidenberg, the Netherlands, in 1638. [Geertruidenberg Marriage Register]

MAIN, JAMES, an army officer in Kedainai and Slutsk, Lithuania between 1637-1664; a Captain of Dragoons at the Battle of Loyew in 1649, and at Kiev in Ukraine in 1651. [SCL.37/157]

MAITLAND, Captain JAMES, of Strathbogie's Regiment, fought at Aberdeen in 1644; later was commissioned by the Marquis of Montrose in Kirkwall to raise a troop of horse to serve under Colonel Gray, on 26 March 1650. [NRS.GD220.3.196]

MAITLAND, JOHN, Captain in Radziwill's army in Lithuania from 1660 until 1669. [SCL.160]

MALCOLM, WILLIAM, a prisoner in Edinburgh Tolbooth, was released to go to Holland as a soldier with Captain Oliphant in 1689. [RPCS.13.573]

MANAN, TIMOTHY, a prisoner in Canongate Tolbooth, was released to go to Holland as a soldier under Captain Robert Reid of Bonakettle on 18 June 1690. [RPCS.XV.713]

MANN, DANIEL, a prisoner of war captured at the Siege of Worcester on 2 September 1651, was transported via London on the John and Sarah of London to Boston in December 1651, landed there in February 1652. [Suffolk Deeds.1/5-6]

MANN, JOHN, a prisoner of war captured at the Siege of Worcester on 2 September 1651, was transported via London on the John and Sarah of London to Boston in December 1651, landed there in February 1652. [Suffolk Deeds.1/5-6]

MANN, PATRICK, a prisoner of war captured at the Siege of Worcester on 2 September 1651, was transported via London on the John and Sarah of London to Boston in December 1651, landed there in February 1652. [Suffolk Deeds.1/5-6]

MANSON, PETER, of the York County Militia, Virginia, in 1701. [TNA.CO5.1312/2]

MARR, JOHN, a soldier of Captain Summer's Company of the Surry County Militia, Virginia, in 1701. [TNA.CO5.1312/2]

MARSHALL, CUTHBERT, a soldier of Captain Jack's Company of Militia in Barbados in 1680. [H.2.123]

MARSHALL, Captain JAMES, in Newporttown, County Fermanagh, Ireland, a divorce, 2 February 1693. [NRS.CC86.57]

MARSHALL, JOHN, a cavalryman in Captain Robinson's Troop of Militia in Barbados in 1679. [H2.203]

MARSHALL, ROBERT, a soldier of Major Waterman's Company of Militia in Barbados in 1679. [H2.160]

MARSHALL, WILLIAM, a soldier of Captain Jack's Company of Militia in Barbados in 1680. [H.2.123]

MARTIN, DANIEL, a prisoner of war captured at the Siege of Worcester on 2 September 1651, was transported via London on the John and Sarah of London to Boston in December 1651, landed there in February 1652. [Suffolk Deeds.1/5-6]

MARTIN, DAVID, a Lieutenant of Mackay's Regiment, in Danish Service in 1626, was killed at Boitzenburg in July 1627. [TGSI.VIII.187]

MARTIN, JOHN, Quartermaster Sergeant of the Scottish Company in Memel, was married there in December 1629 in the St Johann Kirche.

MARTIN, JOHN, from Kirkmichael in Kintyre, Argyll, a soldier in Argyll's Rebellion, was imprisoned in Canongate Tolbooth, banished to the American Plantations on 24 July 1685, then transported via Leith to East New Jersey on the Henry and Francis of Newcastle on 5 September 1685, landed there on 7 December 1685. [RPCS.11.114/129/136/154/330]

MARTIN, PETER, a Scottish soldier in Leiden, Holland, married Griete Jansdaughter from Antwerp, Flanders, in Leiden on 15 March 1591. [Leiden Marriage Register]

MASON, JOHN, a prisoner of war captured at the Battle of Dunbar on 3 September 1650, transported from London on the Unity of Boston to Boston in November 1650, an indentured servant at the Lynn Ironworks in the 1650s. [Suffolk Court Files.1226][LLNV.248]

MATHESON, GEORGE, a Cornet in Marpa's Company of Erskine's in Regiment in Danish Service in 1628. [SAA.118]

MATHESON, Colonel GEORGE, in the Service of the Emperor of All Russia, a will, 17 June 1633, also witnessed the will of Captain Wauchope in Moscow on 29 September 1632. [Suffolk Record Office. S1.1.77.6/9]

MATHIS, MATTHEW, born 1669, enlisted in Captain McKenzie's Company in 1689, fought at the Battle of Killiecrankie, Perthshire, on 27 July 1689. [TNA.WO116.1]

MATHISON, Captain JOHN, of the Cameronian Regiment at the Siege of Dunkeld, Perthshire, on 21 August 1689. [BK.146]

MAULE, GEORGE, Sergeant Major of Forbes of Tullich's Company in Danish Service in 1628. [SAA.ii.121]

MAXTON, ['Muckstone'], NEIL, a prisoner of war captured at the Siege of Worcester on 2 September 1651, was transported via

London on the John and Sarah of London to Boston in December 1651, landed there in February 1652. [Suffolk Deeds.1/5-6]

MAXWELL, ALEXANDER, a prisoner of war captured at the Battle of Dunbar on 3 September 1650, transported from London on the Unity of Boston to Boston in November 1650, settled in Kittery, Berwick, Maine, by 1656, later in York, probate 8 October 1707, Maine. [LLNV.251]

MAXWELL, DANIEL, a prisoner of war captured at the Siege of Worcester on 2 September 1651, was transported via London on the John and Sarah of London to Boston in December 1651, landed there in February 1652. [Suffolk Deeds.1/5-6]

MAXWELL, HUMPHREY, a soldier of Captain Woodward's Company of Militia in Barbados in 1680. [H.2.156]

MAXWELL, J., a soldier of 3rd Company of Cockburn's Regiment in Swedish Service in 1609. [SIS.217]

MAXWELL, Major JAMES, of Glenlaive, a tack, 1682. [Kirkcudbright Deed 162s 735]

MAXWELL, Lieutenant ROBERT, in Ireland in 1624. [CalSPIre]

MAXWELL, Captain ROBERT, subscribed to a bond in Bellicastle, Ireland, in 1666. [Kirkcudbright deeds 741]

MAXWELL, THOMAS, a Sergeant of the 1st Company of Cockburn's Regiment in Swedish Service in 1609. [SIS.217]

MAXWELL, THOMAS, Captain of the Earl of Dunfermline's Regiment in France, a deed, 1676. [NRS.RD2.41.65]

MAXWELL, Lieutenant THOMAS, Commander of a Troop of Horse Militia in Barbados in 1679. [H2.211]

MAXWELL, THOMAS, surgeon of Captain Ely's Company of Militia in Barbados in 1679. [H2.178]

MAXWELL, WALTER, Captain of a Scottish regiment in France, deeds, 1676. [NRS.RD4.39.199; RD4.42.323]

MAXWELL, WILLIAM, soldier of Major Lyte's Company of Militia in Barbados in 1679. [H2.175]

MAXWELL, Lieutenant, in Barbados in 1680. [SPAWI.1680.1336]

MAXWELL, ..., a Sergeant of Fraser's Dragoons in 1646. [TFD.220]

MEGOT, JOHN, son of John Megot of Maistertoun, a Cornet to Alexander Erskine, Captain of a Company of Horse in Dutch Service, a sasine, 19 March 1631. [NRS.RS24.17.161]

MELDRUM, A., a soldier of 1st Company of Cockburn's Regiment in Swedish Service in 1609. [SIS.217]

MELDRUM, JAMES, in Angus, of the Earl of Airlie's Militia in 1670. [NRS.GD16.53.39]

MELDRUM, R., a soldier of 2nd Company of Cockburn's Regiment in Swedish Service in 1609. [SIS.217]

MELDRUM, THOMAS, Colonel in the Service of the King of Norway and Denmark, was admitted as a burgess of Aberdeen on 29 August 1681. [ACA.ABR]

MELVILLE, Colonel ANDREW, an officer in the Service of Duke Georg Wilhelm of Braunschweig- Luneburg in 1665, Commandant of Celle, Saxony, in 1666, later of Gifhorn from 1677 to 1680. [MGIF]

MELVILLE, DAVID, a soldier in Captain McKenzie of Suddie's Company in 1685. [NRS.GD80.171]

MELVILLE, ROBERT, Captain of the Earl of Leven's Regiment in Carrickfergus, Ireland, in 1642. [TNA.SP28.120]

MELVIN, Lieutenant Colonel HENRY, fought and was captured at the Battle of Dunbar on 3 September 1650.

MELVIN, JAMES, of H.M. Guard in France in 1612. [NRS.GD122.2.965]

MENZIES, Major DUNCAN, Ensign of Mar's Regiment of Foot in 1672, Lieutenant in 1685, Captain of Buchan's Regiment in 1688, a Jacobite soldier in 1689. [APS.acc.ix.56]

MENZIES, DUNCAN, Ensign of Major Whyte's company mustered in Glasgow in 1682. [DSA.128]

MENZIES, PAUL, born 1637, son of Sir Gilbert Menzies of Pitfoddels, via Poland to Russia in 1661, a Major in Russian Service, died in Moscow in 1694. [NS.1/1.55]

MENZIES, THOMAS, of Balgownie, a Lieutenant Colonel of the Army of His Imperial Majesty of Russia, was wounded when fighting the Poles at Szudna in 1660, died in the Ukraine. [ACA; birth brief 17.2.1672]

MENZIES, WILLIAM, Corporal of Annandale's Regiment of Horse, was captured by the Jacobites at the Battle of Killiecrankie on 27 July 1689. [RPCS.XIV

MERCER, Sir JAMES, of Aldie, Colonel of a Regiment of Horse in 1643 in the Army of the Covenant. [CA.108]

MERKEL, PETER, from Aberdeen, chief bosun on the Zeeland warship <u>Utrecht</u> around 1665. [ZA.Rekenkamer.c6994]

MERSTOUN, JOHN, formerly of Lord Lindsay's Regiment, then a Lieutenant in Darien, testament, 1707, Comm. Edinburgh. [NRS]

METHIE, JOHN, in Angus, of the Earl of Airlie's Militia in 1670. [NRS.GD16.53.39]

MIDDLETON, Major JAMES, formerly of Wauchope's Regiment, then a Captain of Mar's Regiment of Foot, a Jacobite at the Battle of Killiecrankie on 27 July 1689. [APS.IX.55]

MIDDLETON, JOHN, born 1608, a Lieutenant General in Poland from 1656 to 1658, died in 1674.

MIDDLETON, Lieutenant, a Jacobite captured at the Battle of Cromdale, Strathspey, on 1 May 1690. [RPCS.XV.304]

MILL, ANDREW, a soldier from Caithness, married Catherine Adam from Leith, in Schiedam, Holland, on 26 April 1635. [Schiedam Marriage Register]

MILLER, ALEXANDER, a prisoner of war captured at the Siege of Worcester on 2 September 1651, was transported via London on the John and Sarah of London to Boston in December 1651, landed there in February 1652. [Suffolk Deeds.1/5-6]

MILLER, J., a soldier of 2nd Company of Cockburn's Regiment in Swedish Service in 1609. [SIS.217]

MILLAR, JOHN, from Jedburgh, Roxburghshire, a prisoner in Edinburgh Tolbooth, was released to go to Germany as a soldier under Colonel Sinclair in June 1628. [RPCS.II.333]

MILLAR, ROBERT, of Sir Thomas Livingstone's Regiment in Flanders, testament, 7 June 1697, Comm. Lanark. [NRS]

MILLER, THOMAS, a soldier of Colonel Alexander's Company of the Regiment of Guards, found guilty of theft and plunder, was transported to Barbados in 1668. [RPCS.II.415]

MILLIKEN, JAMES, born near Largs, Ayrshire, in 1669, Major of the Militia in St Kitts. [HS.IX.3]

MILNE, ALEXANDER, a soldier of Hackett's Company in Mackay's Regiment, was killed at the Battle of Killiecrankie, Perthshire, on 27 July 1689. [BK]

MILNE, ANDREW, Lieutenant Colonel of Sir Mungo Campbell of Lawers' Regiment in Temple Patrick, Ireland, in 1642. [TNA.SP28.120]; Lieutenant Colonel of the Edinburgh Foot in 1643, fought at the Battle of Marston Moor and at the Siege of Newcastle in 1644. [CA.133]

MILN, WILLIAM, a Captain of Balfour's Regiment, who was killed at the Battle of Killiecrankie, Perthshire, on 27 August 1689. [BK.207]

MILWARD, JAMES, a prisoner of war captured at the Siege of Worcester on 2 September 1651, was transported via London on the John and Sarah of London to Boston in December 1651, landed there in February 1652. [Suffolk Deeds.1/5-6]

MITCHELL, JAMES, a prisoner of war captured at the Siege of Worcester on 2 September 1651, was transported via London on the John and Sarah of London to Boston in December 1651, landed there in February 1652. [Suffolk Deeds.1/5-6]

MITCHELL, JAMES, a prisoner in Edinburgh Tolbooth, was released to go to Holland as a soldier with Colonel James Douglas on 14 April 1682. [ETR]

MITCHELL, JAMES, a gentleman of the Troop of Guards, his funeral was in Bathgate, West Lothian, in October 1691. [NRS.E99.41.16]

MITCHELL, THOMAS, a soldier from Cupar, Fife, married Iffijen Kry in Haarlem, Holland, in 1597. [Haarlem Marriage Register]

MITCHELL,....., a soldier of Mackay's Regiment, at the Battle of Killiecrankie, Perthshire, on 27 July 1689. [RPCS.XIV][TNA.WO116.1]

MOFFAT, ROBERT, a Captain in the Swedish Army, settled in Sweden, was granted a birth brief in 1672. [RPCS.II.573]

MOFFAT, THOMAS, Major of the Angus Regiment at the Battle of Marston Moor, Yorkshire, on 2 July 1644. [DCW.78][CA.108]

MOIR, JOHN, in Edinburgh, a former archer of the King of France's Guard, testament, 1630, Comm. Edinburgh. [NRS]

MOLLISON, ALEXANDER, a prisoner of war captured at the Siege of Worcester on 2 September 1651, was transported via London on the John and Sarah of London to Boston in December 1651, landed there in February 1652. [Suffolk Deeds.1/5-6]

MOLLISON, Colonel JOHN, Military Governor of Lunenburg, was granted a birth brief in 1674. [RPCS.IV.185] [MAM.153] [MGIF]

MONCREIFF, DAVID, formerly an Ensign of the Earl of Tullibardine's Regiment, Deputy Assistant at Darien, testament, 1707, Comm. Edinburgh. [NRS]

MONCRIEFF, JOHN, Captain of Sir Mungo Campbell of Lawers' Regiment in Temple Patrick, Ireland, in 1642. [TNA.SP28.120]

MONCREIFF, JOHN, Captain of Leven's Regiment at the Battle of Killiecrankie, Perthshire, on 27 July 1689. [BK.96]

MONCREIFF, Captain THOMAS, probate, 1684, Derry.

MONCREIFF, ..., a Captain of Mackay's Regiment, in Danish Service in 1626, in Swedish Service in 1629, was killed at New Brandenburg. [TGSI.VIII.187]

MONCUR, THOMAS, a gunner aboard the Lion of Zeeland in 1631. [ZA]

MONKE, WILLIAM, a soldier, who was sent to Jamaica on the Grantham in 1659. [SPAWI.1659.126]

MONORGAN, J., a soldier of 2nd Company of Cockburn's Regiment in Swedish Service in 1609. [SIS.217]

MONRO, ANDREW, a Sergeant Major of Mackenzie's Company in Danish Service, in 1628. [SAA.ii.124]

MONROE, ANDREW, third son of David Monroe and his wife Agnes, settled in St Mary's County, Maryland, around 1641, an officer in the army of King Charles I during the English Civil War, was captured and transported back to Virginia in 1648, settled in Northumberland County, Virginia, died in 1668. [BAF]

MONRO, ANDREW, a Captain of Fraser's Dragoons, in 1645 [TFD.47]

MONROE, Captain ANDREW, of the Westmoreland County Militia, Virginia, in 1701. [TNA.CO5.1312/2]

MONROE, DANIEL, a prisoner of war captured at the Siege of Worcester on 2 September 1651, was transported via London on

the John and Sarah of London to Boston in December 1651, landed there in February 1652. [Suffolk Deeds.1/5-6]

MONRO, FARQUHAR, a soldier of Mackenzie's Company in Danish Service, was killed at Oldenburg in September 1627. [SAA.ii.124]

MONRO, GEORGE, Lieutenant Colonel of the Earl of Leven's Regiment, in Carrickfergus, Ireland, in 1642. [TNA.SP28.120]

MONRO, GEORGE, a Major General in Ireland, a deed, 1702. [NRS.RD2.104.821]

MONROE, Captain GEORGE, of the Cameronian Regiment at the Siege of Dunkeld on 21 August 1689. [BK.146]

MONRO, HECTOR, of Coull, a Sergeant of Mackenzie's Company in Danish Service, was killed at Oldenburg in September 1627. [SAA.ii.124]

MONRO, Colonel HENRY, of Rosehall, County Down, Ireland, a bond, 1708. [NRS.GD93.303]

MONROE, HUGH, a prisoner of war captured at the Siege of Worcester on 2 September 1651, was transported via London on the John and Sarah of London to Boston in December 1651, landed there in February 1652. [Suffolk Deeds.1/5-6]

MONRO, HUGH, formerly a Lieutenant of Lord Murray's Regiment, an overseer at Darien in 1698, testament, 1707, Comm. Edinburgh. [NRS]

MONRO, JOHN, Major of a Dragoon Regiment of Leven's Army in 1643, Lieutenant Colonel of Fraser's Dragoons at the Battle of Marston Moor, Yorkshire, on 2 July 1644.

MONROE, JOHN, a prisoner of war captured at the Siege of Worcester on 2 September 1651, was transported via London on the John and Sarah of London to Boston in December 1651, landed there in February 1652. [Suffolk Deeds.1/5-6]

MONROE, ROBERT, a prisoner of war captured at the Siege of Worcester on 2 September 1651, was transported via London on the John and Sarah of London to Boston in December 1651, landed there in February 1652. [Suffolk Deeds.1/5-6]

MONRO, ROBERT, Colonel of Major General Monro's Regiment, in Carrickfergus, Ireland, in 1642. [TNA.SP18.120]

MONROE, WILLIAM, Ensign of the Westmoreland County Militia, Virginia, in 1701. [TNA.CO5.1312/2]

MONRO, ..., Captain of the Nansemond County Militia, Virginia, in 1702. [TNA.CO5.1312.

MONTGOMERY, ALEXANDER, from Scotland to the Netherlands in 1586 with 120 soldiers, later commissioned into the Regiment of Bartholemew Balfour. [ARA. Rand van Staat.1524.80]

MONTGOMERY, GEORGE, Captain of Cavalry in Ulster in 1646. [Cal.SPIre]

MONTGOMERY, HENRY, Cornet of Colonel Montgomerie's Regiment, in Linlithgow, West Lothian, in 1645. [NRS.GD76.238]

MONTGOMERY, HUGH, Commander of 120 German cavalry at the Battle of Loyew in 1649, and at Kiev, Ukraine, in 1651, Commandant of Kedainai, Lithuania. [SCL.160]

MONTGOMERIE, Lord Viscount HUGH, Chief of HM Forces in Ulster in 1651. [NRS.GD3.9.7.15]

MONTGOMERY, HUGH, of Borland, formerly a Corporal in the Earl of Eglinton's Troop, later a land officer in Captain Andrew Stewart's Company in Darien, died there. [APS.14.app.114/127]

MONTGOMERIE, Lieutenant JAMES, in Ardstraw, County Tyrone, Ireland, probate, 1618, Derry.

MONTGOMERY, JAMES, Captain of the Earl of Eglinton's Regiment in Bangor, Ireland, in 1642. [TNA.SP28.120]

MONTGOMERY, Colonel JAMES, in Ireland, 1648.
[NRS.GD3.5.420]; in Antrim in 1645. [CalSPIre.260.137]

MONTGOMERY, Sir JAMES, a Cavalry officer in Ulster in 1646.
[Cal.SPIre]

MONTGOMERY, Captain JOHN, in Konigsberg Alstadt, Lithuania, in January 1655. [SCL]

MONTGOMERY, ROBERT, a Trooper under Captain Ury, married Stijn Egberts a widow, in Zwolle, Overijssel, on 19 February 1626. [Zwolle Marriage Register]

MONTGOMERY, ROBERT, Captain of the Earl of Eglinton's Regiment in Bangor, Ireland, in 1642. [TNA.SP28.120]

MONTGOMERIE, Major General ROBERT, of a Regiment of Horse in 1643, with 3 Troops of Cavalry, fought at the Battle of Dunbar on 3 September 1650, [SR.37]; in Tours, France, a letter, 1658. [NRS.GD3.5.553]

MONTGOMERY, ..., Routemaster, in the Service of Duke Janusz Radziwill in Lithuania in the 1660s. [SGB.179]

MONTGOMERY, Captain, of Colonel Cranston's Regiment in the Service of the King of Poland in 1656. [CF.417]

MONTROSE, LAUGHLIN, a prisoner of war captured at the Siege of Worcester on 2 September 1651, was transported via London on the John and Sarah of London to Boston in December 1651, landed there in February 1652. [Suffolk Deeds.1/5-6]

MOODIE, INGRAM, a prisoner of war captured at the Siege of Worcester on 2 September 1651, was transported via London on the John and Sarah of London to Boston in December 1651, landed there in February 1652, an indentured servant at the Lynn Ironworks in 1650s, died 1693, probate Essex County. [Suffolk Deeds.1/5-6][LLNV.248]

MOORE, ALEXANDER, Captain of the Earl of Eglinton's Regiment in Bangor, Ireland, in 1642. [TNA.SP18.120]

MOORE, DONALD, a soldier in Argyll's Rebellion, was transported via Leith to Jamaica in August 1685. [RPCS.11.136]

MOORE, JAMES, a prisoner of war captured at the Siege of Worcester on 2 September 1651, was transported via London on the John and Sarah of London to Boston in December 1651, landed there in February 1652. [Suffolk Deeds.1/5-6][LLNV.248]

MOOR, JOHN, from Leith, a musketeer aboard the Arms of Zeeland in 1644. [ZA]

MOORE, [Muir], JOHN, [1], a prisoner of war captured at the Siege of Worcester on 2 September 1651, was transported via London on the John and Sarah of London to Boston in December 1651, landed there in February 1652. [Suffolk Deeds.1/5-6]

MOORE, [Muir], JOHN, [2], a prisoner of war captured at the Siege of Worcester on 2 September 1651, was transported via London on the John and Sarah of London to Boston in December 1651, landed there in February 1652. [Suffolk Deeds.1/5-6]

MORE, [Muir], ... , a prisoner of war captured at the Siege of Worcester on 2 September 1651, was transported via London on the John and Sarah of London to Boston in December 1651, landed there in February 1652. [Suffolk Deeds.1/5-6]

MORAY, JOHN, son of Moray of Abercairney, a Lieutenant Colonel of the French Army from 1693 to 1701. [NRS.GD24.1.368]

MORCOT, [?], ALEXANDER, a prisoner of war captured at the Siege of Worcester on 2 September 1651, was transported via London on the John and Sarah of London to Boston in December 1651, landed there in February 1652. [Suffolk Deeds.1/5-6]

MORE, JOHN, a soldier in Elbing, [Eblag], East Prussia, in 1681.

MORE, Major PATRICK, from Perth, a cavalry officer in Swedish Service from 1629, Commandant of Buxtehude, near Hamburg, from 1646 to the 1670s; was granted a birth brief in 1663. [MGIF][RPCS][NRS.B59.2.1-3]

MORRISON, DONALD, a soldier in Argyll's Rebellion, was transported via Leith to Jamaica in August 1685. [RPCS.11.136]

MORRISON, JOHN, a soldier of Cockburn's Regiment in Swedish Service in 1609. [SIS.216]

MOOR, JOHN, from Leith, a musketeer aboard the <u>Vere</u> in 1644. [ZA]

MORRISON, JOHN, a prisoner in Edinburgh Tolbooth, was released to go as a soldier with Marshal Schomberg to Holland in 1689. [RPCS.13.548]

MORTON, JOHN, a Scottish soldier, married Elisabeth, widow of Wilhelm Pomerigs, in the Heilger Geist, Elbing, East Prussia, in 1669.

MORTON, PATRICK, a prisoner of war captured at the Siege of Worcester on 2 September 1651, was transported via London on the <u>John and Sarah of London</u> to Boston in December 1651, landed there in February 1652. [Suffolk Deeds.1/5-6]

MORTON, WILLIAM, Captain of the Earl of Lindsay's Regiment in Bangor, Ireland, in 1642. [TNA.SP18.120]

MOUTRAY, THOMAS, a soldier of New Kent County Militia, in Virginia in 1701. [TNA.CO5.1312/2]

MOWAT, ANDREW, Captain of Colonel Murray's Regiment of Foot in Ireland, deeds, 1702. [NRS.RD4.90.829; RD3.99.1.40]

MOWAT, ANDREW, Captain of Major General Murray's Regiment in Dutch Service, testament, 16 December 1706, Comm. Edinburgh. [NRS]

MOWAT, HUGH, an officer of Mackay's Regiment in Danish Service in 1626, in Swedish Service in 1629. [TGSI.VIII.188]

MOWAT, JAMES, a soldier of Colonel Lyne's Company of Militia in Barbados in 1679. [H2.99]

MOWAT, WILLIAM, from Edinburgh, a soldier in Captain George Hume's Company, married Tanneken Jans a widow, in Arnemuiden, Zeeland, on 26 September 1612. [Arnemuiden Marriage Register]

MOWBRAY, FRANCIS, an archer of the Scots Guards in France in the 1560s. [NRS.NRAS.O.143]

MOWBRAY, ROBERT, from Aberdour, Fife, a gunner on the Lion of Zeeland in 1631. [ZA]

MUDIE, PATRICK, a soldier of Lieutenant Colonel Lyne's Company of Militia in Barbados in 1679. [H2.173]

MUDIE, THOMAS, a Captain of Militia in Dundee in 1643. [DCW.1643]

MUIR, HENRY, a soldier from Brechin in Angus, married Elizabeth Lindsay also from Brechin, in Schiedam, Holland, on 7 July 1638. [Schiedam Marriage Register]

MUIR, JAMES, of Bellybraga, formerly a Captain of Lord Cardross's Regiment of Dragoons, deeds, 1689/1691/1693. [NRS.RD2.70.632; RD4.57.617; RD4.72.565]

MUIR, JOHN, a soldier of the Earl of Roxburgh's Company, in the Netherlands in 1650. [GAR.ONA.312.64.103]

MUIR, ROBERT, Captain of 3rd Company of Cockburn's Regiment in Swedish Service in 1609. [SIS.217]

MUIR, ROBERT, a soldier in Argyll's Rebellion, imprisoned in Edinburgh, banished to the American Plantations on 31 July 1685, transported via Leith on the Henry and Francis of Newcastle bound for East New Jersey on 7 July 1685, landed there on 7 December 1685. [RPCS.11.129/130/136/137/330] [NJSA.East Jersey Deeds, liber A, fo.226]

MUIR, WILLIAM, a soldier in Colonel Murray's Company, married Adrieantgen Adriaansdaughter from Goes in Zeeland, in Leiden on 20 December 1597. [Leiden Marriage Register]

MUIR, WILLIAM, a soldier under Captain Balfour in the Ostende Garrison in Flanders, married Jannetgen Jans of Leiden, Holland, there on 15 March 1602. [Leiden Marriage Register]

MULOUNY, TIMOTHY, a prisoner in Canongate Tolbooth, was released to go to Holland as a soldier under Captain Robert Reid of Bonakettle on 18 June 1690. [RPCS.XV.713]

MUNGALL [?], ['Munckbell'], WILLIAM, a prisoner of war captured at the Siege of Worcester on 2 September 1651, was transported via London on the John and Sarah of London to Boston in December 1651, landed there in February 1652. [Suffolk Deeds.1/5-6]

MUNRO, ALEXANDER, a soldier, married Dorothea, widow of Abraham Evert a soldier, in the Burgkirche of Konigsberg, Lithuania, in February 1670.

MUNRO, ALEXANDER, Lieutenant Colonel of Lord Douglas's Regiment, a deed, 1670. [NRS.RD4.26.503]; Lieutenant Colonel of the Earl of Dunfermline's Regiment in France, a deed, 1676, [NRS.RD4.39.199]; Captain of Lord George Douglas's Regiment in France, a deed, 1681. [NRS.RD2.54.535]

MUNRO, ALLEN, a soldier in Captain Sampson's Company of Militia in Barbados in 1680. [H2.150]

MUNRO, ANDREW, a Captain in Mackay's Regiment, in Danish Service, was killed in a duel at Femern. [TGSI.VIII.187]

MUNRO, ANDREW, an officer in Mackay's Regiment, in Danish Service in 1626, in Swedish Service in 1629, was killed at Oldenburg, Saxony. [TGSI.VIII.188]

MUNRO, ANDREW, a Highland soldier, was accused of torturing two witches in North Berwick, East Lothian, in 1652. [NRS.GD17.546]

MUNRO, ANDREW, a soldier in Captain Rawlin's Company of Militia in Barbados in 1679. [H2.117]

MUNRO, DANIEL, a soldier in Captain Liston's Company of Militia in Barbados in 1679. [H2.143]

MUNRO, DAVID, a Major in Mackay's Regiment, in Danish Service, was 'scorched by powder at Eckernfiord, Schlesvig-Holstein. [TGSI.VIII.186]

MUNRO, DAVID, an officer in Mackay's Regiment, in Danish Service, in Swedish Service in 1629. [TGSI.VIII.188]

MUNRO, DENNIS, a soldier in Captain Walley's Company of Militia in Barbados in 1680. [H2.137]

MUNRO, DONALD, son of Robert Munro and his wife Christian Brown, a prisoner of war who was transported to Barbados in 1651. [MT.16]

MUNRO, FARQUHAR, an officer in Mackay's Regiment, in Danish Service, in Swedish Service in 1629, was killed at Oldenburg, Saxony. [TGSI.VIII.188]

MUNRO, Sir HECTOR, of Foulis, Ross and Cromarty, Captain of Mackay's Regiment, in Danish Service, in Swedish Service in 1629, a Colonel in Swedish Service Buxtehude, Germany, in the 1630s, later a Colonel in Dutch Service. [TGSI.VIII.187][RGS.9.112] [SIG.282]

MUNRO, HECTOR, a trooper in Major Stewart's Troop of Horse Militia in Barbados in 1679. [H2.209]

MUNRO, Colonel HENRY, of Rosehall, County Down, Ireland, sasines, 1697. [NRS.RS36.6.430/436]

MUNRO, JOHN, of Obisdell, Ross and Cromarty, Captain of Mackay's Regiment, in Danish Service, in Swedish Service in 1629, later Colonel of a Scottish regiment. [TGSI.VIII.187]

MUNRO, JOHN, from Assynt, Sutherland, a Captain of Mackay's Regiment, in Danish Service, in Swedish Service in 1629. [TGSI.VIII.187]

MUNROE, JOHN, a soldier of the 1st Company of Cockburn's Regiment in Swedish Service in 1609. [SIS.217]

MUNRO, JOHN, a soldier in Captain Helm's Company of Militia in Barbados in 1679. [H2.153]

MUNRO, JOHN, a soldier in Major Waterman's Company of Militia in Barbados in 1679. [H2.160]

MUNRO, JOHN, a soldier in Captain Lyte's Company of Militia in Barbados in 1679. [H2.175]

MUNRO, ROBERT, of Foulis, Ross and Cromarty, Captain of Mackay's Regiment, in Danish Service, in Swedish Service in 1629, later a Colonel in Swedish Service at Ulm, Wurtemberg, in the 1630s, died there on 29 April 1633, buried in the Franciscan church there. [TGSI.VIII.187][RGS.9.112][SS.79] [SIG.282]

MUNRO, ROBERT, of Contullich, Ross and Cromarty, a Colonel in Danish Service, later fought for Sweden in Germany around 1634, at Wittenberg. [TGSI.VIII.185] [RGS.9.111]

MUNRO, THOMAS, a soldier in Captain Burton's Company of Militia in Barbados in 1679. [H2.183]

MUNRO, WILLIAM, a prisoner of war, captured at the Siege of Worcester on 2 September 1651, transported to New England, died in Lexington in 1717. [SG.14.2.46]

MURRAY, Colonel ADAM, officer in charge of Londonderry, Ireland, during the Siege of 1689, originator of 'No Surrender', died in 1706, buried in Old Glendermot Church, Londonderry.

MURRAY, ALEXANDER, a soldier of the 1st Company of Cockburn's Regiment in Swedish Service in 1609. [SIS.217]

MURRAY, ALEXANDER, of Drumdewan, third son of Sir William Murray of Tullibardine, a Colonel in Dutch Service, was killed at Bommel on 19 May 1599. [SP.I.466]

MURRAY, ALEXANDER, a soldier in Colonel Stanfast's Company of Militia in Barbados in 1679. [H2.158]

MURRAY, ALEXANDER, once a soldier of Colonel Hill's Regiment, a blind beggar by 9 May 1695. [NRS.E97.17]

MURRAY, ANDREW, a Sergeant of Murray's Company in Mackay's Regiment, was killed at the Battle of Killiecrankie, Perthshire, on 27 July 1689. [BK]

MURRAY, ANTHONY, a soldier under Captain Murray, married Lintgen Pieter, in Leiden, Holland, on 22 February 1592. [Leiden Marriage Register]

MURRAY, Lieutenant ARCHIBALD, of Skirling, Peebles-shire, bound for Holland with recruits taken from prisons in 1689. [RPCS.XIV]

MURRAY, DANIEL, a soldier in Captain Dent's Company of Militia in Barbados in 1679. [H2.104]

MURRAY, Lieutenant GEORGE, Captain of Dunbarton's Regiment of Foot in 1686, a Jacobite at the Battle of Killiecrankie, Perthshire, on 27 July 1689. [APS.IX.55]

MURRAY, GIDEON, Captain of the Earl of Lothian's Regiment in Carrickfergus, Ireland, in 1642. [TNA.SP18.120]

MURRAY, HUGH, an officer in Mackay's Regiment, in Danish Service, in Swedish Service in 1629. [TGSI.VIII.189]

MURRAY, HUTCHEN, a soldier in Captain Burton's Company of Militia in Barbados in 1679. [H2.183]

MURRAY, JAMES, a soldier from Forres, Moray, married Anna Holmes, in the English Church in Middelburg, Zeeland, on 14 December 1617. [Arnemuiden, Zeeland, Marriage Register]

MURRAY, JAMES, Rear Admiral of the Polish Navy, Commander of the King David at the Battle of the Bay of Gdansk [Danzig] on 28 November 1627, thereafter a Captain in the Polish Army at the Siege of Smolensk. [HS.IX.3]

MURRAY, Colonel JAMES, was authorised to raise infantry for Polish service in Smolensk on 19 October 1633. [Castr. Cracow.58/249]

MURRAY, JAMES, Ensign of the Angus Regiment at the Battle of Marston Moor, Yorkshire, on 2 July 1644. [DCW.78]

MURRAY, JAMES, a prisoner of war captured at the Siege of Worcester on 2 September 1651, was transported via London on the John and Sarah of London to Boston in December 1651, landed there in February 1652. [Suffolk Deeds.1/5-6]

MURRAY, JAMES, a soldier in Captain Johnstone's Company of Militia in Barbados in 1679. [H2.165]

MURRAY, JAMES, from Argyll, a soldier in Argyll's Rebellion, imprisoned in Canongate Tolbooth, transported via Leith on the Henry and Francis of Newcastle to East New Jersey on 5 September 1685, landed there on 7 December 1685. [RPCS.11.330]

MURRAY, Sir JOHN, Captain of the Earl of Lothian's Regiment in Carrickfergus, Ireland, in 1642. [TNA.SP18.120]

MURRAY, Lieutenant JOHN, of Colonel Scott's Regiment, in Linlithgow, West Lothian, in 1648. [NRS.GD76.252]

MURRAY, JOHN, [1], a prisoner of war captured at the Siege of Worcester on 2 September 1651, was transported via London on the John and Sarah of London to Boston in December 1651, landed there in February 1652. [Suffolk Deeds.1/5-6]

MURRAY, JOHN, [2], a prisoner of war captured at the Siege of Worcester on 2 September 1651, was transported via London on

the John and Sarah of London to Boston in December 1651, landed there in February 1652. [Suffolk Deeds.1/5-6]

MURRAY, JOHN, a soldier in Major Fraser's Company of Militia in Barbados in 1680. [H2.134]

MURRAY, JOHN, a soldier in Colonel Lyne's Company of Militia in Barbados in 1679. [H2.100]

MURRAY, JOHN, ['Johannes Morre'], a Scottish soldier in Elbing, East Prussia, in 1681.

MURRAY, JONAS, a prisoner of war captured at the Siege of Worcester on 2 September 1651, was transported via London on the John and Sarah of London to Boston in December 1651, landed there in February 1652. [Suffolk Deeds.1/5-6]

MURRAY, MUNGO, Captain of the Earl of Lindsay's Regiment in Bangor, Ireland, in 1642. [TNA.SP18.120]

MURRAY, Sir MUNGO, Lieutenant Colonel of Barclay's Regiment of Horse in the Army of the Covenant in 1644, fought at the Battle of Philiphaugh on 13 September 1645. [CA.117]

MURRAY, NEIL, a prisoner of war captured at the Siege of Worcester on 2 September 1651, was transported via London on the John and Sarah of London to Boston in December 1651, landed there in February 1652. [Suffolk Deeds.1/5-6]

MURRAY, PATRICK, Quartermaster Sergeant of Forbes of Tullich's Company in Danish Service in 1628. [SAA.ii.121]

MURRAY, PATRICK, Quartermaster of Lord Gordon's Horse, in 1643, at the Siege of Newcastle in 1644. [CA.146]

MURRAY, RICHARD, Captain of a Militia Troop of Horse in County Donegal, Ireland, in 1678. [NRS.GD10.1380]

MURRAY, ROBERT, a Lieutenant General in Dutch Service, Governor of Tournai, [Doornik], Flanders, testament, 18 September 1719, Comm. Edinburgh. [NRS]

MURRAY, W., a soldier in Moscow in 1630. [SSA.50]

MURRAY, WALTER, a Lieutenant in the Service of Holland, testament, 1669, Comm. Edinburgh. [NRS]

MURRAY, Lieutenant Colonel WALTER, in Busch, Brabant, 1669, father of Alexander Murray. [NRS.S/H]

MURRAY, Lieutenant WILLIAM, of Livingstone's Regiment of Dragoons at the Battle of Cromdale, Strathspey, on 1 May 1690. [BK.177]

MURRAY, Lieutenant Colonel, fought and was captured at the Battle of Dunbar on 3 September 1650.

MUSHET, GEORGE, in Angus, of the Earl of Airlie's Militia in 1670. [NRS.GD16.53.39]

MYLNE, Colonel GEORGE, in Angus, of the Earl of Airlie's Militia in 1670. [NRS.GD16.53.39]

NAIRN, Lieutenant ALEXANDER, married the widow of J. Unwin, in the Reformed Church of Peter and Paul in Danzig, [Gdansk], in 1647.

NAIRN, JOHN, Military Governor of Erfurt, Thuringia, in the 1640s and of Leipzig, Saxony, from 1648 to 1649. [MGIF]

NAPIER, ROBERT, Captain of the Foot of the King William County, Virginia, Militia, in 1701. [TNA.CO5.1312/2]

NASMITH, FRANCIS, Ensign of the Cameronian Regiment at the Siege of Dunkeld, Perthshire, on 21 August 1689. [BK.146]

NASMYTH, JOHN, surgeon to the King of France and to the Scots Guards of France, who died in London on 16 September 1613. [Greyfriars gravestone, Edinburgh]

NAYSMITH, JOHN JAMES, [Jan Jacob Nysmit], a midshipman aboard the *Eendracht* bound from the Netherlands to the East Indies in 1668. [GAR.ONA.240.43.61]

NEAL, JOHN, a prisoner of war captured at the Battle of Dunbar on 3 September 1650, transported from London on the Unity of Boston to Boston in November 1650, settled in Kittery, Maine, probate, April 1691, Salem, Massachusetts. [LLNV.251]

NEWLANDS, Captain DAVID, in the Scots Colony in America, a deed, 1701. [NRS.RD3.98.113]

NISBET, JOHN, a Lieutenant of Kenmure's Regiment at the Battle of Killiecrankie, Perthshire, on 27 July 1689, a prisoner of the Jacobites. [BK.121][NRS.GD124.16.76]

NISBET, WILLIAM, born 1596, to Sweden as an army officer, died in Upsalla, Sweden, in 1660. [SHR.IX.274]

OGILVY, ALEXANDER, in Angus, of the Earl of Airlie's Militia in 1670. [NRS.GD16.53.39]

OGILVY, DAVID, of Kinnaltie in Angus, of the Earl of Airlie's Militia in 1670. [NRS.GD16.53.39]

OGILVY, DAVID, in Angus, of the Earl of Airlie's Militia in 1670. [NRS.GD16.53.39]

OGILVIE, Sir DAVID, of Clova, served in Airlie's Troop in 1667, a Lieutenant of an independent Horse Troop in 1674, a Jacobite at the Battle of Killiecrankie, Perthshire, on 27 July 1689. [APS.IX.55]

OGILVY, Corporal GEORGE, in Angus, of the Earl of Airlie's Militia in 1670. [NRS.GD16.53.39]

OGILVY, GEORGE, in Angus, of the Earl of Airlie's Militia in 1670. [NRS.GD16.53.39]

OGILVIE, GEORGE, Military Governor of Speilberg in Moravia, father of Field Marshal George Benedict Ogilvie in 1710. [SIG.316]

OGILVY, JAMES, [1], in Angus, of the Earl of Airlie's Militia in 1670. [NRS.GD16.53.39]

OGILVY, JAMES, [2], in Angus, of the Earl of Airlie's Militia in 1670. [NRS.GD16.53.39]

OGILVY, JAMES, [3], in Angus, of the Earl of Airlie's Militia in 1670. [NRS.GD16.53.39]

OGILVY, Captain JAMES, in Angus, of the Earl of Airlie's Militia in 1670. [NRS.GD16.53.39]

OGILVY, JAMES, in Cortachy in Angus, of the Earl of Airlie's Militia in 1670. [NRS.GD16.53.39]

OGILVY, JAMES, in Ragall in Angus, of the Earl of Airlie's Militia in 1670. [NRS.GD16.53.39]

OGILVY, JOHN, of Peill in Angus, of the Earl of Airlie's Militia in 1670. [NRS.GD16.53.39]

OGILVY, JOHN, in Newton in Angus, of the Earl of Airlie's Militia in 1670. [NRS.GD16.53.39]

OGILVY, JOHN, in Angus, of the Earl of Airlie's Militia in 1670. [NRS.GD16.53.39]

OGILVY, JOHN, a soldier in Oletzko, Prussia, 1680. [SIG.263]

OGILVY, LUDOVICK, in Angus, of the Earl of Airlie's Militia in 1670. [NRS.GD16.53.39]

OGILVIE, PATRICK, Military Governor of Riga, Latvia, in 1657, and of Keksholm in 1660. [MGIF]

OGILVY, PATRICK, in Angus, of the Earl of Airlie's Militia in 1670. [NRS.GD16.53.39]

OGILVY, ROBERT, in Angus, of the Earl of Airlie's Militia in 1670. [NRS.GD16.53.39]

OGILVY, THOMAS, in Angus, of the Earl of Airlie's Militia in 1670. [NRS.GD16.53.39]

OGILVY, WALTER, a soldier from Dundee, married Grietgen Jacobs from France, in Schiedam, Holland, on 21 March 1637. [Schiedam Marriage Register]

OGILVY, Major WALTER, of Lord Gordon's Horse, in 1643, at the Siege of Newcastle in 1644. [CA.146]

OGILVIE, WILLIAM, a Lieutenant at Kedainai, Lithuania, from 1656 to 1664. [SCL.160]

OGILVY, WILLIAM, of Logie in Angus, of the Earl of Airlie's Militia in 1670. [NRS.GD16.53.39]

OGILVY, WILLIAM, in Angus, of the Earl of Airlie's Militia in 1670. [NRS.GD16.53.39]

OGILVY, WILLIAM, Captain of Colonel Hepburn's Regiment, died in battle near Mons, Flanders, in 1709. [NRS.GD77.200.1]

OGILVY, Captain, participated in Sir William Alexander's attempt to colonise Nova Scotia in 1620s, was based at Charles Fort at Port Royal in 1629. [NRS.GD90.sec.3/2]

OGILVY, Captain, a soldier in Memel in 1631. [JSM]

OGILVY, ..., a fourier [assistant Ensign] in Lyck, Eastern Prussia in 1687.

O'NEIL, DANIEL, a prisoner of war captured at the Siege of Worcester on 2 September 1651, was transported via London on the John and Sarah of London to Boston in December 1651, landed there in February 1652. [Suffolk Deeds.1/5-6]

OLIPHANT, DAVID, an officer of Bartholemew Balfour's Regiment in the Netherlands in 1586. [ARA.Rand van Staat.162.79]

OLIPHANT, Captain GEORGE, in Danish Service in 1628. [SAA.ii.143]

OLIPHANT, WILLIAM, Lieutenant of the Cameronian Regiment at the Siege of Dunkeld, Perthshire, on 21 August 1689. [BK.146]

ORCHARDTON, Sir JOHN, son of Sir Andrew Orchardton of Orchardton, Aberdeenshire, and his wife Elizabeth Robertson, a Captain of the Guards in the Swedish Army in 1663. [RGS.II.495]

ORROCK, Captain DAVID, enrolled as an undertaker for Ireland with 2000 acres on 20 July 1609. [RPCS.VIII.324]

OSBURN, Lieutenant WILLIAM, in Edinburgh, a letter, 1654. [NRS.GD219.282]

OTTERBURN, J., a soldier of the 2nd Company of Cockburn's Regiment in Swedish Service in 1609. [SIS.217]

PARKER, WILLIAM, a soldier from Edinburgh, married Annitgen Everts from Rotterdam, in Schiedam, Holland, on 30 June 1635. [Schiedam Marriage Register]

PARGILL, ALEXANDER, a soldier of Lammy's Company in Mackay's Regiment, was killed at the Battle of Killiecrankie, Perthshire, on 27 July 1689. [BK]

PATERSON, DAVID, a prisoner of war captured at the Siege of Worcester on 2 September 1651, was transported via London on the John and Sarah of London to Boston in December 1651, landed there in February 1652. [Suffolk Deeds.1/5-6]

PATERSON, JAMES, a prisoner of war captured at the Siege of Worcester on 2 September 1651, was transported via London on the John and Sarah of London to Boston in December 1651, landed there in February 1652. [Suffolk Deeds.1/5-6]

PATERSON, JAMES, a prisoner of war captured at the Siege of Worcester on 2 September 1651, was transported via London on the John and Sarah of London to Boston in December 1651, landed there in February 1652. [Suffolk Deeds.1/5-6]

PATTERSON, ROBERT, a Corporal in Viscount Claneboy's Troop of Horse in Ireland in 1642. [CalSPIre.260.63]

PATTERSON, Lieutenant Colonel WILLIAM, fortified Slutsk, Lithuania, in 1653, Commandant there. [SCL.185]

PATTON, JAMES, Military Governor of Jama in 1582. [MGIF]

PATOUN, ARCHIBALD, Captain of Leven's Regiment at the Battle of Killiecrankie, Perthshire, on 27 July 1689. [BK.95]

PAUL, JOHN, born 1627, a prisoner of war, who was transported to Boston, an indentured servant at Lynn Ironworks in the 1650s. [SH.16][LLNV.248]

PEEBLES, Captain DAVID, a militia officer in Charles City County, Virginia, in 1655-1656. [VCS.10]

PEEBLES, WILLIAM, a Sergeant of Fraser's Dragoons in 1645. [TFD.220]

PENNYCOOK, WALTER, a musketeer aboard the Dutch ship Aeolus in 1611. [ZA]

PHILLIP, WILLIAM, Military Governor of Demmin in 1656, and of Narva, Estonia, after 1657. [MGIF]

PIRRIE, GEORGE, a prisoner of war captured at the Siege of Worcester on 2 September 1651, was transported via London on the John and Sarah of London to Boston in December 1651, landed there in February 1652. [Suffolk Deeds.1/5-6]

PITCAIRN, Lieutenant JAMES, in Ireland in 1624. [CalSPIre]

PITSCOTTIE, COLIN, Lieutenant Colonel of the Earl of Eglinton's Regiment in Bangor, Ireland, in 1642. [TNA.SP18.120]; Major General Colin Pitscottie, a Brigade Commander who fought at the Battle of Dunbar on 3 September 1650. [SR.37]

PLUMER, WILLIAM, a prisoner in Edinburgh Tolbooth, was released to go to Holland as a soldier in 1689. [RPCS.13.573]

POLSON, MURDOCH, an officer in Mackay's Regiment, in Danish Service in 1626, in Swedish Service in 1629, was killed at Oldenburg, Saxony. [TGSI.VIII.189]

PRESTON, Sir GEORGE, of Valleyfield, an infantry officer who fought at the Battle of Dunbar on 3 September 1650. [SR.37]

PRESTON, Lieutenant ROBERT, of Livingstone's Regiment of Dragoons at the Battle of Cromdale, Strathspey, on 1 May 1690. [BK.177]

PRIMROSE, Lieutenant ARCHIBALD, in Colonel Alexander Leslie's Company in Muscovite Service from 1630 to 1632. [STW.179]

PRINGLE, GEORGE, a Major in the Service of Gustavus Adolphus around 1630, husband of Elizabeth Ruthven, daughter of Sir Patrick Ruthven. [F.2.15]

PRINGLE, GEORGE, Captain of East Lothian's Foot in 1647. [PA.132]

PRINGLE, JOHN, Ensign of the Cameronian Regiment at the Siege of Dunkeld, Perthshire, on 21 August 1689. [BK.146]

PUNN, [?], EDWARD, a prisoner of war captured at the Siege of Worcester on 2 September 1651, was transported via London on the John and Sarah of London to Boston in December 1651, landed there in February 1652. [Suffolk Deeds.1/5-6]

PURDIE, JOHN, a prisoner of war captured at the Siege of Worcester on 2 September 1651, was transported via London on the John and Sarah of London to Boston in December 1651, landed there in February 1652, an indentured servant in the Lynn Ironworks in the 1650s. [Suffolk Deeds.1/5-6][LLNV.248]

PURVIS, FREDERICK, a soldier, a marriage witness in Leiden, Holland, on 25 August 1601. [Leiden Marriage Register]

PURVIS, JOHN, a soldier of the 1st Company of Cockburn's Regiment in Swedish Service in 1609. [SIS.217]

RAE, JAMES, Colonel of the Edinburgh Foot in 1643, fought at the Siege of Newcastle and at the Battle of Marston Moor in 1644. [CA.133]

RAIT, FRANCIS, son of William Rait of Cononsyth, Angus, Standard Bearer to Captain James Ruthven of a Scottish regiment in the Netherlands, a deed, 1680. [NRS.RD2.51.702]

RAMMECK, [Ramage?], WILLIAM, a Scottish lance corporal under Baron von Eiglenburg, married Barbara Miller, widow of Johan Smeling, in the Burgkirche of Koningsberg on 27 June 1667. [Burgkirche Marriage Register]

RAMSAY, Colonel A., in Germany in the service of Gustavus Adolphus, ca.1630. [SIG.282]

RAMSAY, Major General ALEXANDER, Governor of Military Kreuznach from 1632 to 1633. [MGIF] [SIG.282]

RAMSAY, ALEXANDER, in Angus, of the Earl of Airlie's Militia in 1670. [NRS.GD16.53.39]

RAMSAY, DAVID, in Angus, of the Earl of Airlie's Militia in 1670. [NRS.GD16.53.39]

RAMSAY, Major DAVID, in Lithuanian Service from 1664 to 1704, at Vilnius and Zhuprany. [SCL.160]

RAMSAY, DAVID, an Ensign of Colonel Thornhill's Company of Militia in Barbados in 1679. [H2.146]

RAMSAY, GEORGE, a soldier in Captain Hacket's Company of Militia in Barbados in 1680. [H2.128]

RAMSAY, Lieutenant Colonel GEORGE, born 1652, died 1705. [BK.71] [NRS.GD77.189]

RAMSAY, GILBERT, a Jacobite soldier who was killed at the Battle of Killiecrankie, Perthshire, on 27 July 1689. [APS.acc.ix.163]

RAMSAY, Sir JAMES, born 1589, a Major General of the Swedish Army, Military Governor of Hanau, in Bohemia in 1620, died imprisoned in Dillenburg Castle on 11 March 1638. [SHR.IX.45][SS.44][STW.111][MGIF] [SIG.282]

RAMSAY, JAMES, Military Governor Breisach in 1630, and of Colberg in 1631. [MGIF]

SCOTTISH SOLDIERS IN EUROPE AND AMERICA, 1600-1700.

RAMSAY, JAMES, a Scottish Captain, married Maria Gall, in the Reformed Church of Peter and Paul in Danzig, [Gdansk], in 1654.[CRD]

RAMSAY, JAMES, in Angus, of the Earl of Airlie's Militia in 1670. [NRS.GD16.53.39]

RAMSAY, JOHN, a soldier in Captain Rawling's Company of Militia in Barbados in 1679. [H2.118]

RAMSAY, WILLIAM, a soldier in Captain Hacket's Company of Militia in Barbados in 1680. [H2.128]

RAMSAY, ['Ramz'], Major, was enobled in Poland in 1676. [SCA.103][STW.211][BPL]

RATTRAY, Colonel JOHN, of a Scottish regiment in Amiens, France, in 1640. [NRS.GD109.1695]

READ, Captain JAMES, of Tullychin, Killyreagh, County Down, Ireland, born 1675, died 1727. [Killyreagh gravestone]

REDDIE, WILLIAM, a soldier in the Service of the Estates of Holland 'in the Indeans', testament, 6 October 1657, Comm. Edinburgh. [NRS]

REDICO, JOHN, a Scottish soldier, who received six crowns from King Philip IV of Spain in 1623. [NRS.NRAS.0018]

REDPATH, WILLIAM, an archer of the Scots Guards of France in the 1560s. [NRS.NRAS.O.143]

REID, ANDREW, a soldier in Argyll's Rebellion, a prisoner in Edinburgh Tolbooth, was transported via Leith to Jamaica in August 1685. [ROCS.11.328][ETR]

REID, JOHN, a Trooper of Colonel Lambert's Leeward Island Regiment of Militia in 1679. [H.2.199]

REID, Captain ROBERT, recruited men from the prisons of Edinburgh for service as soldiers in Holland in 1690. [RPCS.XV.]

REID, THOMAS, from Edinburgh, gunner aboard the Unicorn bound from Leith to Darien on 14 July 1698, testament, 1708, Comm. Edinburgh. [NRS]

REID, WILLIAM, a Corporal under Captain Scott, was a marriage witness in Leiden, Holland, on 8 January 1604. [Leiden Marriage Register]

RENTON, JOHN, a Major General in Germany in the service of Gustavus Adolphus, around 1630. [SIG.282]

RENTOUN, WILLIAM, Captain of a company of Scottish soldiers in the Service of Danzig, [Gdansk], around 1577. [Cal.SPSot.1.330]

REOCH, WILLIAM, a prisoner in Edinburgh Tolbooth, volunteered to go to Holland as a soldier under Captain Francis Scott on 27 January 1691. [RPCS.XVI.55]

RICHARDSON, ALEXANDER, at the muster at Dungannon, County Tyrone, Ireland, in 1618. [Cal.SPIre.1618.501] [BM.Add.ms18735]

RICHARDSON, JOHN, surgeon of Forbes of Tullich's Company in Danish Service in 1628. [SAA.ii.121]

RICHARDSON, ROBERT, Corporal of Major Whyte's company mustered in Glasgow in 1682. [DSA.128]

RICHARDSON, W., a soldier of the 1st Company of Cockburn's Regiment in Swedish Service in 1609. [SIS.217]

RIDDELL, JAMES, Major of the Earl of Lothian's Regiment in Carrickfergus, Ireland, in 1642. [TNA.SP18.120]

RIDDELL, Sir WALTER, Captain of the Earl of Lothian's Regiment in Carrickfergus, Ireland, in 1642. [TNA.SP18.120]; Lieutenant Colonel of Cranstoun's Foot in 1644. [CA.127]

RIDDELL, Sir WILLIAM, Captain of a Scottish Company in the Service of the United Provinces, testament, 16 October 1676, Comm. Edinburgh. [NRS]

RIDDOCH, ALEXANDER, Lieutenant Colonel of Militia in Barbados in 1679. [H2.159]

RIDDOCH, ESBET [?], a soldier under Captain Robert Scott, married Franchijntgende Rave of Leiden, Holland, there on 27 January 1604. [Leiden Marriage Register]

ROBERTSON, ALEXANDER, of Struan, Perthshire, a Jacobite at the Battle of Killiecrankie, Perthshire, on 27 July 1689. [APS.IX.55]

ROBERTSON, Captain DAVID, in Hamburg, Germany, around 1630. [TNA.SP75.13, fos.233-235]

ROBERTSON, JOHN, a soldier under Captain Nisbet, married Trijnke Jans a widow fron Oudekercke, in Haarlem on 24 April 1594. [Haarlem Marriage Register]

ROBERTSON, JOHN THOMAS, born 1562 in Edinburgh, a soldier who married Elizabeth Peters Tenneson, born 1576 in Dundee, in Breda, Brabant, on 14 March 1598. [Breda Marriage Register]

ROBERTSON, JOHN, from the Shetland Islands, a gunner aboard the Dutch ship Neptunus on 1 May 1645. [ZA]

ROBERTSON, JOHN, a drummer of Captain Dalyell's Company, was mustered at Glasgow in 1682. [DSA.126]

ROBERTSON, PATRICK, a prisoner of war captured at the Siege of Worcester on 2 September 1651, was transported via London on the John and Sarah of London to Boston in December 1651, landed there in February 1652. [Suffolk Deeds.1/5-6]

ROBERTSON, RICHARD, a Corporal of Donaldson's Company in Kenmure's Regiment, was wounded 22 times at the Battle of Killiecrankie, Perthshire, on 27 July 1689. [RPCS.XIV]

ROBERTSON, WILLIAM, a soldier, married Annetgen Aeryaens, in Leiden, Holland, on 20 January 1601. [Leiden Marriage Register]

ROBERTSON, WILLIAM, a Sergeant at Darien in 1699. [DD.262]

ROBINSON, ALESTER, a prisoner of war captured at the Siege of Worcester on 2 September 1651, was transported via London on the John and Sarah of London to Boston in December 1651, landed there in February 1652. [Suffolk Deeds.1/5-6]

ROBINSON, ALESTER, a prisoner of war captured at the Siege of Worcester on 2 September 1651, was transported via London on the John and Sarah of London to Boston in December 1651, landed there in February 1652. [Suffolk Deeds.1/5-6]

ROBINSON, DANIEL, a prisoner of war captured at the Siege of Worcester on 2 September 1651, was transported via London on the John and Sarah of London to Boston in December 1651, landed there in February 1652. [Suffolk Deeds.1/5-6]

ROBINSON, JAMES, a prisoner of war captured at the Siege of Worcester on 2 September 1651, was transported via London on the John and Sarah of London to Boston in December 1651, landed there in February 1652. [Suffolk Deeds.1/5-6]

ROBINSON, JOHN, [1], a prisoner of war captured at the Siege of Worcester on 2 September 1651, was transported via London on the John and Sarah of London to Boston in December 1651, landed there in February 1652. [Suffolk Deeds.1/5-6]

ROBINSON, JOHN, [2], a prisoner of war captured at the Siege of Worcester on 2 September 1651, was transported via London on the John and Sarah of London to Boston in December 1651, landed there in February 1652. [Suffolk Deeds.1/5-6]

RODRIE, THOMAS, a gunner on the Unicorn bound from Leith to Darien on 14 July 1698, testament, 1707, Comm. Edinburgh. [NRS]

ROLLOCK, ANDREW, a Trooper of Colonel Lambert's Leeward Island Regiment of Militia in Barbados in 1679. [H.2.197]

ROLLOCK, JAMES, a Captain of Militia in Dundee in 1644. [DCW.13]

ROLLOCK, Captain, was stationed at Gluckstadt in 1628. [SAA.116]

ROSE, DERMOT, a prisoner of war, probably captured at the Battle of Dunbar on 3 September 1650, was transported to New England, an indentured servant, later on Block Island. [NWI.I.159]

ROSS, ALESTER, a prisoner of war captured at the Siege of Worcester on 2 September 1651, was transported via London on the John and Sarah of London to Boston in December 1651, landed there in February 1652. [Suffolk Deeds.1/5-6]

ROSS, ALEXANDER, a soldier, married Regina Tret in St Elisabeth's, Danzig, [Gdansk], in November 1646.

ROSS, ALEXANDER, Captain of Colonel George Hamilton's Regiment, was admitted as a burgess of Ayr in 1699. [ABR]

ROSS, DANIEL, a prisoner of war captured at the Siege of Worcester on 2 September 1651, was transported via London on the John and Sarah of London to Boston in December 1651, landed there in February 1652. [Suffolk Deeds.1/5-6]

ROSS, DANIEL, master gunner of Edinburgh Castle from 1677 to 1680. [NRS.GD20.1.818]

ROSS, DANIEL, a soldier of Captain Morrell's Company of Militia in Barbados in 1680. [H.2.152]

ROSS, DAVID, son of Alexander Ross of Invercarron, an officer in Mackay's Regiment, in Danish Service in 1626, in Swedish Service in 1629. [TGSI.VIII.189]

ROSS, DAVID, a prisoner of war captured at the Siege of Worcester on 2 September 1651, was transported via London on the John and Sarah of London to Boston in December 1651, landed there in February 1652. [Suffolk Deeds.1/5-6]

ROSS, GEORGE, a soldier of Captain Bowcher's Company of Militia in Barbados in 1679. [H.2.112]

ROSS, HUGH, of Priesthill, a Lieutenant of Mackay's Regiment, in Danish Service in 1626, in Swedish Service in 1629. [TGSI.VIII.187]

ROSS, HUGH, a soldier of Mackay's Regiment, was wounded at the Battle of Killiecrankie, Perthshire, on 27 July 1689. [RPCS.XV.151]

ROSS, JAMES, a Lieutenant in Danzig, [Gdansk], was accused of being a Swedish spy in the 1620s. [SAP.98]

ROSS, Lieutenant JAMES, was buried in St Elisabeth's, Danzig, [Gdansk], in 1643. [CRD]

ROSS, JAMES, [1], a prisoner of war captured at the Siege of Worcester on 2 September 1651, was transported via London on the John and Sarah of London to Boston in December 1651, landed there in February 1652. [Suffolk Deeds.1/5-6]

ROSS, JAMES, [2], a prisoner of war captured at the Siege of Worcester on 2 September 1651, was transported via London on the John and Sarah of London to Boston in December 1651, landed there in February 1652. [Suffolk Deeds.1/5-6]

ROSS, JOHN, [1], a prisoner of war captured at the Siege of Worcester on 2 September 1651, was transported via London on the John and Sarah of London to Boston in December 1651, landed there in February 1652. [Suffolk Deeds.1/5-6]

ROSS, JOHN, [2], a prisoner of war captured at the Siege of Worcester on 2 September 1651, was transported via London on the John and Sarah of London to Boston in December 1651, landed there in February 1652. [Suffolk Deeds.1/5-6]

ROSS, JOHN, a prisoner of war captured at the Battle of Dunbar on 3 September 1650, transported via London probably on the Unity of Boston in November 1650, settled in Kittery, Berwick, Maine, in 1656. [CEB]

ROSS, JOHN, a soldier of Captain Woodward's Company of Militia in Barbados in 1679. [H.2.156]

ROSS, JOHN, a soldier of Captain Thornhill's Company of Militia in Barbados in 1679. [H.2.151]

ROSS, JOHN, a soldier of Captain Bowcher's Company of Militia in Barbados in 1679. [H.2.112]

ROSS, JOHN, a soldier of Major Williams's Company of Militia in Barbados in 1679. [H.2.103]

ROSS, JONAS, a prisoner of war captured at the Siege of Worcester on 2 September 1651, was transported via London on the <u>John and Sarah of London</u> to Boston in December 1651, landed there in February 1652. [Suffolk Deeds.1/5-6]

ROSS, NICHOLAS, a Captain of Mackay's Regiment, in Danish Service in 1626, in Swedish Service in 1629. [TGSI.VIII.187]

ROSS, RICHARD, a soldier of the New Kent County Militia, Virginia, in 1701. [TNA.CO5.1312/2]

ROSS, Captain ROBERT, of Grant's Regiment of Infantry at the Battle of Cromdale, Strathspey, on 1 May 1690. [BK.177]

ROSS, WILLIAM, in Angus, of the Earl of Airlie's Militia in 1670. [NRS.GD16.53.39]

ROSS, WILLIAM, a soldier of Captain Merrill's Company of Militia in Barbados in 1679. [H.2.152]

ROSS, WILLIAM, a soldier of the New Kent County Militia, Virginia, in 1701. [TNA.CO5.1312/2]

ROSS, Ensign, a Jacobite captured at the Battle of Cromdale, Strathspey, on 1 May 1690. [RPCS.XV.304]

ROSS, Lieutenant, of James City County Militia, Virginia, in 1702. [TNA.CO5.1312/2]

ROUCHE, JOHN, Captain of Lord Sinclair's Regiment in Carrickfergus, Ireland, in 1642. [TNA.SP18.120]

ROW, JAMES, a prisoner of war captured at the Siege of Worcester on 2 September 1651, was transported via London on the <u>John and Sarah of London</u> to Boston in December 1651, landed there in February 1652. [Suffolk Deeds.1/5-6]

ROY, DONALD, a prisoner of war captured at the Siege of Worcester on 2 September 1651, was transported via London on the John and Sarah of London to Boston in December 1651, landed there in February 1652. [Suffolk Deeds.1/5-6]

ROY, PATRICK, a Jacobite captured at the Battle of Cromdale, Strathspey, on 1 May 1690. [RPCS.XV.304] . [SAA.116]

RUSSELL, DAVID, Captain of a Danish Regiment of Foot in 1625, Captain of the Scanian National Foot 1628-1629

RUSSELL, JAMES, a soldier of Major Lyte's Company of Militia in Barbados in 1679. [H.2.175]

RUSSELL, JAMES, a soldier of Captain Burrow's Company of Militia in Barbados in 1679. [H.2.181]

RUSSELL, SIMON, a prisoner of war captured at the Siege of Worcester on 2 September 1651, was transported via London on the John and Sarah of London to Boston in December 1651, landed there in February 1652. [Suffolk Deeds.1/5-6]

RUSSELL, THOMAS, a soldier of the 1st Company of Cockburn's Regiment in Swedish Service in 1609. [SIS.217]

RUSSELL, WILLIAM, a Captain in Lithuanian Service from 1652 to 1696, served in Birzai, Kedainai, and Vilnius. [SCL.160]

RUSSELL, Captain, a soldier in Memel in 1631. [JSM]

RUTHERFORD, ADAM, a soldier under Captain Nesbit, married Grietge Frerix from Dyepeveen, in Haarlem, Holland, on 17 April 1594. [Haarlem Marriage Register]

RUTHERFORD, ANDREW, later Earl of Teviot, a General in Germany under Gustavus Adolphus, 1630. [SIG.282]

RUTHERFORD, Lord ANDREW, a Lieutenant General in the Service of the King of France in 1661. [RGS.XI.32]

RUTHERFORD, E., a soldier of the 1st Company of Cockburn's Regiment in Swedish Service in 1609. [SIS.217]

RUTHVEN, Sir J. a Colonel in Germany in the service of Gustavus Adolphus, around 1630. [SIG.282]

RUTHVEN, JAMES, Captain of a Scottish regiment in Holland, a deed, 1680. [NRS.RD2.51.702]

RUTHVEN, JAMES, Captain of Colonel Francis Collingwood's Regiment of Foot, died on Nevis, West Indies, probate 1699, PCC. [TNA]

RUTHVEN, JOHN, a Captain in Danish Service at Gluckstadt in 1628. [GAA.116]

RUTHVEN, JOHN, Captain of the Earl of Dunfermline's Regiment in France, a deed, 1676, [NRS.RD4.39.199]

RUTHVEN, Sir PATRICK, born 1573, a soldier in Swedish Service from 1606 to 1609, fought in Livonia and Russia, Swedish Quartermaster in 1615, Colonel of the Kalmar Regiment in 1623, knighted on the battlefield by Gustavus Adolphus the King of Sweden, the Commander of a Scottish regiment in Elbing and Memel from 1629 to 1630, Military Governor of Ulm from 1632 to 1633, in Paris from 1631 to 1635, defeated the Saxons at Domitz in 1635, returned to Britain in 1636, a General under King Charles I, was created Earl of Forth and Brentford, died on 2 February 1651. [Monifieth, Angus, gravestone] [SHR.IX.47] [SS.41] [NRS.GD16.312] [SIG.282]

RUTHVEN, Sir THOMAS, of Freeland, an infantry officer who fought at the Battle of Dunbar on 3 September 1650. [SR.37]

RUTHVEN, Captain, was killed in Danzig, [Gdansk], in 1599. [RPCS.VI.856]

RUXTON, JOHN, a prisoner of war captured at the Battle of Dunbar on 3 September 1650, transported via London probably on the Unity of Boston in November 1650, an indentured servant at Lynn Ironworks in 1650s. [Suffolk Court Files.1226]

SANDELANDS, Sir JAMES, from Slamannan, Stirlingshire, a Sergeant Major under Colonel Broggs, in the Service of the United Provinces in 1629. [NRS.GD84.2.177]

SANDILANDS, JAMES, a soldier, quit rent in Delaware, 1668, and 1670, died 1692. [New York Historical ms. Dutch, xx/xxi.28]

SANDILANDS, Sir WILLIAM, a Captain in Dutch Service in 1665. [JCP.I.136]

SANDERSON, ALEXANDER, from Scotland, a cavalry officer in Poland, died in Ireland during 1633. [Desertcreat gravestone, County Tyrone, Ireland]

SANDERSON, Captain ALEXANDER, of Tulligun, County Tyrone, Ireland, deeds, 1677, 1678. [NRS.RD2.45.142; RD2.47.387]

SANDERSON, HANNIBAL, a gunner aboard the Lion of Zeeland in 1631. [ZA]

SANDERSON, JOHN, Sergeant of Forbes of Tullich's Company in Danish Service in 1628. [SAA.ii.121]

SANDERSON, ROBERT, a Lieutenant Colonel in Antrim, Ireland, in 1645. [CalSPIre.260.137]

SANDERSON, Captain ROBERT, of Balvie and of Castle Sanderson in County Cavan, Ireland, deeds, 1684, 1706, [NRS. RD4.55; RD3.108.395-8], a sasine, [NRS.RS.59.2.225]

SANDERSON, WILLIAM, a Corporal in Danish Service in 1629. [SAA.116]

SANDERSON, WILLIAM, from Kinghorn in Fife, an Ensign who died at Darien in 1699, testament, 1707, Comm. Edinburgh. [NRS]

SAUNDERS, WALTER, from Prestonpans, Midlothian, a musketeer aboard the Dutch ship Zeeridder in 1647. [ZA]

SAUNDERSON, Captain, at muster in Dungannon, County Tyrone, Ireland, in 1618. [CalSPIre.1618.501]

SCOTT, BENJAMIN, a soldier of Lieutenant Maxwell's Company of Militia in Barbados in 1679. [H.2.211]

SCOTT, EDWARD, a soldier of Captain Ely's Company of Militia in Barbados in 1679. [H.2.177]

SCOTT, Captain FRANCIS, bound for Holland with recruits in January 1691. [RPCS.3.XVI.55]

SCOTT, GEORGE, a soldier under Captain Robert Scott, married Stijntgen Joppen in Leiden, Holland, on 2 February 1604. [Leiden Marriage Register]

SCOTT, GEORGE, a soldier of Colonel Bayley's Company of Militia in Barbados in 1679. [H.2.131]

SCOTT, GEORGE, born 1622, an old soldier, latterly on garrison duty in Edinburgh and Dunbarton Castles in 1691. [RPCS.XV.228]

SCOTT, HUGH, son of Hugh Scott of Gala in Selkirkshire, an Ensign who died at Darien, testament, 1707, Comm. Edinburgh. [NRS]

SCOTT, JAMES, a Colonel in Swedish Service from 1606, Governor of Riga, Latvia, in 1632, and of Narva, Estonia, in 1634. [KAS Muster Roll.1632.8.9][MGIF]

SCOTT, JAMES, a soldier of Captain Woodward's Company of Militia in Barbados in 1679. [H.2.156]

SCOTT, JAMES, a prisoner in Edinburgh Tolbooth, was released to go to Holland as a soldier under Captain Thomas Hamilton on 11 March 1684. [RPCS.8.403/683]

SCOTT, JOHN, chaplain to Major General Monro's Regiment in Ireland in 1642. [FI.48]

SCOTT, JOHN, a prisoner of war captured at the Siege of Worcester on 2 September 1651, was transported via London on the John and Sarah of London to Boston in December 1651, landed there in February 1652. [Suffolk Deeds.1/5-6]

SCOTT, JOHN, a soldier of Captain Hall's Company of Militia in Barbados in 1679. [H.2.136]

SCOTT, JOSEPH, of the Surrey County Militia, Virginia, in 1701. [TNA.CO5.1312/2]

SCOTT, MATTHEW, a soldier of Lieutenant Colonel Affleck's Company of Militia in Barbados in 1679. [H.2.148]

SCOTT, PHILIP, a Trooper of Colonel Lambard's Leeward Island's Militia in Barbados in 1679. [H.2.199]

SCOTT, RICHARD, a Captain of Militia in Barbados in 1679. [H2.170]

SCOTT, ROBERT, in Swedish Service from 1623 - 1628, Swedish Quartermaster General, in Danish Service from 1628 as Master General of Artillery, died 1631. SAA.116]

SCOTT, ROBERT, of the Surrey County Militia, Virginia, in 1701. [TNA.CO5.1312/2]

SCOTT, THOMAS, Lieutenant of Militia in Dundee in 1643. [DCW.13]

SCOTT, THOMAS, a soldier of Captain Harrison's Company of Militia in Barbados in 1679. [H.2.141]

SCOTT, WALTER, Lieutenant Colonel of the Earl of Lothian's Regiment in Carrickfergus, Ireland, in 1642. [TNA.SP18.120]

SCOTT, Colonel WALTER, with 5 [?] Troops of Cavalry, fought at the Battle of Dunbar on 3 September 1650. [SR.37]

SCOTT, WALTER, a Colonel in Dutch Service in 1665. [JCP.I.136]

SCOTT, Captain WALTER, of Major Farmer's Troop of Horse Militia in Barbados in 1679. [H.2.199]

SCOTT, W., a soldier of the 2d Company of Cockburn's Regiment in Swedish Service in 1609. [SIS.217]

SCOTT, WILLIAM, [Willem Schots], a Sergeant of Captain Philip Balfour's Company at Schiedam, Holland, in 1640. [GAR.ONA.328.293.3601]

SCOTT, WILLIAM, Cornet of Militia of Essex County, Virginia, in 1701. [TNA.CO5.1312/2]

SCOUGALL, Major PATRICK, of Balcarres's Regiment of Horse, Army of the Covenant in 1644. [CA.114]

SCRYMGEOUR, Sir JAMES, Viscount Dudhope, Colonel of the Angus Regiment in 1644, he was killed at the Battle of Marston Moor, Yorkshire, on 2 July 1644. [DCW.77]

SCRYMGEOUR, WILLIAM, Major of the Angus Regiment at the Battle of Marston Moor, Yorkshire, on 2 July 1644. [DCW.78][CA.108]

SEATON, Captain ALEXANDER, in Danish Service in 1626, wounded at Oldenburg in 1627, Military Governor of Stralsund in 1628. [MGIF]. SAA.120]

SEATON, DAVID, Captain of Lord Sinclair's Regiment in Newry, Ireland, in 1642. [TNA.SP18.120]

SEATON, LACHLAN, a Sergeant of the Scots Footguards in Flanders, a deed, 1695. [NRS.RD4.77.261]

SEATON,........, an Ensign of Mackay's Regiment in Swedish Service in 1629, was killed at Stralsund. [TGSI.VIII.188]

SEMPLE,........, an officer of Mackay's Regiment, in Danish Service in 1626, in Swedish Service in 1629. [TGSI.VIII.189]

SENNOTT, WILLIAM, a Major of Mackay's Regiment, in Danish Service in 1626, in Swedish Service in 1629, died of the plague in Stettin. [TGSI.VIII.186]

SESSOR, [?], DANIEL, a prisoner of war captured at the Siege of Worcester on 2 September 1651, was transported via London on the <u>John and Sarah of London</u> to Boston in December 1651, landed there in February 1652. [Suffolk Deeds.1/5-6]

SETON, ALEXANDER, Lieutenant Colonel of Mackay's Regiment in Swedish Service in 1629. [TGSI.VIII.185]

SETON, GEORGE, a Captain of the Earl of Dunfermline's Regiment in France, a deed, 1676. [NRS.RD4.39.199]

SETON, JAMES, Earl of Dunfermline, an Ensign in Mar's Regiment of Foot in 1687, a Jacobite at the Battle of Killiecrankie, Perthshire, on 27 July 1689. [APS.IX.55]

SETON, Sir JOHN, of Carchunoth, a soldier in Bohemia 1619-1620, [STW.111]; Military Governor of Trebon from 1620 to 1622. [MGIF]

SEYTOUN, JOHN, Captain of the King of France's Guard in 1627. [NRS.GD7.2.33]

SHAIRP, ROBERT, son of Thomas Shairp of Hustoun, an Ensign who died at Darien in 1699, testament, 1707, Comm. Edinburgh. [NRS]

SHARP, Captain WALTER, a field officer in Flanders in 1659. [NRS.GD30.867]

SHAIRP, WALTER, Captain of the Scots Fusiliers in Flanders in 1697, a Colonel by 1709. [NRS.GD30.780]

SHARP, Lieutenant Colonel WILLIAM, a field officer in Flanders in 1659. [NRS.GD30.867]

SHAW, ALEXANDER, a prisoner in Edinburgh Tolbooth, was released to go to France as a soldier under Lieutenant John McCulloch on 4 February 1676. [RPCS.IV.668]

SHAW, ANGUS, a soldier of Captain Boune's Company of Militia in Barbados in 1679. [H.2.130]

SHAW, JAMES, a prisoner in Edinburgh Tolbooth, was released to go to France as a soldier under Lieutenant John McCulloch on 4 February 1676. [RPCS.IV.668]

SCHAW, MATTHEW, of the Surrey County Militia, Virginia, in 1701. [TNA.CO5.1312/2]

SHAW, ROBERT, a Corporal of Oliphant's Company in Danish Service, in 1628. [SAA.ii.143]

SHAW, ROBERT, a prisoner in Edinburgh Tolbooth, was released to go to France as a soldier under Lieutenant John McCulloch on 4 February 1676. [RPCS.IV.668]

SHERON, [?], ANSELL, [?], a prisoner of war captured at the Siege of Worcester on 2 September 1651, was transported via London on the John and Sarah of London to Boston in December 1651, landed there in February 1652. [Suffolk Deeds.1/5-6]

SHIVAS, SAMUEL, a prisoner of war captured at the Siege of Worcester on 2 September 1651, was transported via London on the John and Sarah of London to Boston in December 1651, landed there in February 1652. [Suffolk Deeds.1/5-6]

SHONE, [?], JAMES, a prisoner of war captured at the Siege of Worcester on 2 September 1651, was transported via London on the John and Sarah of London to Boston in December 1651, landed there in February 1652. [Suffolk Deeds.1/5-6]

SHURON, [?], DANIEL, a prisoner of war captured at the Siege of Worcester on 2 September 1651, was transported via London on the John and Sarah of London to Boston in December 1651, landed there in February 1652. [Suffolk Deeds.1/5-6]

SIBBALD, DAVID, son of John Sibbald of Keir and his wife Janet Strachan, a Lieutenant Colonel in Swedish Service, was killed in Germany in September 1641. [ACA. APB.2.5.1642]

SIBBALD, JOHN, son of John Sibbald of Keir and his wife Janet Strachan, a soldier in Swedish Service who fought in Germany, later in Prussia, a birth brief, 2 May 1642. [ACA.APB]

SIBBALD, WILLIAM, a soldier in Edinburgh Castle from 1680 until 1708. [NRS.GD20.1.818]

SIMMONS, WILLIAM, a Scottish soldier, married Elisabeth Moritz in St Elisabeth's, Danzig, [Gdansk], on 22 May 1633.

SIMPSON, ALESTER, a prisoner of war captured at the Siege of Worcester on 2 September 1651, was transported via London on the John and Sarah of London to Boston in December 1651, landed there in February 1652. [Suffolk Deeds.1/5-6]

SIMPSON, ALEXANDER, a prisoner of war captured at the Siege of Worcester on 2 September 1651, was transported via London on the John and Sarah of London to Boston in December 1651, landed there in February 1652. [Suffolk Deeds.1/5-6]

SIMPSON, ANDREW, formerly a shipmaster in Leith, then Commander of the Navy of the Czar of Russia, a deed, 1706. [NRS.RD3.69.311]

SIMPSON, CHRISTOPHER, a soldier of Colonel Leslie's Company in Muscovite Service from 1630 to 1632. [STW.179]

SIMPSON, DANIEL, [1], a prisoner of war captured at the Siege of Worcester on 2 September 1651, was transported via London on the John and Sarah of London to Boston in December 1651, landed there in February 1652. [Suffolk Deeds.1/5-6]

SIMPSON, DANIEL, [2], a prisoner of war captured at the Siege of Worcester on 2 September 1651, was transported via London on the John and Sarah of London to Boston in December 1651, landed there in February 1652. [Suffolk Deeds.1/5-6]

SIMPSON, DAVID, a Quartermaster of Fraser's Dragoons, at the Battle of Marston Moor, Yorkshire, on 2 July 1644. [TFD.47]

SIMPSON, DAVID, a prisoner of war captured at the Siege of Worcester on 2 September 1651, was transported via London on the John and Sarah of London to Boston in December 1651, landed there in February 1652. [Suffolk Deeds.1/5-6]

SIMPSON, GEORGE, in Angus, of the Earl of Airlie's Militia in 1670. [NRS.GD16.53.39]

SYMSON, M., in Angus, of the Earl of Airlie's Militia in 1670. [NRS.GD16.53.39]

SIMPSON, PATRICK, a prisoner of war captured at the Siege of Worcester on 2 September 1651, was transported via London on the John and Sarah of London to Boston in December 1651, landed there in February 1652. [Suffolk Deeds.1/5-6]

SIMPSON, WILLIAM, a soldier who married Elisabeth Moritz in St Elisabeth's, Danzig, [Gdansk], on 22 May 1633. [CRD]

SINCLAIR, ADAM, from the Shetland Islands, a musketeer aboard the Dutch ship Neptunus on 1 May 1645. [ZA]

SINCLAIR, ANDREW, born 1614, to Sweden as a musketeer in Colonel Robert Stuart's Regiment in 1635, a Regimental Commander by 1678, enobled in 1689, died in 1689. [SHR.IX.276]

SINCLAIR, DAVID, to Sweden in 1651, a Cavalry officer who was killed at the Battle of Warsaw in 1656. [SHR.IX.275]

SINCLAIR, FRANCIS, son of James Sinclair of Murkle, a Major of Mackay's Regiment, in Danish Service in 1626, in Swedish Service in 1629, a Colonel in Germany in the service of Gustavus Adolphus, ca.1630, was enobled in 1645.
[TGSI.VIII.186][SHR.IX.275]

SINCLAIR, JAMES, from the Shetland Islands, a musketeer aboard the Dutch ship Neptunus on 1 May 1645. [ZA]

SINCLAIR, JOHN, third son of George Sinclair the 5th Earl of Caithness, a Major of Mackay's Regiment, a Colonel in Swedish Service in 1629, was killed at Newmarke in the Upper Palatinate in 1632. [TGSI.VIII.185][SHR.IX.51] [SIG.282]

SINCLAIR, Lord JOHN, Colonel of the College of Justice Foot, 1644. [CA.124]

SINCLAIR, PATRICK, Captain of Lord Sinclair's Regiment in Newry, Ireland, in 1642. [TNA.SP18.120]

SINCLAIR, RICHARD, a Sergeant of Captain Scott's Company of Militia in Barbados in 1679. [H2.190]

SINCLAIR, THOMAS, from Edinburgh, a soldier under Captain Montgomery, married Maricken Jans from Gouda, Holland, in Dordrecht, Holland, on 8 February 1587. [Dordrecht Marriage Register]

SINCLAIR, WILLIAM, from the Shetland Islands, a musketeer aboard the Dutch ship de Meermine in 1633. [ZA]

SKED, GEORGE, a soldier was buried in Greyfriars, Edinburgh, in 1698.

SKEEN, ANDREW, from the Shetland Islands, a seaman aboard the Zeeland Admiralty warship Wapen van Zeelant in 1664-1665. [ZA.Rekenkamber.c6985]

SLOANE, JOHN, a soldier of the Westmoreland County Militia, Virginia, in 1701. TNA.CO5.1312/2]

SMITH, ALEXANDER, a Corporal of Viscount Claneboy's Troop of Horse in Ireland in 1642. [CalSPire.260.63]

SMITH, SAMUEL, a prisoner in Edinburgh Tolbooth, was released to go to Holland as a soldier in 1689. [RPCS.13.573]

SINCLAIR, SOLOMON, a prisoner of war captured at the Siege of Worcester on 2 September 1651, was transported via London on the John and Sarah of London to Boston in December 1651, landed there in February 1652. [Suffolk Deeds.1/5-6]

SMALL, JAMES, Lieutenant of the Angus Regiment at the Battle of Marston Moor, Yorkshire, on 2 July 1644. [DCW.78]

SMEATON, JOHN, was admitted as a burgess of Stirling, having served in the burgh's company of soldiers, on 31 May 1648. [SBR]

SMISON, PATRICK, a prisoner of war captured at the Siege of Worcester on 2 September 1651, was transported via London on the John and Sarah of London to Boston in December 1651, landed there in February 1652. [Suffolk Deeds.1/5-6]

SMITH, HENRY, a prisoner of war captured at the Siege of Worcester on 2 September 1651, was transported via London on

the John and Sarah of London to Boston in December 1651, landed there in February 1652. [Suffolk Deeds.1/5-6]

SMITH, JAMES, a Scottish soldier married Ursula .... in St Marien Kirche in Danzig, [Gdansk], on 15 January 1612.

SMITH, JAMES, a drummer of Captain Dalyell's Company, was mustered at Glasgow in 1682. [DSA.126]

SMITH, JOHN, a Scottish soldier, father of Christina who was baptised in the Polish church in Steindamm, Prussia, on 17 February 1636.

SMITH, MALCOLM, a Quartermaster of Fraser's Dragoons, at the Battle of Marston Moor, Yorkshire, on 2 July 1644. [TFD.47]

SOMERVILLE, Major of Callendar's Foot in 1643, of the Army of the Covenant in 1646. [CA.119]

SOMERVILLE, JAMES, son of George Somerville and his wife Agnes Scoon in Dalkeith, assistant armourer, from Leith on the Unicorn bound for Darien on 14 July 1698, testament, 1707, Comm. Edinburgh. [NRS]

SPEEDY, PETER, a soldier from Forres, Moray, married Maertge Frerix in Schiedam, Holland, on 14 June 1636. [Schiedam Marriage Register]

SPENS, JAMES, third son of William Spens, settled in Sweden, a General of the Swedish Army in Germany, was appointed as the Swedish Ambassador to England in 1612, died in 1632. [SHR.IX.276][SS.25]

SPENS, JAMES, son of James Sens in Edinburgh, a Drum Major in Swedish Service in Doesburg, Riga, Amsterdam, and Batavia from 1617 to 1632. [NRS.RH9.2.231-242]

SPENS, ROBERT, a soldier in Warsaw, Poland, in July 1582. [STW.197]

SPIDMAN, ANDREW, was admitted as a burgess of Stirling, having served in the burgh's company of soldiers, on 31 May 1648. [SBR]

SPIDIMAN, PATRICK, a soldier from Forres, Moray, married Janiken Hutson in Schiedam, Holland, on 13 June 1637. [Schiedam Marriage Register]

STEEL, JOHN, was admitted as a burgess of Stirling, having served in the burgh's company of soldiers during the 'present expedition, on 17 January 1644. [SBR]

STEEL, Captain NINIAN, of the Cameronian Regiment at the Siege of Dunkeld, Perthshire, on 21 August 1689. [BK.146]

STENHOUSE, ANDREW, a Sergeant of Fraser's Dragoons in 1644. [TFD.219]

STEPHENSON, JOHN, Captain of the Cameronian Regiment at the Siege of Dunkeld, Perthshire, on 21 August 1689. [BK.146]

STEPHENSON, ROBERT, a Sergeant of Fraser's Dragoons in 1644. [TFD.219]

STEPHENSON, ……, Ensign of the Cameronian Regiment at the Siege of Dunkeld, Perthshire, on 21 August 1689. [BK.146]

STEVENS, JOHN, a soldier from Crail, Fife, married Immitge Lucas, in Delft, Holland, in 1601. [Delft Marriage Register]

STEVENSON, Captain ALEXANDER, in Dublin, Ireland, a deed, 1698. [NRS.RD4.98.129]

STEEL, JAMES, was admitted as a burgess of Stirling, having served in the burgh's company of soldiers, on 31 May 1648. [SBR]

STEVENSON, JAMES, a thief, possibly from Paisley, Renfrewshire, a prisoner in Edinburgh Tolbooth, was released to go to Flanders or Holland as a soldier with Captain Thomas Hamilton on 28 March 1684. [ETR][RPCS.8.691]

STEVENSON, WILLIAM, a soldier of Hackett's Company in Mackay's Regiment, was killed at the Battle of Killiecrankie, Perthshire, on 27 July 1689. [BK]

STEWART, ABRAHAM, a soldier of Captain Brown's Company of Militia in Barbados in 1679. [H2.106]

STEWART, ALEXANDER., a soldier of the 2d Company of Cockburn's Regiment, a brother of the Earl of Traquair, a Lieutenant of Mackay's Regiment, in Danish Service in 1626, died in October 1627 after Oldenburg, Saxony. [TGSI.VIII.188]

STEWART, ALEXANDER, a soldier from Glasgow, married Elizabeth Dempster from Brechin, Angus, in Schiedam, Holland, on 24 July 1635. [Schiedam Marriage Register]

STEWART, Colonel ALEXANDER, of Lawers Brigade, who was killed at the Battle of Dunbar on 3 September 1650. [SR.37]

STEWART, ALEXANDER, of Ballachan, a Jacobite soldier in 1689. [APS.acc.ix.57]

STEWART, ANDREW, Lord Ochiltree, at a muster in Dungannon, County Tyrone, Ireland, in 1618. [CalSPIre.1618.501]

STEWART, ARCHIBALD, a prisoner in Edinburgh Tolbooth, was released to go to Holland as a soldier under Captain William Douglas on 6 March 1683. [ETR]

STEWART, AUSTIN, a prisoner of war captured at the Siege of Worcester on 2 September 1651, was transported via London on the John and Sarah of London to Boston in December 1651, landed there in February 1652. [Suffolk Deeds.1/5-6]

STEWART, A., a soldier of the Westmoreland County, Virginia, 1701. [TNA.CO5.1312/2]

STEWART, CHARLES, a prisoner of war captured at the Siege of Worcester on 2 September 1651, was transported via London on the <u>John and Sarah of London</u> to Boston in December 1651, landed there in February 1652. [Suffolk Deeds.1/5-6]

STEWART, DAVID, a Lieutenant of Kenmure's Regiment at the Battle of Killiecrankie, Perthshire, on 27 July 1684, a prisoner of the Jacobites. [BK.207]

STEWART, FREDERICK, a soldier of the 2nd Company of Cockburn's Regiment in Swedish Service in 1609. [SIS.217]

STEWART, GABRIEL, soldier of Captain Lewgar's Company of Militia in Barbados in 1679. [H2.77]

STEWART, GEORGE, Captain of Mackay's Regiment, in Danish Service in 1626, in Swedish Service in 1629, later Lieutenant Colonel of Conway's Regiment. [TGSI.VIII.187]

STEWART, JAMES, of Cardonnell, former Captain of the Scots Guards in France, died on 5 January 1584. [Paisley Abbey gravestone]

STEWART, JAMES, a soldier from St Andrews, Fife, married Janneke Anthonis in Bergen-op-Zoom in 1586. [Bergen-op-Zoom Marriage Register]

STEWART, JAMES, Ensign of the 2nd Company of Cockburn's Regiment in Swedish Service in 1609. [SIS.217]

STEWART, JAMES, at a muster in Strabane, County Tyrone, Ireland, in 1618. [CalSPIre.1618.501]

STEWART, Ensign JAMES, in Ireland in 1625. [CalSPIre., 1625]

STEWART, JAMES, Corporal of Forbes of Tullich's Company in Danish Service in 1628. [SAA.ii.121]

STEWART, JAMES, Quartermaster of Viscount Claneboy's Troop of Horse in Ireland in 1642. [CalSPIre.260.63]

STEUART, JAMES, a Lieutenant at the fortress of Weichselmunde, married Gertrud, daughter of Arndt Uphage, in the Reformed Church of Peter and Paul in Danzig, on 20 November 1656.

STEWART, JAMES, a Sergeant of Captain Scott's Company of Militia in Barbados in 1679. [H2.191]

STEWART, JOHN, a soldier under the Marquis of Montrose in 1640s, a prisoner of war captured at the Battle of Dunbar on 3 September 1650, transported from London on the <u>Unity of Boston</u> to Boston in November 1650, an indentured servant at Lynn Ironworks in 1650s. [Suffolk Court Files. 1226][LLNV.248]

STEWART, JOHN, of Appin, a Jacobite at the Battle of Killiecrankie, Perthshire, on 27 July 1689. [APS.IX.55]

STEWART, JOHN, a prisoner in Dundee Tolbooth, was released to go to Holland as a soldier under Lieutenant Alexander Murray of Skirling on 13 September 1689. [RPCS.XIV.619]

STEWART, JOHN, Lieutenant of the Cameronian Regiment at the Siege of Dunkeld, Perthshire, on 27 August 1689. [BK.146]

STEWART, JOHN, of Kingarrochie, a soldier who died at Darien in 1699, testament, 1707, Comm. Edinburgh. [NRS]

STEWART, J., Lieutenant of the 2nd Company of Cockburn's Regiment in Swedish Service in 1609. [SIS.217]

STEWART, Ensign LUDOVIC, in Ireland in 1625. [Cal.SP.Ireland, 1625]

STEWART, NEIL, a prisoner of war captured at the Siege of Worcester on 2 September 1651, was transported via London on the <u>John and Sarah of London</u> to Boston in December 1651, landed there in February 1652. [Suffolk Deeds.1/5-6]

STEWART, PATRICK, a cannoneer, married Neelttgen Adriaens from Dordrecht, Holland, in Aardenburg, Holland, on 2 January 1610. [Ardenburg Marriage Register]

STEWART, R., Lieutenant of the 1st Company of Cockburn's Regiment in Swedish Service in 1609. [SIS.217]

STEWART, ROBERT, Lieutenant of Mackay's Regiment, in Danish Service in 1626, in Swedish Service in1629, later Colonel of Lumsden's Pikemen. [TGSI.VIII.188]

STEWART, Colonel ROBERT, in Antrim, Ireland, in 1645. [Cal.SPIre.260.137]

STEWART, ROBERT, [1], a prisoner of war captured at the Siege of Worcester on 2 September 1651, was transported via London on the John and Sarah of London to Boston in December 1651, landed there in February 1652. [Suffolk Deeds.1/5-6]

STEWART, ROBERT, [2], a prisoner of war captured at the Siege of Worcester on 2 September 1651, was transported via London on the John and Sarah of London to Boston in December 1651, landed there in February 1652. [Suffolk Deeds.1/5-6]

STEWART, ROBERT, a Jacobite soldier in 1689. [APS.acc.ix.56]

STEWART, SAMUEL, Captain of Robert Home of the Heugh's Regiment in Carrickfergus, Ireland, in 1642. [TNA.SP18.120]

STEWART, Lieutenant THOMAS, on Lord Ochiltree's expedition to Cape Breton, landed there on 1 July 1629, was captured by the French on 10 September 1629 and taken to Dieppe, France. [CSP.Col.1574-1660, fo.104]

STEWART, WILLIAM, the younger of Galston, archer of the Scots Guards in France in the 1560s. [NRS.NRAS.O.143]

STEWART, Captain WILLIAM, in Ulster in 1611. [CalSPIre.1611.251]

STEWART, WILLIAM, from Islay, Argyll, who had gone as a soldier to aid in the relief of La Rochelle, France, in 1627, was admitted as a burgess of Glasgow in 1627. [GBR]

STEWART, WILLIAM, brother of the Earl of Traquair, Lieutenant Colonel of Mackay's Regiment in Swedish Service in 1626. [SHR.IX.51][TGSI.VIII.185]; a Colonel in Germany in the service of Gustavus Adolphus, ca.1630. [SIG.282]

STEWART, Sir WILLIAM, a Cavalry officer in Ulster in 1646. [CalSPIre.]

STEWART, Colonel WILLIAM, with two Troops of Cavalry, fought at the Battle of Dunbar on 3 September 1650. [SR.37]

STEWART, WILLIAM, a prisoner of war captured at the Siege of Worcester on 2 September 1651, was transported via London on the John and Sarah of London to Boston in December 1651, landed there in February 1652. [Suffolk Deeds.1/5-6]

STIRLING, Captain ALEXANDER, of the Edinburgh Foot in 1644. [CA.133]

STIRLING, ALEXANDER, of Achyle, formerly a Lieutenant of the Earl of Tullibardine's Regiment, a soldier who died at Darien in 1699. testament, 1707, Comm. Edinburgh. [NRS]

STIRLING, DAVID, a prisoner of war captured at the Siege of Worcester on 2 September 1651, was transported via London on the John and Sarah of London to Boston in December 1651, landed there in February 1652. [Suffolk Deeds.1/5-6]

STIRLING, JOHN, a prisoner of war captured at the Siege of Worcester on 2 September 1651, was transported via London on the John and Sarah of London to Boston in December 1651, landed there in February 1652. [Suffolk Deeds.1/5-6]

STIRLING, ROBERT, Sergeant of the Militia of Dundee in 1643. [DCW.13]

STIRLING, Sir ROBERT, a Royalist Army officer in Ireland from 1641 to 1648. [CalSPIre.1660]

STITT, Sergeant JOHN, Commissary of the Train of Artillery, 1688. [DSA.166]

STRACHAN, ALEXANDER, of Thornton, Lieutenant Colonel of the Earl of Balcarres's Regiment of Horse in 1644, fought at the Siege of Newcastle, the Siege of York, and the Battle of Marston Moor. [CA.11]

STRACHAN, Colonel ARCHIBALD, with Troops of Cavalry, fought at the Battle of Dunbar on 3 September 1650. [SR.37]

STRACHAN, Lieutenant JAMES, in Angus, of the Earl of Airlie's Militia in 1670. [NRS.GD16.53.39]

STRACHAN, JAMES, a Sergeant Captain of the Angus Regiment in 1644. [DCW.78]

STRACHAN, Captain, with a Troop of the Scots Greys in Stranraer, Wigtonshire, from 1681 to 1702. [NRS.E100.5.88]

STRATON, WILLIAM, in Angus, of the Earl of Airlie's Militia in 1670. [NRS.GD16.53.39]

STUART, Lieutenant HENRY, of the Cameronian Regiment at the Siege of Dunkeld, Perthshire, on 21 August 1689. [BK.146]

STUART, JAMES, archer of the Scots Guards in France in the 1560s. [NRS.NRAS.O.143]

STUART, Lieutenant JAMES, husband of Gertrude Uphagen who was buried in St Elisabeth's, Danzig, [Gdansk], in 1658. [CRD]

STUART, J., a soldier of the 1st Company of Cockburn's Regiment in Swedish Service in 1609. [SIS.217]

STUART, JOHN, a soldier, in Pillau, married Lubbertin, widow of Hans Meyhunder, in the Burgkirche, Konigsberg, on 19 May 1670.

STUART, JOHN, a soldier of the Albany Garrison, was killed near Albany, New York, in 1671. [CMA.13.333]

STUART, PATRICK, a soldier from the Highlands, married Lijsbeth Davids from Dordrecht, Holland, there on 30 January 1647. [Dordrecht Marriage Register]

STUART, Sir ROBERT, a Cavalry officer in Ulster in 1646. [CalSPIre]

STUART, THOMAS, archer of the Scots Guards in France in the 1560s. [NRS.NRAS.O.143]

SCOTTISH SOLDIERS IN EUROPE AND AMERICA, 1600-1700.

STUART, Lieutenant, in Memel in 1631. [JSM]

STURROCK, DAVID, a soldier from Dundee, married Josijntie Pieters in Hulst, the Netherlands, on 24 August 1657. [Hulst Marriage Register]

SUTHERLAND, 'ANSELL', a prisoner of war captured at the Siege of Worcester on 2 September 1651, was transported via London on the John and Sarah of London to Boston in December 1651, landed there in February 1652. [Suffolk Deeds.1/5-6]

SUTHERLAND, HENRY, from the Shetland Islands, a musketeer aboard the Dutch ship Neptunus on 1 May 1645. [ZA]

SUTHERLAND, ISAAC, a soldier of Lieutenant Colonel Tidcomb's Company of Militia in Barbados in 1679. [H2.132]

SUTHERLAND, PATRICK, a prisoner of war captured at the Siege of Worcester on 2 September 1651, was transported via London on the John and Sarah of London to Boston in December 1651, landed there in February 1652. [Suffolk Deeds.1/5-6]

SUTHERLAND, ROGER, a soldier of Lieutenant Colonel Lyne's Company of Militia in Barbados in 1679. [H2.101]

SUTHERLAND, THOMAS, a soldier of Colonel Colleton's Company of Militia in Barbados in 1679. [H2.119]

SUTHERLAND, ..., Lieutenant of Mackay's Regiment, in Danish Service in 1626, in Swedish Service in 1629, later in Ruthven's Regiment. [TGSI.VIII.188]

SWAINE, ALEXANDER, from Dysart, Fife, a gunner on the Zeeland warship Utrecht in 1665. [ZA.Rekenkamer.c6994]

SWINTON, ALEXANDER, son of William Swinton and his wife Jean Wright in Glasgow, an Ensign who was killed at Darien on 6 February 1699, testament, 1707, Comm. Edinburgh. [NRS]

SYDSERF, PATRICK, Sergeant Major in Colonel Sir James Ramsay's Regiment in Germany, dead by May 1634. [NRS.NRAS.0028.8.1]

TAILFAIR, JOHN, a Captain in the Service of the Scottish India and Africa Company, in St Kitts in 1700. [NRS.GD84.sec.1.22.9b]

TAIT, ROBERT, Lieutenant of the Cameronian Regiment at the Siege of Dunkeld, Perthshire, on 21 August 1689. [BK.146]

TAIT, W., a soldier of the 2nd Company of Cockburn's Regiment in Swedish Service in 1609. [SIS.217]

TANNIELL, [?], JOHN, a prisoner of war captured at the Siege of Worcester on 2 September 1651, was transported via London on the John and Sarah of London to Boston in December 1651, landed there in February 1652. [Suffolk Deeds.1/5-6]

TARRES, JAMES, a soldier, from Elgin, Moray, to Tangiers in 1678. [RPCS.VII.135]

TARRES, JOHN, in Danish Service at Gluckstadt from 1627 to 1629. [SAA.117]

TAYLOR, ANDREW, from Wemyss, Fife, a gunner on the Arms of Zeeland in 1644. [ZA]

TAYLOR, DAVID, a prisoner of war captured at the Siege of Worcester on 2 September 1651, was transported via London on the John and Sarah of London to Boston in December 1651, landed there in February 1652. [Suffolk Deeds.1/5-6]

TAYLOR, EDWARD, a prisoner of war captured at the Siege of Worcester on 2 September 1651, was transported via London on the John and Sarah of London to Boston in December 1651, landed there in February 1652. [Suffolk Deeds.1/5-6]

TAYLOR, EUAN, a prisoner of war captured at the Siege of Worcester on 2 September 1651, was transported via London on the John and Sarah of London to Boston in December 1651, landed there in February 1652. [Suffolk Deeds.1/5-6]

TAYLOR, JAMES, a prisoner of war captured at the Siege of Worcester on 2 September 1651, was transported via London on the John and Sarah of London to Boston in December 1651, landed there in February 1652, an indentured servant at Lynn Ironworks in the 1650s. [Suffolk Deeds.1/5-6][LLNV.248]

TAYLOR, JOHN, a prisoner of war captured at the Siege of Worcester on 2 September 1651, was transported via London on the John and Sarah of London to Boston in December 1651, landed there in February 1652. [Suffolk Court Deeds.1226]; probate 23 February 1691, Maine.

TAYLOR, WILLIAM, from the Shetland Islands, a soldier in Amsterdam, married Margaret Duncanson from Stirling, in the Oudekirk, Amsterdam, on 6 February 1639. [Amsterdam Marriage Register][NYGBR.128.15]

TAYLOR, WILLIAM, a prisoner of war captured at the Siege of Worcester on 2 September 1651, was transported via London on the John and Sarah of London to Boston in December 1651, landed there in February 1652. [Suffolk Deeds.1/5-6]

TENLER, [?], DAVID, a prisoner of war captured at the Siege of Worcester on 2 September 1651, was transported via London on the John and Sarah of London to Boston in December 1651, landed there in February 1652. [Suffolk Deeds.1/5-6]

TENLER, [?], JOHN, a prisoner of war captured at the Siege of Worcester on 2 September 1651, was transported via London on the John and Sarah of London to Boston in December 1651, landed there in February 1652. [Suffolk Deeds.1/5-6]

THILGER, [Telfer?], ANDREW, a soldier from Aberdeen, married Margaret Kirkwood from Edinburgh, in Schiedam, Holland, on 29 December 1641. [Schiedam Marriage Register]

THOMPSON, ALEXANDER, a prisoner of war captured at the Siege of Worcester on 2 September 1651, was transported via London on the John and Sarah of London to Boston in December 1651, landed there in February 1652. [Suffolk Deeds.1/5-6]

THOMPSON, ['Jempson'], ANDREW, a prisoner of war captured at the Siege of Worcester on 2 September 1651, was transported via

London on the John and Sarah of London to Boston in December 1651, landed there in February 1652, an indentured servant at Lynn Ironworks. [Suffolk Deeds.1/5-6][LLNV.248]

THOMSON, CHARLES, in Angus, of the Earl of Airlie's Militia in 1670. [NRS.GD16.53.39]

THOMSON, DAVID, a soldier with the Dutch, married Christina, daughter of Wilhelm Schmitt in the Reformed Church of Peter and Paul in Danzig, [Gdansk], on 28 October 1657.

THOMSON, DAVID, from Dysart, Fife, a gunner on the Zeeland warship Utrecht in 1665. [ZA.Rekenkamer.c6994]

THOMSON, Colonel DAVID, in France, deeds, 1674, 1676. [NRS.RD4.39.797; RD4.36.233; RD4.40.84, etc.]

THOMSON, DONALD, from Argyll, a soldier in Argyll's Rebellion, imprisoned in Edinburgh, was transported from Leith on William Arbuckle's ship bound for New England in July 1685. [RPCS.11.94]

THOMSON, DONALD, from Argyll, a soldier in Argyll's Rebellion, was transported via Leith to Jamaica in August 1685. [RPCS.11.329]

THOMSON, DUNCAN, from Argyll, a soldier in Argyll's Rebellion, was transported via Leith to Jamaica in August 1685. [RPCS.11.130]

THOMSON, GEORGE, a Sergeant of Fraser's Dragoons in 1645. [TFD.220]

THOMSON, GEORGE, a prisoner of war captured at the Battle of Dunbar on 3 September 1650, transported from London on the Unity of Boston to Boston in November 1650, an indentured servant at Lynn Ironworks in 1650s. [Suffolk Court Files. 1226] [LLNV.248]

THOMSON, JAMES, from Aberdeen, a soldier in Colonel Brock's Company, married Lijsbet van der Mole, in Schiedam, Holland, on 14 January 1635. [Schiedam Marriage Register]

THOMSON, JAMES, a prisoner of war captured at the Battle of Dunbar on 3 September 1650, transported from London on the <u>Unity of Boston</u> to Boston in November 1650, an indentured servant at Lynn Ironworks in 1650s. [Suffolk Court Files. 1226] [LLNV.248]

THOMSON, Captain JOHN, in the Service of Hamburg in 1660. [JTA.102]

THOMSON, JOHN, from Argyll, a soldier in Argyll's Rebellion, a prisoner in Edinburgh, was transported via Leith to New England on 6 July 1685. [RPCA.11.94]

THOMSON, NEIL, from Argyll, a soldier in Argyll's Rebellion, was transported via Leith to Jamaica in August 1685. [RPCS.11.329]

THOMSON, NICHOLAS, a prisoner in Edinburgh Tolbooth, released to go to Holland as a soldier under Lieutenant Colonel Gordon in 1689. [RPCS.13.573]

THOMSON, THOMAS, Colonel of the Scots Guards of France in the 1560s. [NRS.NRAS.0.143]S

THOMSON, THOMAS, Military Governor of Hagelburg in 1638. [MGIF]

THOMSON, THOMAS, Colonel of the King of France's Guards, a deed, 1663. [NRS.RD4.7.837]

THOMSON, WILLIAM, a prisoner of war captured at the Battle of Dunbar on 3 September 1650, transported from London on the <u>Unity of Boston</u> to Boston in November 1650, settled in Kittery, Berwick, Maine, in 1656. [CEB][LLNV.252]

TINDALL, DAVID, Sergeant of the Militia of Dundee in 1643. [DCW.13]

TOSH, JAMES, born 1629, a prisoner of war, transported to New England, an indentured servant at Lynn Ironworks in the 1650s. [Suffolk Court Files.1226]

TOSH, JOHN, a prisoner of war captured at the Battle of Dunbar on 3 September 1650, transported from London on the Unity of Boston to Boston in November 1650, an indentured servant at Lynn Ironworks in the 1650s. [Suffolk Court Files.1226][LLNV.248]

TOSH, THOMAS, a Captain of Militia in Dundee in 1651. [DCW.54][CBRD.174]

TOSH, WILLIAM, a prisoner of war, captured at the Battle of Dunbar on 3 September 1650, transported to New England, an indentured servant on Block Island. [NWI.I.159]

TOSSACH, ALEXANDER, a chapman imprisoned in Dundee Tolbooth, was released to go to Holland as a soldier with Captain Dundas in July 1689. [RPCS.XIII.569]

TOUGH, ALESTER, a prisoner of war captured at the Siege of Worcester on 2 September 1651, was transported via London on the John and Sarah of London to Boston in December 1651, landed there in February 1652. [Suffolk Deeds.1/5-6]

TOURS, JOHN, Major of Barclay's Regiment of Horse in the Army of the Covenant in 1644, fought at the Battle of Philiphaugh on 13 September 1645. [CA.117]

TOURS, Colonel JOHN, brother of Major Robert Tours, of the Scots Guards in France, a deed, 1666. [NRS.RD2.15.556]

TOWER, PATRICK, a prisoner of war captured at the Siege of Worcester on 2 September 1651, was transported via London on the John and Sarah of London to Boston in December 1651, landed there in February 1652. [Suffolk Deeds.1/5-6]

TOWER, THOMAS, a prisoner of war captured at the Battle of Dunbar on 3 September 1650, transported from London on the Unity of Boston to Boston in November 1650, an indentured servant at Lynn Ironworks in the 1650s. [Suffolk Court Files.1226] [LLNV.248]

TRAILL, Lieutenant Colonel JAMES, died on 18 May 166-. [Killyreagh gravestone, County Down, Ireland]

TRENT, MORRIS, a militiaman in Barbados in 1679. [H2.171]

TROTTER, Lieutenant WILLIAM, of Captain Dalyell's Company, was mustered at Glasgow in 1682. [DSA.126]

TRUMPETT, JOHN, in Angus, of the Earl of Airlie's Militia in 1670. [NRS.GD16.53.39]

TULLOCH, ALEXANDER, Captain of Mackay's Regiment, in Danish Service in 1626, in Swedish Service in 1629. [TGSI.VIII.187][SIG.282]

TURNBULL, A., a soldier of the 2nd Company of Cockburn's Regiment in Swedish Service in 1609. [SIS.217]

TURNBULL, ROBERT, a Lieutenant of the Darien Company, at Fort St Andrew, Darien in 1699, returned to Scotland by July 1701. [SHR.XI.404]

TURNBULL, THOMAS, a soldier in Argyll's Rebellion, a prisoner in Edinburgh Tolbooth, was transported from Leith to Jamaica in August 1685. [RPCS.11.330][ETR.369]

TURNER, JAMES, Major of Lord Sinclair's Regiment in Newry, Ireland, in 1642. [TNA.SP18.120]

TWEEDIE, THOMAS, a prisoner in Edinburgh Tolbooth, released to go to Holland as a soldier under Lieutenant John McCulloch on 4 February 1676. [RPCS.4.668]

TWEEDIE, ..., Quartermaster of Fraser's Dragoons in 1645. [TFD.220]

TYRIE, ALEXANDER, Sergeant of the Militia of Dundee in 1643. [DCW.13]

TYRIE, ALEXANDER, a soldier of New Kent County Militia, in Virginia in 1701. [TNA.CO5.1312/2]

TYRIE, ANDREW, one of the 25 archers of the King's Guard at Fontainbleu, France, testament, 17 June 1608, Comm. Edinburgh. [NRS]

TYRIE, JAMES, a soldier of New Kent County Militia, in Virginia in 1701. [TNA.CO5.1312/2]

URQUHART, JOHN, Governor of Birsen in 1655. [MGIF]

URQUHART, PATRICK, in Angus, of the Earl of Airlie's Militia in 1670. [NRS.GD16.53.39]

URQUHART, THOMAS, a Quartermaster of Fraser's Dragoons, in 1645. [TFD.47]

URQUHART, …, formerly a Captain in the Darien Company Service, 1707. [APS.14.app.114]

VEECH, JOHN, a Corporal of Fraser's Dragoons in 1645. [TFD.220]

VEITCH, SAMUEL, born 1668, Lieutenant, of the Cameronian Regiment at the Siege of Dunkeld, Perthshire, on 21 August 1689, died 1732. [BK.71/146][NRS.GD77.189]

VETCH, JAMES, in Angus, of the Earl of Airlie's Militia in 1670. [NRS.GD16.53.39]

VETCH, WILLIAM, formerly a Lieutenant of the Earl of Angus's Regiment, later in Darien, died on the Hope in 1699, testament, 1709, Comm. Edinburgh. [NRS]

WADDELL ,……, Lieutenant of Leven's Regiment at the Battle of Killiecrankie, Perthshire, on 27 July 1689. [BK.96]

WALE, ANDREW, a soldier in Oletzko, Prussia, 1681. [SIG.263]

WALKER, DONALD, a farmer in Otter, Argyll, a soldier in Argyll's Rebellion, a prisoner in Edinburgh Tolbooth, was transported from Leith to Jamaica in August 1685. [ETR.373]

WALKER, DUNCAN, a soldier in Argyll's Rebellion, was transported from Leith to Jamaica in August 1685. [RPCS.11.136]

WALKER, JOHN, a soldier of the garrison at Dordrecht, Holland, married Marytgen Jans from Leiden, Holland, there on 21 April 1589. [Leiden Marriage Register]

WALKER, WILLIAM, a soldier in Argyll's Rebellion, was transported from Leith to Jamaica in August 1685. [RPCS.11.136]

WALLACE, Major HUGH, of the Earl of Glencairn's Foot, at the Siege of Newcastle in 1644, and the Battle of Kilsyth in 1645. [CA.143]

WALLACE, JAMES, Captain of Major General Monro's Regiment in Carrickfergus, Ireland, in 1642. [TNA.SP18.120]

WALLACE, NICHOLAS, a prisoner of war captured at the Siege of Worcester on 2 September 1651, was transported via London on the <u>John and Sarah of London</u> to Boston in December 1651, landed there in February 1652. [Suffolk Deeds.1/5-6]

WALLACE, THOMAS, a soldier of the 1st Company of Cockburn's Regiment in Swedish Service in 1609. [SIS.217]

WALLACE, WILLIAM, Military Governor of Jama in 1580. [MGIF]

WALLACE, Sir WILLIAM, of Craigie, Captain of the King's Regiment of Horse in 1686, a Jacobite soldier in 1689. [APS.acc.ix.56]

WALLACE, ..., a Corporal in Danzig, [Gdansk], in 1599. [RPCS.VI.856]

WALLACE, Lieutenant Colonel, fought and was captured at the Battle of Dunbar on 3 September 1650.

WALSH, Lieutenant, of the Cameronian Regiment at the Siege of Dunkeld, Perthshire, on 21 August 1689. [BK.146]

WARDROP, D., a soldier of the 2nd Company of Cockburn's Regiment in Swedish Service in 1609. [SIS.217]

WARREN, JAMES, a prisoner of war captured at the Battle of Dunbar on 3 September 1650, transported from London on the <u>Unity of Boston</u> to Boston in November 1650, probate, 24 December 1702, Maine. [LLNV.282]

WATSON, ALEXANDER, a soldier of Colonel Leslie's Company in Muscovite Service from 1630 to 1632. [STW.179]

WATSON, ALEXANDER, the younger, Sergeant of the Militia of Dundee in 1643. [DCW.13]

WATSON, JAMES, a soldier in Moscow in 1630. [SSA.50]

WATSON, JACK, a soldier under Captain Mowbray, married Susanna Caddell a Scottish widow, in Aardenburg, Holland, on 2 January 1610. [Aardenburg Marriage Register]

WATSON, WILLIAM, a Captain of Militia in Dundee in 1650. [CBRD.174]

WATSON, WILLIAM, from Islay, Argyll, a soldier in Argyll's Rebellion, was transported from Leith to Jamaica in August 1685. [RPCS.11.136]

WATT, ALEXANDER, a soldier in Captain Bowcher's Company of Militia in Barbados in 1679. [H2.16]

WATT, ALEXANDER, soldier of Captain Sleigh's Company, possibly in Dundee, was accidentally shot and killed by James Yeaman, a soldier of the same Company in 1689. [NRS.GD26.9.219

WATT, DAVID, a soldier in Colonel Lyne's Company of Militia in Barbados in 1679. [H2.77]

WATT, JOHN, armourer, bound from Leith to Darien on the Caledonia on 14 July 1698, testament, 1707, Comm. Edinburgh. [NRS]

WATT, WILLIAM, a Lieutenant of the Foot Guards in Flanders, deeds, 1692. [NRS.RD4.70.356/563]

WAUCHOPE, EDWARD, Ensign of a Scottish regiment in the Service of the King of France in 1688. [DSA.159]

WAUCHOPE, Major Francis, of the Grenadier Company, of a Scottish regiment in the Service of the King of France in 1688. [DSA.159]

WAUCHOPE, GILBERT, a Captain of the Swedish Army, via Leith to Sweden in 1607. [RPCS.7.420]

SCOTTISH SOLDIERS IN EUROPE AND AMERICA, 1600-1700.

WAUCHOPE, JAMES, a Lieutenant of Captain Alexander Hamilton's Regiment in Danish Service from 1627-1629. [SAA.117]

WAUCHOPE, Captain JAMES, in Moscow, will dated 29 September 1632. [Suffolk Record Office.S1.77.6/9]

WAUCHOPE, PHILIP, a Lance Corporal of Captain Andrew Gray's Company in Danish Service 1627-1628. [SAA.117]

WAUCHOPE, ROBERT, Captain of Major General Monro's Regiment in Carrickfergus, Ireland, in 1642. [TNA.SP18.120]

WAUCHOPE, Captain JOHN, of a Scottish regiment in the Service of the King of France in 1688. [DSA.159]

WAUGH, ALEXANDER, a Cornet of the Stafford County Horse Militia, Virginia, in 1701. [TNA.CO5.1312/2]

WAUGH, JOHN, jr, of the Stafford County Horse Militia, Virginia, in 1701. [TNA.CO5.1312/2]

WAUGH, JOSEPH, of the Stafford County Horse Militia, Virginia, in 1701. [TNA.CO5.1312/2]

WEDDERBURN, ALEXANDER, of Kingennie, Angus, a Captain of Militia in Dundee in 1643. [DCW.13]

WEDDERBURN, ALEXANDER, of Easter Powrie, Angus, Lieutenant of Militia in Dundee in 1643. [DCW.13]

WEDDERBURN, GEORGE, from Prestonpans, Midlothian, a musketeer aboard the Dutch ship *Vere* in 1644. [ZA]

WEETHS, [?], GEORGE, a soldier married Lijntgen Frederick, in Leiden, Holland, on 28 May 1593. [Leiden Marriage Register]

WEIR, GEORGE, Captain of Buchan's Regiment in Flanders, testament, 27 July 1703, Comm. Edinburgh. [NRS]

WEIR, JOHN, a soldier in Argyll's Rebellion, was transported from Leith to Jamaica in August 1685. [RPCS.11.130]

WEIR, ..., of Kirkfield, Ensign of Belhaven's Troop of Horse at the Battle of Killiecrankie, Perthshire, on 27 July 1689. [BK.96]

WELSH, ANDREW, a soldier in Captain Burrow's Company of Militia in Barbados in 1679. [H2.181]

WELSH, Captain GEORGE, at Six Mile Quarter, Ireland, in 1653. [OB.83]

WELSH, WALTER, a soldier in Captain Liston's Company of Militia in Barbados in 1679. [H2.143]

WEMYSS, JAMES, a soldier who arrived in Moscow in 1628 via Holland and Sweden, later in Novgorod. [SSA.49]

WEMYSS, [WEEMS], JAMES, raised and landed in New York with his company before 4 November 1697, [SPAWI.1697.29]; the muster roll of Captain Weems' Company at Albany, New York, on 28 July 1698, [SPAWI.1698.835]; Captain of Fusiliers at Albany, New York, on 7 February 1699, [SPAWI.1699.384.xv]

WEMYSS, JAMES, an Ensign who died at Darien in 1699, testament, 1707, Comm. Edinburgh. [NRS]

WEMYSS, Sir PATRICK, with 62 horsemen in Ireland in 1647. [CalSPIre.265.41-47]

WHYTE, Major ANDREW, with his company mustered in Glasgow in 1682. [DSA.128]

WHITE, JAMES, a Scottish soldier, married Elizabeth Daniels from Edinburgh, in Utrecht, Holland, on 24 October 1613. [Utrecht Marriage Register]

WHYTE, THOMAS, Corporal of Major Whyte's company mustered in Glasgow in 1682. [DSA.128]

WHYTE, MALCOLM, a soldier in Argyll's Rebellion, was transported from Leith to Jamaica in August 1685. [RPCS.11.126]

WHITEHEAD, Lieutenant Colonel JAMES, of Major General Holburne's Regiment, 15 July 1656. [NRS.GD76.272]

WICHTON, GEORGE, Sergeant of the Militia of Dundee in 1643. [DCW.13]

WILLIAMS, ALISTER, a soldier of Captain Woodward's Company of Militia in Barbados in 1679. [H2.156]

WILLIAMS, JAMES, a soldier from Dundee, married Elsken Adolfs, in Dordrecht, Holland, on 26 April 1587. [Dordrecht Marriage Register]

WILLIAMS, Cornet, of Livingstone's Regiment of Dragoons at the Battle of Cromdale, Strathspey, on 1 May 1690. [BK.177]

WILLIAMSON, ALEXANDER, from the Orkney Islands, a seaman aboard the Zeeland warship Swanenburgh in 1665. [ZA.Rekenkamer.c6984]

WILLIAMSON, GEORGE, from Prestonpans, Midlothian, a musketeer aboard the Zeeland warship Sandenburch in 1645. [ZA]

WILLIAMSON, JOHN, a soldier under Captain Slater, married Maritgen Jacobsdaughter of Leiden, Holland, there on 5 July 1576. [Leiden Marriage Register]

WILLIAMSON, JOHN, a soldier under Captain Gabriel de la Nyvelle, married Trijn Jans from Oudenaarde, Flanders, in Leiden, Holland, on 20 January 1601. [Leiden Marriage Register]

WILLIAMSON, JOHN, from Leith, a gunner's mate aboard the Zeelandia in 1665. [ZA.Rekenkamer.c6984]

WILLIAMSON, JOHN, from Dysart, Fife, a gunner's mate aboard the Zeeland warship Utrecht in 1665. [ZA.Rekenkamer.c6994]

WILSON, ADAM, a soldier from Edinburgh, married Janneken Pieterzoon from Groningen, in Dordrecht, Holland, on 21 March 1593. [Dordrecht Marriage Register]

WILSON, ANDREW, a prisoner of war captured at the Siege of Worcester on 2 September 1651, was transported via London on the John and Sarah of London to Boston in December 1651, landed there in February 1652. [Suffolk Deeds.1/5-6]

WILSON, ARCHIBALD, Ensign of the Cameronian Regiment at the Siege of Dunkeld, Perthshire, on 21 August 1689. [BK.146]

WILSON, CHRISTOPHER, a prisoner of war captured at the Siege of Worcester on 2 September 1651, was transported via London on the John and Sarah of London to Boston in December 1651, landed there in February 1652. [Suffolk Deeds.1/5-6]

WILSON, E., a soldier of fortune, a prisoner in Edinburgh Castle, requested to go to Holland as a soldier in 1685. [NRS.GD26.9.222]

WILSON, Lieutenant Colonel EDWARD, a prisoner on the Bass Rock, in the Firth of Forth, was released to go to Holland on 21 March 1690. [RPCS.XV.162]

WILSON, JAMES, a Scottish soldier, father of Else who was baptised in St Marien Kirche in Danzig, [Gdansk], on 27 July 1612.

WILSON, JOHN, [1], a prisoner of war captured at the Siege of Worcester on 2 September 1651, was transported via London on the John and Sarah of London to Boston in December 1651, landed there in February 1652. [Suffolk Deeds.1/5-6]

WILSON, JOHN, [2], a prisoner of war captured at the Siege of Worcester on 2 September 1651, was transported via London on the John and Sarah of London to Boston in December 1651, landed there in February 1652. [Suffolk Deeds.1/5-6]

WILSON, JOHN, an officer in the Service of the Prince of Lunenburg at Winsen in 1672. [NRS.GD29.2152]

WILSON, JOHN, Ensign of the Cameronian Regiment at the Siege of Dunkeld, Perthshire, on 21 August 1689. [BK.146]

WILSON, NICOLAS, from Glasgow, a gunner aboard the Lion of Zeeland in 1631. [ZA]

WILSON, THOMAS, a soldier from Glasgow, married Maritghe Willems in Delft, Holland, on 26 January 1592. [Delft Marriage Register]

WILSON, ..., Major of Mackay's Regiment in Danish Service in 1626, in Swedish Service in 1629. [TGSI.VIII.186]

WINDRAM, THOMAS, a government soldier, was killed at the Battle of Killiecrankie, Perthshire, on 27 July 1689. [RPCS.XIV]

WISHART, ANDREW, a soldier in Major Foster's Company of Militia in Barbados in 1679. [H2.134]

WISHART, GEORGE, born 1599, chaplain to a Scottish regiment in Dutch Service around 1650, died in 1671. [NRS.NA17027]

WISHART, Major GEORGE, wrote from Dundee requesting remission for James Yeaman, a soldier of Captain Sleigh's Company, who had accidentally shot and killed Alexander Watt, a soldier of the same Company, letter dated 28 June 1689. [NRS.GD26.9.219]

WISHART, PATRICK, in Angus, of the Earl of Airlie's Militia in 1670. [NRS.GD16.53.39]

WISHART, ROBERT, in Angus, of the Earl of Airlie's Militia in 1670. [NRS.GD16.53.39]

WISHART, WILLIAM, in Angus, of the Earl of Airlie's Militia in 1670. [NRS.GD16.53.39]

WOOD, EDWARD, a prisoner in Edinburgh Tolbooth, released to go to Holland as a soldier under Lieutenant Middleton in 1689. [RPCS.13.573]

WOOD, GEORGE, in Angus, of the Earl of Airlie's Militia in 1670. [NRS.GD16.53.39]

WOOD, JAMES, in Angus, of the Earl of Airlie's Militia in 1670. [NRS.GD16.53.39]

WOOD, JOHN, was commissioned into the Russian Army in 1632. [SSA.48]

WOOD, JOHN, a Gentleman at Arms in Gordon's Company in the Service of King Louis XIII of France in 1625. [NRS.RH1.2.447]

WOOD, ROBERT, a poor soldier in Rotterdam in 1697. [NRS.RH4.17.1]

WOODALL, JOHN, [1], a prisoner of war captured at the Siege of Worcester on 2 September 1651, was transported via London on the John and Sarah of London to Boston in December 1651, landed there in February 1652. [Suffolk Deeds.1/5-6]

WOODALL, JOHN, [2], a prisoner of war captured at the Siege of Worcester on 2 September 1651, was transported via London on the John and Sarah of London to Boston in December 1651, landed there in February 1652. [Suffolk Deeds.1/5-6]

WORD, EDWARD, a prisoner in Edinburgh Tolbooth, was released to go to Holland as a soldier under Lieutenant Middleton in 1689. [RPCS.XIII.573]

WRIGHT, JAMES, from Musselburgh, Midlothian, a soldier of Colonel Livingstone's Company, married Trijnje Aryens from Schiedam, Holland, there on 22 January 1639. [Schiedam Marriage Register]

WRIGHT, WILLIAM, a soldier in Lyck, Eastern Prussia, in 1681.

YEAMAN, JAMES, a soldier of Captain Sleigh's Company, possibly in Dundee, accidentally shot and killed Alexander Watt, a soldier of the same Company in 1689. [NRS.GD26.9.219

YOUNG, ABRAHAM, Captain of the Scottish soldiers in the Service of the King of Poland in 1604, [Acta Consularia Craco.519]

YOUNG, ALEXANDER, a Corporal, a witness to a marriage in Leiden, Holland, on 9 February 1585. [Leiden Marriage Register]

YOUNG, ROBERT, Captain of Colonel Graham's Regiment of Foot in Flanders, testament, 29 March 1694, Comm. Edinburgh. [NRS]

www.ingramcontent.com/pod-product-compliance
Lightning Source LLC
Chambersburg PA
CBHW062026220426
43662CB00010B/1497